Valentino

Also by David Bret and published by Robson Books

The Piaf Legend
The Mistinguett Legend
Maurice Chevalier
Marlene, My Friend
Morrissey: Landscape of the Mind
Gracie Fields
Tallulah Bankhead: A Scandalous Life
Living on the Edge: The Freddie Mercury Story
Maria Callas: The Tigress and the Lamb

Valentino

A Dream of Desire

David Bret

First published in Great Britain in 1998 by Robson Books Ltd, Bolsover House, 5–6 Clipstone Street, London W1P 8LE

British Library Cataloguing in Publication Data
A catalogue record for this title is available from the British Library

ISBN 1 86105 123 9

Photoset in Sabon by Derek Doyle & Associates, Mold, Flintshire.
Printed in Great Britain by WBC Book Manufacturers Ltd., Bridgend, Mid-Glamorgan.

This book is dedicated to
BARBARA
(1930–1997)
La plus grande chanteuse de
notre age, et Les Enfants de Novembre.
N'oublie pas . . .
La vie sans amis c'est comme
un jardin sans fleurs.

Contents

Acknowledgements

Writing this book would not have been possible had it not been for the inspiration, criticism and love of that select group of individuals whom I still regard as my true family and *autre coeur*: Barbara, Irene Bevan, Marlene Dietrich, Montserrat Caballé, René and Lucette Chevalier, Jacqueline Danno, Hélène Delavault, Tony Griffin, Roger Normand, Joop van Dijk, Betty Paillard, Annick Roux, Caroline Clerc, Monica Solash, John and Anne Taylor, Terry Sanderson, François and Madeleine Vals. God bless you all!

Very special thanks to Gerald McKee, Diana McLellan, Damia. Heartfelt appreciation to my agent, David Bolt, and to the team at Robson Books, and most especially to my wife, Jeanne, still the keeper of my soul.

Introduction

A powder vending machine! In a men's washroom! Homo Americanus! Why didn't someone quietly drown Rudolph Guglielmi, alias Valentino, years ago? . . . It is time for a matriarchy if the male of the species allows such things to persist. Better a rule by masculine women than by effeminate men. Man began to slip when he discarded the straight razor for the safety pattern. We shall not be surprised when we hear that the safety razor has given way to the depilatory. Who or what is to blame is what puzzles us. Is this degeneration into effeminacy a cognate reaction with a pacifism to the virilities and realities of the war? Are pink powder and parlour pinks in any way related? And how does one reconcile masculine cosmetics, sheiks, floppy pants and slave-bracelets with a disregard for law and an aptitude for crime more in keeping with the frontier of half a century ago than a 20th century metropolis? Do women like the type of 'man' who pats pink powder on his face in a public washroom and arranges his coiffure in a public elevator? Do women at heart belong to the Wilsonian era of 'I Didn't Raise My Boy To Be A Soldier'? What has become of the old caveman line?

This quite unwarranted attack on Rudolph Valentino, accusing him of singlehandedly 'effeminising otherwise normal, healthy, red-blooded American males', appeared in the *Chicago Tribune* in July 1926, under the banner headline: PINK POWDER PUFFS.

Five weeks later, the man who had achieved fame as the World's Greatest Lover was dead.

The 'disregard for law' statement in the article referred to Rudy's failure to heed – or more likely his genuine belief that Hollywood stars really *were* beyond reproach – the fact that California law demanded a full year between divorce and remarriage. This oversight was milked for all it was worth by the Hays Office and the press, and resulted in the actor's arrest and imprisonment on a bigamy charge. The other passages, needless to say, alluded to Rudy's steadfast refusal to conform to media ideology regarding the behaviour and appearance of the stereotypical, all-American hero, as portrayed by contemporary 'family favourites' such as Tom Mix, John Barrymore, Douglas Fairbanks, and the majority of the nation's sporting heroes. Faced with a passionate, unpredictable Latin who was wholly incapable of suppressing emotions which, many thought, should have been kept to himself, moralists and cynics simply did not know what to make of him, so they lampooned and attacked.

That Valentino was gay by natural inclination, and bisexual in his early years through financial pressure, cannot be denied. He does not, however, appear to have been deliberately indiscreet or any more promiscuous than many of his heterosexual contemporaries. Initially, he saw sex as means of survival rather than an actual pleasure, taking a succession of partners with whom he would never have exchanged a second glance, had it not been for the incentive of hard cash. Later, of course, love-making became an art form. Rudy plucked his eyebrows, glossed his lips with Vaseline, cut his sideburns at a rapier-point angle, shaved his chest and sleeked back his hair with brilliantine until it resembled black patent leather. Towards the end of his life, he was rarely seen in public without his platinum slave-bracelet. He wore brightly-coloured shirts, elaborate hats and chinchilla coats, and favoured heavy perfumes. He posed in swimwear which had been especially, though it would seem unnecessarily, fashioned 'up front' to display to admirers and envious detractors that he was 'bigger than the other boys'. One of the former commented wryly, 'Rumour has it that Rudy wielded a weapon that was longer than his name!' He also boasted that the visible scar on his left cheek – his one physical flaw which, despite his vanity, he refused to cover with makeup in his films – had been aquired during a duel with swords, from which he had, of course, emerged victorious. In fact, the injury had been caused by a cut-throat razor when, at the age of seven, he had tried to shave like his father!

And yet, Valentino was not as effeminate or illiterate as many of his attackers would have us believe. He excelled at most sports, in particular boxing, horseriding, swimming and athletics. He drove fast, exotic and expensive cars and collected rare first editions. He spoke several languages fluently, and was a skilled mechanic and cameraman. In effect, he was considerably more 'butch' and intellectual than most of his American colleagues, not one of whom came within a whisker of matching his appeal. When Valentino bared his chest and flexed his muscles on the screen, let alone narrowed his gaze, female cinemagoers across the world swooned in droves, gay fans fought to conceal their necessarily closeted emotions, and those who disliked him for whatever reason gritted their teeth.

Rudolph Valentino remains, without any doubt, the most alluring, charismatic and *beautiful* man to have ever appeared on celluloid, a man who said more with his eyes than most would have dared put into words. The simplest of gestures from him, today, would act every single one of our so-called 'superstars' off the screen.

1
The Dream of Desire

'No matter how poor an Italian family may be, it never suffers a shortage of names.'

He was born Rodolpho Alfonso Raffaelo Pierre Filibert di Valentina d'Antonguolla, at three in the morning of 6 May 1895, in Castellaneta, a small town 23 miles from the port of Taranto, in Southern Italy. And despite popular belief, he did not come from an impoverished or inconsequential background. The d'Antonguolla is alleged to have alluded to his family's rights to a number of small royal properties, which the actor once seriously considered tracking down – until he became so wealthy in his own right that he lost interest. The di Valentina was a defunct papal title, apertaining to lands the family had held during the late-17th century, and one which they had stubbornly refused to relinquish. Guglielmi, Rudy's paternal grandfather, was a civil engineer responsible for designing some of Italy's most famous railway bridges. His father, Giovanni Guglielmi, was a captain with the Italian cavalry who resigned this well-paid position when, around 1890, Guglielmi senior died, bequeathing him a not inconsiderable fortune. It had always been Giovanni's ambition to become a vet, in civilian life, but he was suddenly struck by wanderlust and joined a travelling circus. For the next two years, studying every textbook he could lay his hands on, he looked after the animals. Then, having seen enough of the world, Giovanni returned to Castellaneta to fall in love with a local teacher; Gabrielle Bertin, the daughter of an eminent Parisian surgeon, Pierre-Filibert Bertin (hence two of Valentino's other first names) who had recently arrived in the town to teach French at a local school. The couple married in 1893 after a brief courtship, and using what was left of his fortune, Giovanni purchased a small farm and founded a flourishing veterinary practice. This was contained in a flat-topped, white-painted house at the corner of the Via Roma, near the town square.

The Guglielmis had four children: in descending order these were Alberto, Rodolpho, Maria, and Beatrice who did not survive infancy. From the very beginning, Alberto and Maria were their father's favourites, and Rudy was the mother's boy. Two years after Valentino's death, Hiram Kelly Moderwell, a reporter with the *Chicago Tribune*, was dispatched to Castellaneta to probe into the actor's childhood, and some of the facts he unearthed – unpublished at the time, for obvious reasons – are quite startling. Supplementing this information was the evidence collected by the actor-dance bandleader Chaw Mank who, in the early twenties, spent some time as Rudy's secretary and helped set up his first fanclub.

Apparently, Gabrielle spoiled her child rotten, even going so far as to dress Rudy in girls' clothes, so much so that from very early on his father grew to despise him. Apart from succumbing to violent outbursts of temper – a trait which would be passed on to Rudy – Giovanni would also thrash the boy black and blue for the most trifling misdemeanour, then lock him in the darkened broom cupboard for hours on end, sometimes overnight. Solace would then come in the form of hugs and tidbits from his mother.

By the age of ten, Rudy had become completely out of control. Already tall and strong for his age, as well as hefty, he and his tomboy sister, Maria, headed a gang of thugs which soon became the scourge of the neighbourhood. Rudy would later attribute his waywardness to brotherly neglect, saying, 'Alberto was two years my senior and considered himself far too important to associate with me. Thus, Maria and I became partners in nefarious undertakings. I used to think that I led and Maria followed, but looking back with the wisdom of years, it would appear that Maria did the leading. At least she led me into a lot of difficulty!'

Rudy is said to have terrorised some of the weaker boys into submission by dangling them by the feet over a balcony, and threatening to drop them on to the concrete courtyard twenty feet below, unless they handed over their pocket money. He was particularly aggressive and troublesome if his father had beaten him the night before, and besides stealing from local shops he once attempted to drown a boy who had insulted Gabrielle in the town square fountain. He also had the habit of exposing himself in church, and it was this singularly despicable act which brought about the possibility of his expulsion from school. Before this could happen, however, in the spring of 1907, Giovanni Guglielmi died. For some months, he had been investigating a malaria epidemic which had been wiping out cattle in the district, and whilst trying to formulate a vaccine he succumbed to the disease himself. According to Rudy, his father's lasts words to him and Alberto were, 'My boys, love your mother – and above all, love your country.' Later, Rudy wrote in his memoirs, 'There was something very close and beautiful between my mother and my father. Theirs was one of the world's great loves.'

For Rudy, however, his father's death was a relief; now there would be no more beatings. Giovanni's brother moved into the house on the Via Roma for several months and helped out until Gabrielle had decided what to do with the business. Ultimately, she opted to sell the practice, and at the end of the year she and her children relocated to Taranto, where she had relatives. Rudy's reputation had preceded him, however, and as no ordinary school would accept him, Gabrielle enrolled him as a fee-paying student at the Collegio Dante Alighieri, the equivalent of a British grammar school. Here, he was only slightly less unruly than he had been in Castellaneta, though over the next eighteen months he made some progress with his studies. However, his appalling manners and his utter disregard for discipline got him into trouble on the day the Italian king, Victor Emmanual III, visited Taranto. Rudy had been confined to the dormitory after perpetrating some mischief or other, with strict instructions to stay put. As an extra precaution, he had been stripped to his underclothes, and had all his other clothes removed – not that this stopped him. 'I was far too inflamed by desire for this real contact with a real figure of achievement to be stopped by bolts and bars, or by the lack of garments,' he recalled, explaining how he had found a uniform several sizes too big for him and, as all the best horses had been spoken for, he had 'borrowed' a donkey from the stables and proudly ridden forth to salute his sovereign – holding up the royal cortège as it passed through the main street of the town. Victor Emmanuel may well have appreciated the gesture, but the Dante Alighieri's principal did not: Rudy was sent home in disgrace.

A few weeks later, Gabrielle enrolled Rudy at the Collegio della Sapienza, a military school for the sons of doctors, in Perugia. Here, though he did well in French, Spanish and mathematics, his main interests were football, dancing and learning to play the piano. 'It was called a "college of savants",' he recalled. 'Though what optimist or liar gave it that name I cannot imagine. For I was surely not a savant when I went in, and just as surely no savant when I came out.' Unhappy in Perugia, a few weeks before his fifteenth birthday, in 1910, he applied to join the Royal Naval Academy, and set off for Venice to sit his entrance examination. He passed with flying colours, only to fail the medical on account of his acute myopia, and his chest measurement which, even at 39 inches, was an inch short of the legal requirement.

For the first time in his life, Rudy doubted his manhood, setting a precedent which, in later years, would border on the paranoid. To his surprisingly primeval way of thinking, a man could not possibly be regarded as such unless he possessed the 'three basic components of manliness': a perfect, blemish-free, power-packed body; a cast iron constitution on land, sea and air; and a predilection for over-indulgence in exercise, eating, and sex! 'I wanted to die,' he said afterwards. 'I felt that I had drunk the very dregs of humiliation. I contemplated the canal . . . and might have accomplished the dread deed had it not been that another boy found himself in the same position. We found mutual consolation, and decided to go on with life . . .'

According to several of Rudy's friends, the 'mutual consolation' almost certainly refers to some sort of experimental homosexual involvement. This was not necessarily an actual affair, but one which at least enabled him to *determine* his sexuality – that is, if he had not already done so – and begin learning how to cope with it in a world which was almost totally homophobic. Even so, Rudy did not allow himself to get *too* attached to the young man, and his next move was to secure himself a place at the Royal Academy of Agriculture, near Genoa. Although he could do nothing about his eyesight other than wear spectacles – something his vanity would *never* have allowed – he did begin weight-lifting and working out in the Academy's gymnasium, and quickly developed a powerful physique. By the time he was eighteen and standing his full height of 5 feet 11 inches, Rudy tipped the scales at 180 pounds.

Although he did well at the Agricultural Academy, emerging from his studies with a diploma which would, if he so wished, enable him to pursue a career in scientific farming, Rudy was still not sure what to do with his life. Besides football and body-building, he spent much of his time dreaming of what life must be like in America. His father had left him a sizeable inheritance, but he could not touch this until he was twenty-one, so he pestered his mother to advance him some of the money to finance a trip to New York. Gabrielle flatly refused to have anything to do with this idea, but she did suggest a compromise. Because Rudy had done so well in his studies, she agreed to personally finance a month-long trip to Paris where, she reasoned, as well as visiting some of her relatives, he would also pick up a little culture and lose his rough edge, maybe sow a few wild oats, but above all forget about his infatuation with America.

Paris proved a revelation for Rudy's rebellious and bohemian spirit. He never looked up his relatives and, only interested in the city's seamier side, eschewed the wealth of tourist attractions for spit-and-sawdust establishments such as the Alcazar and the Jockey Club, and the more upmarket Concert-Damia in Montmartre. Although he may not have known initially that these catered for an almost exclusive homosexual clientele, once he discovered this fact, he visited them time and time again.

Sex, however, was the last thing on Rudy's mind when he was at the Concert-Damia, founded by the former dancer who was by this time starting out on a new, fabulous career as France's greatest *chanteuse-réaliste*, a position she would retain until the early-forties. In 1910, three years before her meeting with Valentino, Damia had created the *valse chaloupée*, or the apache, as it was known in England and America, with Max Dearly. Rudy first saw it performed at the Concert-Damia by the husband and wife act, Martin et Coco, and one evening after the pair had come off the stage, he marched up to their table and asked them if they would teach him the routine *they* had perfected! Impressed by the young man's audacity, Martin readily agreed.

The apache was an impassioned piece in which traditional dance steps gave way to sensual body movements, and of course it perfectly suited Rudy's already potent virility and his leanings towards sado-masochism. The scenario is a low dive in Paris, where several customers are clustered around the bar. The *fille de joie* enters, hoists up her skirt, and tucks the night's takings into the top of her stocking just as the *voyou* comes in. He looks menacing and, drawing the knife from his belt, he grabs the girl and demands the money. When she refuses, he thrashes her. Beating her fists against his chest, she tries to get away and he swings her around and flings her to the floor like a rag. He pulls her to her feet and they dance a little. She attempts to get away again, and he tosses her over his shoulder, then under his legs. Again they dance, then she slaps him, and knees him between the legs. This infuriates him beyond belief . . . grasping an ankle and an arm, he spins her around and around in circles, up and down, missing the floor by a hair's breadth, and this time when he lets her go she crashes into the bar, scattering the customers. Finally, tossing her over his shoulder and sticking the knife between his teeth, he carts her off to face her fate, whatever this may be!

Rudy learned the apache quickly, and excelled at it, so much so that within the week, when Martin et Coco announced that they were leaving Paris to tour the provinces, Rudy was offered their spot at the Concert-Damia. Circumstances, however, prevented him from accepting the engagement, for also appearing on the bill was the forty-three-year old chansonnier, Claude Rambeau, who suddenly developed a crush on Rudy.

Rudy became so confused by his sexuality, unable to choose between the still-handsome Rambeau and the somewhat sluttish Coco – with whom he had experienced an erection whilst rehearsing the apache – that the virulently homophobic Martin attempted a 'cure' by loaning Rudy his wife for the night. What had happened on the dance floor, however, failed to take place in the bedroom. Fleeing from Coco with his virginity still intact, Rudy had let Rambeau have his way with him, though if what he recounted to Chaw Mank is anything to go by, this first sexual encounter with a man was not much to write home about:

> He had kept drinking all night, because once he had found out that it did not hurt as much as he had feared, he had become bored with it all. Claude had been at him until nearly dawn . . . Back in his room, [Rudy] had spent several minutes in front of the mirror accusing himself of unnatural acts, obscenities and eternal persecution, but he had failed to make himself feel humiliated or cheapened, to awaken any feelings of remorse or guilt. Neither had he, however, found a sexual nirvana.

Rudy had no hesitation, a few evenings later, when two young men closer to his own age – *and* Italian – visited the Concert-Damia. 'Abruptly, I became a mendicant who received scant favours,' he later confessed, and after spending the night with them, he bade Paris farewell and drove with them to Monte Carlo, where in the course of the next week he gambled and lost what little remained of the money given to him by his mother. Not to be daunted, Rudy 'earned' his ticket home by selling himself to a wealthy, middle-aged businessman – setting a precedent which would see him through the dark days of the not too distant future.

Upon his return to Taranto, Rudy finally succeeded in convincing his mother that, if she gave him his inheritance so that he could go off in search of his dream, this would prove cheaper than forking out for the rest of his education. This time, Gabrielle called a family meeting and it was decided, taking into account all the trouble Rudy had caused in the past, that it might not be a bad idea to get him out from under everybody's feet. In addition, he would not be totally isolated from the family whilst in New York; the Guglielmis had distant relatives who lived in the city's Italian quarter, off West 49th Street, and it was arranged that he should stay with them. Rudy's family even clubbed together to pay for his fare – but only one-way, and the very cheapest immigrant class at that. If he wanted to return to Italy – and most of them hoped never to see him again – then he would have to do so under his own steam. On 8 December 1913, with only his mother to accompany him to the railway station and shed tears at his departure, Rudy set off on the first leg of his journey to the docks at Hamburg. At dawn the next day, with his worldly possessions neatly packed in a battered old trunk, he set sail for New York on the *Cleveland*.

2
Beauty's Acknowledgement

'My ambitions vaulted high above the earth and fastened themselves to the immemorial stars. I wanted fame and I wanted LOVE! I shall never go home, I said to myself, until I can go home SOMEBODY!'

Rudy could not have arrived in New York at a worse time or under less favourable circumstances. He had spent the greater part of the voyage below deck, playing poker, but repeating the bad luck he had experienced earlier in Monte Carlo, he had lost every last cent of his travelling allowance to cardsharps. Therefore, because he had been unable to settle his bill for on-board expenses, the purser had impounded his luggage.

It was two days before Christmas, bitterly cold, and pouring with rain. Contrary to his admissions to the press some years later, however, Rudy did not arrive in the United States a pauper. His mother had transferred $4,000 to Brown Brothers Bank on Wall Street, besides paying for his travelling clothes: a fine blue serge suit and matching flat cap, two white shirts and a V-necked pullover, assorted ties and underwear, and a pair of strong brogues. What Gabrielle had not reckoned on was the cold, and Rudy had kept warm whilst at sea by wrapping newspapers next to his chest, under his vest. One of the first things he bought in New York, after spending eight desperate hours finding the bank and returning to the ship to pay the purser and reclaim his trunk, was a thick overcoat.

Although he spoke passable French and Spanish, Rudy knew only a few very basic phrases in English, yet he had made up his mind before leaving Taranto that he would not be staying anywhere near New York's Italian quarter, where he assumed his relatives would only delight in relaying details of his every movement back to his family in Italy. He had slightly amended his plans, however, whilst aboard the *Cleveland*, having been befriended by a young Italian couple – most likely the same couple who appear in the photographs, taken on the ship, which turned up some years after Valentino's death. They had given him the address of an Italian family, the Giolottis, who ran a restaurant and rented out rooms. The only snag was that this was still on West 49th Street, though when Rudy saw how *long* the streets were in New York, he assumed that his relatives would never find him ... not that he imagined they would even try.

Never one to do things by halves, Rudy rented a furnished suite from the Giolottis, albeit a small one, comprising one bedroom, a bathroom and a sitting room. His first weeks in this strange new environment were understandably miserable – not on account of language problems, as has been stated, but because he was so lonely at a time when he had been used to being surrounded by dozens of Guglielmis who had flocked to his mother's house each festive season. This changed, however, in the new year. Rudy had his agricultural diploma and a letter of introduction to the Commissioner of Immigration, two documents which would almost certainly have guaranteed him work as a landscape gardener, but because he had money in the bank, he was not in any particular hurry to tie himself down when there was so much to see and explore. He loved riding the subway, eating hamburgers and chewing gum – such things were as yet unheard of in Italy – and he spent hours looking around the big department stores, the likes of which he had never imagined. By night he frequented the Continental-style dance clubs and cafés, such as Bustanoby's, where the staff and most of the customers were French, a language he could at least converse in.

In those days Bustanoby's was a meeting place for professional *bon-vivants*, mostly bisexual gigolos who were perfectly willing to sleep with anyone so long as the price was right – and with one another when there were no takers. Among such individuals were Counts Otto and Alexandre Salm, who with their society pal, Georges Ragni, very quickly inducted the inquisitive Italian into the world of *thés-dansants*, tangos and paid-for sex. Alexandre Salm, then in his late-twenties, had formerly been the lover of the famous tango-singer, Carlos Gardel, and it was this and the fact that Salm was reputedly the foremost exponent of the dance which precipitated Rudy into having an affair with him. For the time being, he was not interested in selling his body to the highest bidder. 'I finally pinned Alex to the wall one day and told him that I would never let him go until he had taught me the tango,' he wrote in his diary.

Alexandre Salm would have done anything to hang on to the most beautiful man he had ever seen – even when Rudy demanded that, in order for him to get used to dancing the tango in public, their first lesson should take place in front of the ape-house, at the Bronx Zoo! What the Frenchman did not reckon on was Rudy's almost uncanny knack of picking up even the most complicated routine in a matter of hours. Within days, *Rodolpho Guglielmi* had become the best tango-dancer in New York, and Alexandre Salm had been unceremoniously dispensed with as a teacher *and* a lover.

Rudy's outings with his rich society friends had severely depleted his inheritance, and he now realised that he would have to begin looking for a job. To cut down on his expenses, he moved out of the Giolotti's apartment block and took a room in a boarding house where *English* was the only language spoken. Again, he learned quickly, though he would always speak the language with a marked accent, and a few weeks later, armed with his diploma and letter of introduction, he went to see the Commissioner of Immigration. Here, he was in luck. Cornelius Bliss, the millionaire, had just moved into his newly-built mansion in Jericho, Long Island, and he was looking for a landscape gardener to supervise the laying out of his grounds in the Italian style.

Rudy was but one of many applicants interviewed by Bliss for the position, and he was hardly qualified to take on the responsibility of head gardener. However, the tycoon was a 'connoisseur' of good-looking young men, and with his recently acquired moustache Rudy looked a good deal older than eighteen. Not only did he get the job, Bliss also allowed him to live rent-free, in a modest garret over the stables.

In Jericho, Rudy never got around to doing much gardening. The grounds were frozen solid, so whilst awaiting the thaw he helped feed the horses and cleaned out the stables, one job that he considered *way* beneath him. Cornelius Bliss never allowed his staff to ride the horses, a rule which Rudy completely ignored – though when his employer observed how well he could handle even the most stubborn beast, he relaxed the rule. The last straw came, however, when Rudy went joy-riding on the carpenter's motorcycle, wrapping it around a tree and walking away from the scene unscathed, but writing off the machine. Bliss, who had made the mistake of getting involved with Rudy, was terrified of firing him in case he opened his mouth, so instead he told him that his wife had changed her mind about the Italian gardens – she now wanted a golf course.

Rudy's recompense was a handsome pay-off from Bliss, and a letter of recommendation for a job on another estate in New Jersey. When this turned out to be picking bugs off rose bushes, a task he found more contemptible than mucking out horses, he stuck it out for the obligatory first two weeks to get his wages, before returning to Long Island to give Cornelius Bliss a piece of his mind, threatening to expose their relationship unless Bliss did something about his plight. The millionaire used his considerable influence to secure Rudy an apprenticeship with the New York Park Commission as an apprentice landscape gardener. And, as an incentive to ensuring Rudy kept silent, he also agreed to pay him a generous monthly allowance.

The prospects for the new position were good: at the end of a one-month trial period, Rudy would sit a routine examination, and if he passed this, his name would be added to the City's permanent payroll. Rudy worked hard and passed the examination, only to be informed that the City would not be able to take him on full-time until he had become an American citizen – a procedure which would take another five years.

Furious, and perhaps with good reason, Rudy vented his spite on Cornelius Bliss, but this time his bluff was called. Bliss calmly warned him that although a scandal such as the one Rudy was threatening would almost certainly ruin him, the repercussions on an under-aged, immigrant male prostitute would also be dire. He told Rudy to expect immediate incarceration in one of the state's most notorious jails, amongst every type of hardened, desperate criminal while the authorities bided their time acquiring a deportation order.

Rudy returned to New York. He had virtually no money, and he was compelled to do whatever he felt was necessary to afford a decent meal and a bed for the night – emptying dustbins, sweeping yards, washing dishes at a cheap restaurant, polishing cars. The first time he could not afford a room, he slept in a hostel for down-and-outs, an experience which so sickened him that he spent the next few nights, fortunate that the weather was clement, on a public bench in Central Park. His clothes had started to wear out and the more unkempt he became, the less fussy he became about his choice in bedfellows. And yet his family back in Italy knew nothing about his struggle, for he had filched a quantity of headed notepaper from the Waldorf Astoria, so as far as Gabrielle was concerned, *this* was where her son was staying.

As a last resort, Rudy solicited help from Alexandre Salm, who was understandably reluctant to have anything to do with him, at first. In any case, this was September 1914, and with the war raging in Europe, Salm's allowance had been cut off and he too was close to the breadline. He was, however, reminded of all the money and favours Rudy had lavished on *him*, not so long before, so he loaned Rudy the use of a razor and his bathroom, gave him a little cash, and allowed him to stay the night.

The next day, Salm introduced Rudy to his friend, the French music-hall star, Jules Raucourt, who, having enjoyed considerable success in Europe occasionally partnering Gaby Deslys – in 1915, the pair would triumph in London with *Rosy Rapture* – was about to open on Broadway. Raucourt made it very clear, however, that he would only help Rudy in return for sex. The young man obliged – there was no denying that the entertainer was almost as handsome as he was, and he had already developed a passion for Frenchmen which would last the rest of his life. Raucourt took him to one of the best tailors in town, and when Rudy studied his reflection in his benefactor's bedroom mirror, and observed how clean and tidy he looked, he made up his mind that he would *never* submit to manual work again.

A few days later, Rudy read in a newspaper that Maxim's, the famous restaurant, were looking for 'white-button boys' – lithe young dancers who earned huge amounts of money by partnering the wealthy women who attended the establishment's afternoon *thés-dansants* either alone, or with escorts who could not dance. Rudy decided that he had nothing to lose and he went for an audition. Luck was on his side. The Master of Ceremonies was a former head waiter from Bustanoby's, and having witnessed the effect the young Italian had had on his clientele, he engaged him on a trial basis for two afternoons a week. Rudy was warned, however, that his activities with partners should not progress beyond the dance floor, and that he should refrain from making eyes at their escorts. For this, once he had completed his 'apprenticeship', he would be paid $20 a week, he would be allowed to keep any tips, and all his meals and a room would be provided free of charge by Maxim's.

For a month, Rudy supplemented his income by working as an errand boy for the Giolottis' restaurant – a job which saw him delivering considerably more than pizzas if any of the clients were attractive and sufficiently well-heeled to pay for whatever else was on offer. Such was his stamina, that he was capable of 'servicing' several customers each evening, and still having enough energy left to dance the tango at Bustanoby's until the early hours of the morning.

For Rudy, the irrepressible flirt, Maxim's was *the* mecca for easy pickings. As with some of the great gay icons of the future – such as Johnnie Ray and Liberace – middle-aged women in particular found him irresistible. On first exploring the New York dance scene he had been astonished by the openness and independence enjoyed by the city's female population. In Taranto, only the wrong kind of woman ventured out on her own after dark, or frequented bars, and although he had seen women selling sex on street corners before, he had never imagined that somewhere in the world there were places where a *man* could be paid for having fun. If, indeed, sex *could* be considered wholesome between an eighteen-year old youth and a sixty-year old matron, he reminded himself. He soon forgot his misgivings about this when he realised how wealthy some of the women were, shoving one and five-dollar bills into his top pocket whilst they were swirling around the dance floor ... and this was *before* the real action began! 'I had to *learn* how to dance,' Rudy told Chaw Mank. 'But fucking came naturally, and as I was being constantly reminded how good I was in that department, I milked it for all it was worth!'

After his first month at Maxim's, Rudy was able to afford a two-roomed apartment on the more opulent East 61st Street, and a wardrobe which might have been the envy of any matinee idol. Here, for thirty minutes each morning, he would sit in front of his dressing-table mirror, preening himself and practising the infamous, myopic stare which would send shivers down the spines of his admirers and bring scoffs from detractors.

Much as he would have loved to have danced the Turkey Trot or the apache and really shown his clients what he could do, Rudy's speciality was the tango, and when someone complimented him on his small, perfectly-formed tight buttocks, he exaggerated this part of his anatomy by wearing a corset. Next, he had the waist of his trousers taken in by two inches at the back, 'so that everything was moved forward and up', shocking many women, who nevertheless still fought amongst themselves to be partnered by the man who had already earned himself the nickname, 'The Italian Stallion', and who exuded charm by *always* stooping to kiss the lady's hand after he had escorted her back to her seat.

Such was Rudy's popularity that the manager of Maxim's supplied him with a gramophone and a selection of Carlos Gardel recordings, and for a percentage of the profits he was allowed to give private dancing lessons, on a one-to-one basis, when the establishment was closed. On more than one occasion he got to dance the tango with Harry Pilcer, then the most famous dancer in America, and a man who was almost as handsome as he was. Pilcer, then aged twenty-eight, later confessed that Rudy had asked him, point-blank, to go to bed with him, but that he had refused because at the time he had been enjoying a secret liaison with the then little-known Al Jolson. Rudy was, however, granted a kiss and offered some sound advice ... to shave off his ungainly moustache! Rudy did this, and he also copied Pilcer's 'truc' of exaggerating his staggering profile by sleeking back his thick dark hair with a liberal application of brilliantine. One week later, the penultimate stage of Rudy's metamorphosis occurred when an admirer complained that the name Rodolpho Guglielmi was too much of a mouthful. Drawing upon his impressive array of titles, he became Rudolfo di Valentina.

In June 1915, a few weeks after his twentieth birthday, Rudy embarked on his first *real* love affair with a woman, as opposed to the hurried, paid-for sex sessions with either gender, which usually filled in the two-hour gap before the end of the tea-dance and the start of the client's evening schedule.

Some of Hollywood's biggest stars would frequently drop in on a Maxim's tea-dance when they were working in New York. Rudy had already partnered Lillian Gish, Constance Talmadge, Mary Pickford and even Marie Dressler, treating each of them with the same courtesy as his society regulars, but showing no preference because of their status. Mae Murray, the *coqueluche* or darling of the largely closeted homosexual community, had gone out of her way to befriend him, initially so that she could boast to friends of her prowess in having bedded and, she claimed, 'reformed' the young Italian. However once she had become aware that Rudy was capable of making love to either sex with equal passion, she had begun respecting him. It was Mae Murray who had earlier introduced Rudy to the heart-throb actor, William Boyd, a man with an alleged loathing of homosexuals until Rudy had charmed him into spending at least one night with him ... and now, it was through her that he got to know the wealthy, very beautiful heiress, Bianca de Saulles.

Around five years Rudy's senior, Bianca Errazuriz had fallen for the rugged, virile ex-Yale quarterback turned businessman, Jack de Saulles, five years earlier when he had visited her native Chile, and after a whirlwind romance the pair had married in Paris. Their marriage, however, had begun to disintegrate as soon as they returned from their honeymoon on account of de Saulles' thuggish behaviour in the bedroom and his insatiable appetite for chorus girls.

Upon hearing some of these stories, Rudy immediately decided that he would become Bianca's knight in shining armour and rescue her from her 'louse of a husband', from whom she had already started divorce proceedings. He began monitoring de Saulles' movements, but because he could not afford a private detective, personally followed him on his romantic assignations ... unaware that de Saulles, who had both the police department and the vice-squad in his employ, had hired someone to keep tabs on *him*.

Rudy's relationship with Bianca soon began affecting his work at Maxim's, particularly as she was now spending virtually every afternoon at the establishment. Those bejewelled matrons for whom a twirl around the dance floor had suddenly taken on a new meaning did not take kindly to some dusky foreigner hogging their man – that *Rudy* was a foreigner, of course, was immaterial! – and they complained to the management. The house-rules stated that there was to be no over-fraternisation with the customers or accepting tips in excess of five dollars. Rudy was found guilty on both counts and reprimanded in front of his fellow button-boys, which, of course, he took as an affront to his dignity. He told Mae Murray that he would begin looking for a new job at once.

Mae Murray, who was probably feeling responsible for Rudy's plight, salvaged Rudy's badly dented pride a few evening later by introducing him to the exhibition dancer, Bonnie Glass. With her partner, the outrageous, priggish Clifton Webb, Bonnie had become the toast of New York's elite dance-society, but in July 1916 she was left in the lurch when, after a fierce argument with Webb, he stormed out of her life to make an even more successful assault on the stage, and later in film comedies. Only days earlier, Glass and Webb had been booked to open at the New York Roof, one of the city's most exclusive nightclubs and Bonnie told Rudy, whilst they were dancing the tango, that if he agreed to partner her, she would pay him $50 a week. This was less than he was making at Maxim's, but at least he would be performing before a paying audience and, Bonnie added, immediately after the New York Roof there was to be a season at the Winter Garden, followed by a summer tour. Rudy did not take much persuading, though he might not have been too pleased had he known that the key rule in Bonnie Glass's book had always been that her partners should be gay, minimising the risk of physical involvement. In addition, he believed that now was as good a time as any to be seen in the company of another woman; Bianca had finally filed for divorce, and he was terrified that there might be repercussions. He had already been heavied by one of Jack de Saulles' henchmen and told what would happen to him, should he continue the affair.

The di Valentina-Glass partnership was an instant success, and after wowing New York audiences for three months, the pair were offered an all-expenses tour of nightclubs along the Eastern seaboard. The programme included a selection of cakewalks, waltzes and foxtrots, and of course, the tango. The tour culminated with a 'command' performance at the White House before President Wilson – this was filmed, and the fragment which survives, of the pair dancing the apache, is thought to be Valentino's earliest appearance on celluloid.

On the strength of her association with Rudy, Bonnie Glass opened two clubs of her own in New York – the Montmartre, in the basement of the former Boulevard Café, and Chez Fisher, on 55th Street. Their partnership ended soon afterwards, however, when she retired from the stage to marry the millionaire, Ben Ali Haggin.

Each week, whilst he had been touring with Bonnie Glass, Rudy had written to his mother in Taranto, always enclosing what few dollars he could spare. Italy had now entered the war, and there was a severe food shortage. He had even begun taking flying lessons, declaring that if the crunch came, he would return home and enlist in the flying corps. He shelved the idea, however, when he became amorously involved with another trainee pilot, a good-looking, twenty-three-year old aspiring actor named Norman Kaiser who, as Norman Kerry, would enjoy considerable success in films playing opposite Mary Pickford.

Meanwhile, Rudy was invited to partner another hugely successful exhibition dancer, Joan Sawyer, and even feigned having an affair with her – ignoring her frequent homophobic outbursts – hoping to extricate himself from the de Saulles divorce case. He then hit upon the audacious idea of introducing Sawyer to Jack de Saulles – via an intermediary, of course – and even arranged for witnesses to state, under oath, that the pair had been conducting a clandestine affair! Incredibly, the ruse worked, and Bianca cited Sawyer as co-respondent, though when the dancer discovered what Rudy had done, she dissolved their partnership and saw to it that he was subpoenaed to give evidence.

Rudy's machinations, not to mention his perjury at telling the court that he too had several times seen Sawyer and de Saulles in compromising situations, enabled Bianca to obtain a divorce, on grounds of adultery, on 15 July 1916. The understandably irate de Saulles, however, wasted little time in exacting his revenge, particularly as his own investigation had unearthed a few unsavoury revelations about Rudy's past. It was bad enough his wife having conducted an affair with an Italian, de Saulles declared to all and sundry, but the fact that she had cheated on him with a known 'pederast' was a gross affront to his own virility. Therefore, when de Saulles discovered that Rudy had reverted to his old ways by visiting an apartment-house owned by a Mrs Georgia Thym – one which supplied prostitutes of both sexes and, it was alleged, also traded in white slavery – he informed his friends in the vice-squad.

Mrs Thym's house was raided within the hour, and though Rudy's imminent fame would result in the 'loss' of the subsequent police report, details of the raid have survived in print. 'Many persons of means, principally social climbers, had been blackmailed after discreet visits to [Mrs Thym's] house', declared the *New York Times*, listing several names, including, 'One handsome fellow who goes by the name of Rudolpho Guglielmi, and who calls himself a marquis.' The press also delivered their first attack on Rudy's manhood – revealing to readers whom they knew would be 'shocked' that when arrested, he had been wearing 'the latest ornament of effeminacy amongst men' ... a wristwatch!

Whether Rudy was buying or selling at Mrs Thym's has never

been established, though he did spend two days in the notorious Tombs Prison on a licentious behaviour charge – an indictment which almost certainly would have led to his deportation, had the police known that he had been visiting the brothel since April, when he had still been a minor.

This incident effectively ended Rudy's relationship with Bianca de Saulles, and he marked the occasion by inviting Norman Kerry to move into his East 61st Street apartment. There was another reason for this besides the obvious one – although he had returned to the *thés-dansants* and was giving the occasional exhibition performance, without a big-name partner Rudy was not making enough money to pay the rent. Kerry too, at this stage of his career, was earning very little.

Salvation for both men came with the grim tidings, on 3 August 1917, that Bianca de Saulles had been arrested after shooting her husband dead during a fracas over who should have custody of their child. By sheer coincidence, Norman Kerry had recently been offered a substantial part in *The Masked Model*, a musical revue which, after a successful season in New York, was about to tour across the country to San Francisco. Kerry was so infatuated with Rudy that he had seriously considered turning the part down rather than leave him behind, but now an ideal situation had presented itself. Terrified of being summoned as a witness for Bianca's trial and having his past raked up again, Rudy had decided to relocate to California, where an Italian-run vineyard was taking on large numbers of expatriate labourers.

In desperation, Kerry told Rudy that there was another solution: the producer of *The Masked Model* was desperately in need of two dancers for the chorus. Rudy went along to an audition, and was promptly engaged on a salary of $75 a week. Despite the enthusiasm of the New York critics, however, the revue attracted poor reviews out in the provinces, and closed in Ogden, Utah, leaving most of the players stranded without means of financial support.

Norman Kerry was distraught. He had just enough money to pay his train fare back to New York where, he declared, he would find himself a regular job and forget all about acting. Rudy persuaded him to change his mind and take the train with him in the opposite direction. The Californian weather was reputed to be glorious, he argued, and working in a vineyard would do them both a power of good, and maybe add a few pounds of muscle to his lover's lanky frame! Yet no sooner had the pair arrived in San Francisco than they learned that another theatre company was auditioning for bit-parts and dancers for the musical-comedy, *Nobody Home*. Both men were successful, and though this show also folded after just sixteen performances, with tremendous luck they got into the chorus of *The Passing Show*, then in the middle of a sell-out tour, and about to embark for Los Angeles. Its leading players were Al Jolson ... and Harry Pilcer.

Rudy could not have been more thrilled. Since dancing the tango with the ethereal-looking Pilcer at Maxim's, Rudy had been longing to meet him again and now, despite Norman Kerry, he became preoccupied with having an affair with Pilcer. Sadly, his attempts at seduction would only lead to disappointment. Although a promiscuous bisexual in his younger days – his conquests had included the then-unknown Mae West, Nora Bayes, and even Al Jolson who, incredibly, would always get away with singing Pilcer's signature tune, 'I'm Just Wild About Harry' – Pilcer had recently flung himself into what would be remembered as one of the most volatile showbusiness love-affairs of the first half of this century. In short, he was besotted with the mercurial French star Gaby Deslys who, it was rumoured, would be joining the cast of *The Passing Show* at the end of the year.

In Los Angeles, Rudy and Kerry moved into the Alexandria Hotel, an establishment much-favoured by the acting fraternity, and as yet one which tended not to frown upon two young men sharing the same, one-bed room. The two men also dropped out of *The Passing Show*. Attending his first Hollywood audition, Norman Kerry was hired to star opposite Mary Pickford in a film, and Rudy, having been twice rejected by Harry Pilcer, decided not to tempt emotional turmoil by working with him.

Encouraged by Kerry, who assured him that he had absolutely nothing to lose, Rudy began joining the queues which formed every morning outside the gates of the film studios, hoping to be taken on as an extra. Most evenings he could be found in downtown dance-halls, earning tips by partnering wealthy socialites, or giving the occasional exhibition. His first big break occurred when he met the director Emmett Flynn, who hired him as a 'crowd-player' for First National's *Alimony*, starring Josephine Whittel and Lois Wilson. Flynn paid him $15 for three days' work, and in the film – which is mediocre, at best – Rudy is seen very briefly in two ballroom scenes, dancing the tango.

It was a start, though for Rudy, who had hoped to follow Kerry's example and be offered a romantic lead immediately, the next two months were disappointing. Emmett Flynn told him that, as most directors would consider him too foreign-looking, he would rarely progress beyond bit-parts as the heavy, or a lounge lizard. Norman Kerry, on the other hand, was offered $100 a week by Pickford Productions to appear in *The Little Princess*, but when Mary Pickford awarded him a rise in salary halfway through shooting, Rudy became so incensed that he came close to ending their relationship. Only the fact that he was entirely dependent on Kerry prevented this, though he did march up to Pickford one day and *demand* to be told why Norman Kerry, who was far less good-looking than he was, could be earning so much when he himself was virtually broke. The actress known as 'The World's Sweetheart' shrugged her shoulders and retorted haughtily, 'Keep sending in the pictures, pretty boy, and who knows? *Somebody* might want you!'

Mary Pickford's acid comments and Rudy's jealousy of his lover's success did push him in another direction, however. He had become pally with several of the extras he had met on the First National lot, including the then unknown Rod La Roque – and the twenty-three-year old Richard Barthelmess, the man with whom he now began cheating on Norman Kerry. After years as a child star in the theatre, Barthelmess had been given his Hollywood break in 1916 in two films – *War Brides* and *Snow White* – and at a party after a private showing of the latter, Mae Murray, who appears to have had a brief fling with him, had introduced him and his female escort to Rudy as 'Snow White and the Seven Inches'.

Many of these mostly kept young men were known to congregate at least once a week at the Torch Club, a former mansion house which possessed every facility that the closeted Hollywood gay could wish for. There were four scented 'bareback' pools, ten cocktail bars, and forty air-conditioned apartments where even the ugliest of patrons could realise their wildest sexual fantasies. Membership did not come cheap – between $100 and $1,000 a month, depending on whether one found one's own entertainment or selected from the large selection of well-endowed studs whose favours were listed alongside the prices on the menu. Rudy, who in those days was so poor yet willing to go a whole day without food so that he could purchase a shirt which had taken his fancy, had no difficulty getting into the Torch Club. The unsuspecting Norman Kerry was footing the bill.

Rudy's first visit to the Torch Club, accompanied by a blond actor referred to only as Rob, ended in humiliation. Obviously attracted to his hunky young escort, he allowed himself to be led into one of the numerous massage-rooms off the pool area, where he came face to face with one of the most unattractive directors in Hollywood. His name was Joe Maxwell, and Rudy later confessed to his friend Chaw Mank that Maxwell, squatting stark naked on a slab, had barked, 'Get down on your knees, pretty boy!' Whether Rudy complied is not known ... a few days later, however, Maxwell offered him $50 a week to play a 'new-style heavy' in *The Married Virgin*, a poor film which, on account of litigation between Maxwell and his cameraman, was not released until 1922. Then, allegedly so as not to offend Valentino in view of his unconsummated marriage, its title was changed to the only slightly less acerbic Frivolous Wives.The rushes for the film were seen by Emmett Flynn, who hired Rudy to play 'an Italian Bowery tough' in *Virtuous Sinners*. The stars of the film were Wanda Hawley ... and Norman Kerry. Again, the salary was only $50 a week, though Rudy was earning money most evenings, alternating between partnering Katherine Phelps at the Hotel Maryland, and Marjorie Tain at Watt's Tavern, an actors' watering-hole just outside Los Angeles.

The incident at the Torch Club had done nothing to curb Rudy's visits to the establishment, and over the next two years he would 'partake' of several future major Hollywood stars, including Gary Cooper, Charles Farrell, Milton Sills and Richard Arlen. Its most notorious feature was Room 23, a small suite which had a large two-way mirror on the ceiling over the bed, so that those clustered in the room above could spy on arguably the hottest show in town. It was the club's best-kept secret. First-time visitors, especially attractive ones, were usually told that Room 23 was the only one available that night, though when Rudy was informed that his 'debut performance' with Richard Barthelmess had been watched and accorded top marks, he demanded the suite time and time again. It is said that the most frequently-asked question of the Torch Club's studio-supplied doorman was, 'Will Rudy be *coming* tonight?' His nocturnal activities were, however, soon brought to the attention of the disapproving Norman Kerry: there was a furious quarrel, and Rudy left the Alexandria Hotel to move into a tiny apartment over a downtown café in Santa Monica.

Another Torch Club regular was Paul Powell, a director with Universal who paid Rudy $125 a week to appear in two films: *A Society Sensation* and *All Night*, both starring the fifteen-year old starlet, Carmel Myers. Production on these was hampered by the presence of Myers' domineering mother who, having heard of Rudy's alleged reputation, told Powell that she had no intention of allowing her little girl to be 'deflowered' by a foreigner. In fact, Myers was not as innocent as everyone assumed. She pestered Rudy to have sex with her, and became unpleasant towards him when he refused, even going so far as to have the director change one of the key scenes in *A Society Sensation*. Instead of Rudy rescuing *her* from drowning, *she* saves him, an act which would have his detractors sharpening their quills upon the film's re-release a few years later.

Rudy's unexpected rise in salary enabled him to put down a deposit on his first car, a $750 second-hand Mercer which he hoped might give him a certain prestige. It did not. His next two parts saw him dancing the apache in *A Rogue's Romance*, and most of the footage he shot for *The Homebreaker* with Dorothy Dalton ended up on the cutting-room floor.

It was now that Mae Murray re-entered Rudy's life, entirely by chance, when she saw him dancing one evening at the Vernon Club. Rudy had recently transferred here because of the women he partnered were infinitely wealthier than those at the Hotel Maryland. Murray was a regular visitor to the club with her husband, Robert Z Leonard, who directed most of her films. A slim, vivacious blonde, famous for her 'bee-stung' lips, she was nevertheless a difficult, highly-strung woman whose status between 1917–30 as one of the world's highest-paid stars enabled her to demand and get her own way, without compromise, in everything she did. Fanatical about dancing, she always had an orchestra close at hand so that she could get the 'feel' of her scenes, although they were silent, of course, or a gramophone next to which there would be a pile of Carlos Gardel or jazz records. She also insisted that a dance-sequence be featured in every one of her films, sometimes at the most ridiculous, inopportune moment. Therefore, when Mae Murray told her husband that she wanted Rudolpho di Valentina to appear in her next feature, *The Big Little Person*, the under-the-thumb director – who could not stand 'that damned faggot gigolo', as he always referred to Rudy – had little choice but to hire him.

Mae Murray was so infatuated with Rudy that even before shooting began on *The Big Little Person* she had ordered Robert Z Leonard to sign him up for her next film, *The Delicious Little Devil*, in which he played Jimmie Calhoun, the tough but likeable son of an Irish millionaire. It was whilst he was making this film that Rudy met a twenty-year old hustler named José-Ramon Samaniegos, of whom more later – but if the sexual chemistry *was* there, it was tempered momentarily in favour of the ravenous Murray, who was nightly picking up the tab at glitter-palaces such as Branstatters, and the Ship's Café in Santa Monica ... besides paying him to have sex with her in his cramped apartment each afternoon after the shoot. What *she* did not know was that during his lunch-breaks Rudy was also 'servicing' Dorothy Gish, with whom he had been contracted to appear in D W Griffith's *Out Of Luck* – *and* still spending his nights with Richard Barthelmess! Robert Z Leonard, though, *was* told of the lusty young Italian's affair with his wife, and decided to confront him about it, boasting to friends that he would shame him into leaving Hollywood for good. In fact, it was Rudy who humiliated *him* ... by describing in the minutest detail all that he and Mae Murray had done in boudoirs, dressing rooms, and even in the back of her car.

There should have been a third film with Mae Murray, but for once Leonard stood up to his wife – even though the monstrous row they had over Rudy signalled the beginning of the end, so far as their marriage was concerned – and Rudy found himself out of work and counting the pennies again. The first casualty of his renewed misfortune was his greatest possession apart from his wardrobe – his Mercer. Because he could not now afford to keep up with the payments, the car was repossessed by the finance company, an event which broke Rudy's heart but which brought a huge sigh of relief from Hollywood's motorists: Rudolpho di Valentina may not yet have been a big name in movies, but he was the film-capital's most notorious road-hog!

Adding to his misery, a few days after losing his car, a letter arrived from Taranto informing Rudy that his mother had died of cancer, aged only forty-nine. He was devastated. Only recently he had begun making arrangements for Gabrielle to emigrate to America, and he later said that had he been aware of her illness, he would have returned to Italy to care for her. It was for *exactly* this reason that Gabrielle had kept her condition to herself. Rudy's letters home had been regular, but misleading, telling his mother how well he was doing, of how he had a beautiful car and a luxurious apartment. How much of this she had actually believed was another matter, but Gabrielle had certainly nurtured no desire to drag her son away from his new life to one of renewed drudgery in post-war Italy.

The sad news left Rudy at a low ebb, and he fell victim to the Spanish flu epidemic which had ravaged almost the whole world, claiming even more casualties than the war. Because he had a horror of doctors – he had never taken a pill or been prescribed medicine in his life – he believed self-cure to be the best remedy, but his reluctance to undergo treatment could have cost him his life.

3
Vanity's Excuse

'It is my great ambition to make pictures that will constitute great screen art.'

Rudy's 'type' was still working against him in the autumn of 1919, when the legendary D W Griffith began casting for *Scarlet Days*. Dorothy Gish was to play the lead, but Griffith had tremendous difficulty trying to find someone to play her lover in the film – a Spaniard. When Gish suggested Rudy, however, the director would have nothing to do with him, declaring that he looked 'too foreign' ... then promptly hiring the American star, Richard Barthelmess! Rudy *was* allowed to watch, but he was unimpressed by the pair's on-screen clinch, and quipped, 'They could have done better than that. I should know because I've had them both!' He was, however, hurt by such blatant prejudice, and made his feelings known to the director, whose compromise was to pay him $100 a week to partner his mistress, Carol Dempster, in an exhibition prologue when another of his films, *The Greatest Thing In Life*, opened for a season at the Los Angeles Auditorium. Most of the critics declared that the dancing had been far superior to the film; ironically a few weeks later, Rudy and Dempster danced at the premiere of *Scarlet Days*.

For Rudy, two more bit-parts followed: *Eyes Of Youth*, with Clara Kimball Young, and *The Cheater*, his debut venture for MGM, which led to him giving his first press-conference. Rudy loved nothing more than talking about himself, though he was a great fabricator of stories and often told completely different versions of the same anecdote, sometimes in the same day. And, of course, had the press been made aware of the real Rudy, he would quickly have been hounded out of Hollywood.

Most of the reporters who interviewed Rudy were of the opinion that he was a sensitive, likeable if morose young man, but one with very little sense of humour, completely unpredictable, often scathing towards the Hollywood society which he considered to be inarticulate and insincere, and above all arrogant. This latter trait was, of course, subterfuge for his tremendous insecurity, at least in his formative days in Hollywood. He had left Italy on the assumption that there would be no turning back, and though acting and dancing had not been part of his original plan, the iron-clad determination had always been there to become *someone*. Now, he was convinced that he was well on his way. When a reporter asked him where he had lived before coming to Hollywood, he replied in broken English, 'Taranto, in Italy – a family palace!' Henceforth, he was able to reinvent his background far more efficiently than any Hollywood public-relations office. He had driven a 120 horsepower Fiat in a race between Naples and Rome, only to come a disappointing second! He had flown an aircraft for the US preparatory, which was at least partly true. He had written a screenplay, which may have been true. He had left the Perugia Military Academy with a Certificate of Distinction, which was a lie – he had been expelled for misconduct! And he had recently signed a contract which, he predicted, would bring him worldwide fame!

The film was *An Adventuress* starring Julian Eltinge, the most acclaimed female impersonator of his day, but all it brought Rudy was scorn. If this was the only kind of film he could be bothered to appear in, one critic declared after seeing a preview, then he might just as well kiss his Hollywood career goodbye. Fortunately, most of Rudy's fans never saw the film, which went out on limited release. When it was finally reissued in 1922 as *The Isle Of Love*, he had achieved his greatest goal elsewhere, and the press were only interested in another of its bit-players, Virginia Rappe, whose death the previous September, after the Fatty Arbuckle rape-orgy, had made headline news across the world.

It was at around this time that questions started being raised concerning Rudy's sexuality – or rather why, unlike the rest of the young-blood actors, he was never seen about town with a girl on his arm. He was criticised for his taste in clothes: brightly-hued shirts, hats and cravats and ivory cigarette-holders may have been regarded as the height of playboy sophistication in Mediterranean countries, the critics declared, but to wear them in Hollywood meant *only* one thing.

Rudy was also a member of the privileged Los Angeles Athletic Club, and it was here, in October 1919, that he met George O'Brien, a nineteen-year old budding actor from San Francisco. Tall, powerfully-built and devastatingly handsome, like Rudy, George was very much the sporting fanatic. At high school he had been top in his class at swimming, diving, football and basketball: he was also an expert oarsman and rider, and he excelled at lawn tennis. His biggest obsession, however, was boxing, a sport which he had learned during a recent stint with the American Navy, and which ostensibly led to him and Rudy becoming an item. Indeed, Rudy's and George O'Brien's fighting skills were *so* phenomenal that after seeing them together just once in the ring, the legendary Jack Dempsey offered to manage their careers, should they decide to turn professional. Rudy was too bitten by the acting bug to even consider such a dramatic change of direction, though George was tempted. Unfortunately, he was still legally a minor, and his plans were quickly scuppered by his mother who, for years, had been encouraging him to take up medicine.

Once Rudy had ascertained that George O'Brien was his 'type' – it is not known if the younger man had had any homosexual experiences before Rudy – he lost no time in taking him to the Torch Club, where for obvious reasons George was awarded the nickname, 'Big Swinger'. Rudy was apprehensive when George invited him to Sunday lunch with his parents: his father was San Francisco's Chief of Police! George insisted, however, and in years to come the O'Briens would proudly boast of how Valentino had been a regular visitor to their home. They were also *told*, in time, the truth about the young men's relationship, and what is more they are said to have reacted compassionately.

Shortly after becoming Rudy's lover, George O'Brien – whose seemingly endless list of talents also included photography – was taken on by Tom Mix as his second assistant cameraman. He later said he had found the work itself immensely rewarding, but that it had been an ordeal having to contend with the cowboy star's oversized ego and frequent tantrums. He therefore began working as a lifeguard, and most mornings before his shift could be seen sprinting with Rudy along the beach at Santa Monica – both men wearing skin-tight shorts which left absolutely nothing to the imagination. But if female admirers found themselves swooning over these handsome, extroverted slabs of perfectly-proportioned beefcake, their jealous escorts only sneered.

George O'Brien and Rudy were never faithful to one another, however, setting a precedent which would continue throughout both their lives. Both would enjoy numerous relationships at the same time, with lovers who for reasons of availability were strategically positioned across the United States and Europe, with absolutely no strings attached and, it would appear, no problems, despite the countless one-night stands and chance encounters dotted haphazardly between what George termed 'the serious stuff'.

It had always been Rudy's opinion that his personal life should remain his own affair, and though he often gave the impression that he was incredibly thick-skinned, he was effectively a sensitive man who quickly took offence. He was livid when the director, Douglas Gerrard – a man who, incredibly, would also become a lover – asked him point-blank if the rumours of his being a 'fairy' were true. He was equally perturbed by the fact that, in order to survive in a contrived environment where double standards were almost a way of life, one had to pretend to be something one could never be – as, indeed, Gerrard himself was doing at the time.

The last straw came when Alla Nazimova, MGM's biggest star at the time, threw a party at the Ship's Café to celebrate the completion of her latest film, *Stronger Than Death*. Hollywood's most notorious lesbian ever, who as an 'immigrant outsider' herself should have known better, behaved appallingly when Rudy arrived at the bash as the guest of the actress Dagmar Godowsky, screaming at the top of her voice in front of two hundred people, 'How *dare* you bring that gigolo, that *sodomite* into the presence of Nazimova?' Most of the guests at the party expected Rudy to at least stand his ground, though such was this woman's power that no one *ever* answered her back without fear of the severest reprisal. Unfortunately, he only made matters worse by suddenly bursting into tears and fleeing from the room.

Terrified that his reputation may have been reduced to tatters, Rudy submitted to the all too familiar 'normalisation' programme by accepting a more or less obligatory invitation to attend a party which Douglas Gerrard had arranged at the Sunset Boulevard home of the actress Pauline Frederick where, the director assured him, there would be dozens of beautiful girls from which he would be able to take his pick. Here, however, was the greatest irony of all – Pauline Frederick's friends were almost exclusively lesbian.

Still grieving for his mother, Rudy was in no mood for having fun, and he arrived at the party dressed from top to toe in black. He spent much of the evening sitting alone in a darkened corner of the sitting-room, ignoring everyone's pleas to join in with the festivities which had spilled out on to the verandah and into the garden ... until he was befriended by one of the guests, who was doubling as a waitress. Jean Acker was a boyish but pretty actress-dancer with Metro, and though she and Rudy were as unalike as chalk and cheese, she did manage to drag him out of his doldrums with her witty, sparkling conversation.

Rudy was at an all-time low. 'I was unutterably lonely,' he said afterwards, 'I longed for a great and real friend.' Acker had only recently broken up with another actress, though Rudy did not know this at the time, and he allowed himself to fall for her. So too she seemed to fall in love with him, and over the next week the pair were inseparable. Then, on their eighth day together, he hired a horse and trap and took her for an evening drive along the coast, where he asked her to marry him in the romantic moonlight setting.

From this point, events moved very quickly. Richard Rowland, the head of Hollywood Metro, was about to leave for New York to take over as the company's chief there, and a farewell party had been arranged for the following evening. Douglas Gerrard suggested that it would be practical if this could be turned into a double celebration, so this is what happened. A special licence was obtained, and the wedding took place the very next day: 5 November 1919.

The di-Valentina-Acker marriage was no more than a sham which provided a convenient cover for the bride's lesbian activities. Such an arrangement – known in Hollywood as a 'twilight tandem' – could of course have worked well for Rudy, had it not been for what happened next. For when the couple returned to their bridal suite at the Hollywood Hotel, Jean Acker slammed the door in Rudy's face.

For several minutes, unaware that the scene was being observed by some of the other guests, Rudy gently pleaded with Jean Acker to open the door. When this failed to work, he began banging his fists against it and demanding his rights as a husband and to be let inside the room. This brought him an even bigger audience of onlookers, whose curiosity was well and truly satisfied when the new wife began screaming from the other side that it had all been a terrible mistake, and that she did not want Rudy anywhere near her, not even in the same building. Rudy fled at once, and their 'nuptuals' were spent at opposite ends of the town – Acker leaving the hotel minutes later to spend the night at Nazimova's Sapphic conclave on Sunset Boulevard, and Rudy flinging himself upon the mercy of Norman Kerry who, though he may have thought he had been duped far too often by this flighty Italian, found it impossible *not* to take him in when he witnessed Rudy's distress.

One good thing emerged from this mess, however, for it was Jean Acker who persuaded Rudy to change his name to Rudolph Valentino.

Had he taken the time to delve into his wife's past – she seems to have known about his – Rudy would have reconsidered before taking this monumental step which, within a few months, would make him an even bigger laughing-stock than he was right now. Norman Kerry promised that he would help him all he could, financially, and by providing him with a roof over his head until he could get back on his feet – but he added point-blank that in no way would the pair ever be lovers again.

Rudy flung himself into his work. Universal offered him a small part in the ironically titled *Once To Every Woman* – particularly as shooting finished on 6 December, the day the newspapers carried the story of his official separation from Jean Acker. Norman Kerry then pulled the strings to get him a slightly better one in his own film, *Passion's Playground*, playing Kerry's brother.

Whilst shooting this film, Rudy was introduced to a good-looking, nineteen-year old French cameraman named Paul Ivano, to whom he felt immediately attracted. Ivano told him a little about himself: he had been born Paul Ivano Ivanichevitcz in Nice, of Russian parents, and during the war he had joined the French Signal Corps, only to be gassed soon after being sent to the Front, and discharged from the army. In August 1919, still suffering from his ordeal, he had been sent by his family to recuperate in Palm Springs. He had decided to make America his home, and soon afterwards he had moved to Hollywood, hoping to make a name for himself.

The most important part of his story, however, Ivano kept to himself until he and Rudy had enjoyed a one-night stand in Rudy's Santa Monica apartment – for several months, the cameraman had been having a secret affair with the horrendous Nazimova who, he confessed, was not averse to sharing her bed with a man every now and then. Rudy was furious, and told Ivano that he never wanted to see him again. As shall be seen, such was the chemistry between these two young men, even after a single night, that not even the ubiquitous Nazimova would be able to keep them apart.

Rudy's brief but inconsequential role in MGM's *The Cheater*, directed by Henry Otto and starring May Allison, introduced him to the young actress, Viola Dana, who was filming on an adjacent lot. Many years later, Viola – one of the leading lights with MGM and a brilliant, bubbly comedienne of the silent era whose career sadly petered out with the advent of sound – disclosed her story to the world with such sincerity that she, and the thousands of Valentino fans who were listening to the interview, could only rue the fact that he had so few close friends of her calibre. 'He was the most perfect gentleman I ever knew,' she said. 'Who gives a *damn* what anybody else thought? *I* knew him!'

Their friendship began with a muttered felicitation from Rudy, on Christmas Eve 1919, as he was passing Viola's dressing-room. She asked him, by way of small talk, what he was doing over the festive season, but when he replied that he was doing nothing and that he had nowhere to go, and when she observed how pasty and undernourished he looked, she invited him to spend the holidays at the home she shared with her sister and brother-in-law.

The relationship between Rudy and Viola Dana was very intense, but strictly platonic. The actress was, however, warned by friends and studio bosses against socialising with such a man. To be seen dancing with Valentino, she was told, could damage her reputation as one of the most respected women in Hollywood – but to have him in her house, overnight, even if twelve members of her family *were* there, would be career suicide. Viola used her own judgement. She did not feel sorry because of the situation with Jean Acker. Their common bond was a search for a soul-mate in that they had both recently lost a loved one – in Viola's case her fiancé, the stunt-flyer Ormer Locklear, who had died when his light plane had crashed into an oil-well during the shooting of *The Skywayman*.

At Viola's house, Rudy was asked to dress up as Santa Claus and hand out the presents. Astonishingly, the gift from his hostess was the first he had received since coming to America, and needless to say this gesture moved him to tears. 'A lot of people came forward after he died, saying how well they knew Rudy,' Viola said. 'All those so-called friends saying what they'd done for him. But there was one Christmas when *nobody* wanted to know the poor boy. They never talk about *that*! And I could cry even now, thinking about him being alone at that time of year.'

It was Viola Dana who introduced Rudy to Lewis Selznick, the Kiev-born movie mogul and the father of the better-known David, who had started life in America as a door-to-door jewellery salesman. Initially, Selznick did not know what to make of the young man's alternating moods of melancholy and mirth, but after spending two days in his company he was able to form his own opinion about Valentino, the *actor*, as opposed to the caricature nurtured by the cynics and scandal-mongers. He decided to take a risk by offering Rudy second-lead to Martha Mansfield and Eugene O'Brien in *The Wonderful Chance*, which was scheduled to begin shooting in New York at the end of January 1920.

Meanwhile, directly after the holiday period, Rudy bumped into Paul Ivano again, and this time the outcome was infinitely more rewarding. Ivano had had a huge row with Nazimova, and now *he* was looking for a shoulder to cry on. Rudy considered his options. His future suddenly was looking brighter. His salary for the Selznick picture was to be $300 a week – an almost unprecedented sum in those days for a relative unknown. And now, with three weeks to go before his departure for New York, he was faced with another brief but cripplingly lonely sojourn in the Santa Monica apartment – George O'Brien was now working in films, albeit only as an extra, and as yet terrified of living openly with another man – or a risky relationship with a man who was inextricably linked with one of the most powerful, neurotic and *talkative* women about town.

Inevitably, Rudy chose Ivano, a decision which he would not regret in years to come. For three weeks the pair were inseparable. By day they hired horses and rode off into the picturesque, then unspoilt Santa Monica mountains, while their evenings were spent curled up in front of a log fire, reading to one another or swapping stories about their respective youths in Europe. The pair shared the chores at Ivano's little bungalow, and saw only their closest friends. Ivano cleaned, shopped and washed the dishes; Rudy cooked the meals. An accomplished chef, he naturally served up only Italian dishes, and was particular about his ingredients. Ivano later spoke of the little delicatessen in downtown Hollywood which supplied them with full-length spaghetti, carefully packed in cardboard boxes, and not cheap. 'Rudy considered it bad luck to break the spaghetti, or cut it once it was cooked,' he recalled. 'So in order to lower it into the pan of boiling water, he would stand on a stepladder. Then, at dinner, you were expected to wind six feet of the stuff onto your fork!'

This romantic idyll was interrupted – albeit only temporarily, for Paul Ivano would remain one of Rudy's 'regulars' until the end – when Rudy left for New York. He was of course sad to be leaving behind one of the few men who had ever tried to understand him, but nevertheless looking forward to once again meeting old friends such as Alexandre Salm, and revisiting some of his former stomping grounds, and even getting to partner a few old clients.

Fortunately, perhaps, there would be no time for socialising. Much of *The Wonderful Chance* was to be shot on location, but this was held up by adverse weather. However, the fact that someone as important as Lewis Selznick had considered Rudy worthy of a high salary was enough to make at least one studio boss wonder if this young man, ingloriously dubbed by one hack as 'that accursed dago whore', had something going for him after all. He was approached by the director of Pioneer Films and offered what was for him a fortune – $400 a week to play a Brazilian opportunist in James Vincent's *Stolen Moments*, opposite the now-forgotten Marguerite Namara. The film was shot whilst the cast and crew of *The Wonderful Chance* were hanging around waiting for the weather to improve.

Rudy had only completed his first day's shooting on the Selznick film when he received a call from Richard Rowland, the head of Metro, who demanded that he report to his office without delay. Rudy assumed that Rowland wished to discuss the 'Acker business' with him, or at best offer him the part of yet another routine heavy – his latest role was that of a spivvish gangster who spent much of his screen time sporting a straw boater and twirling his moustache.

To his utter amazement, he was offered the part of Julio Desnoyers, one of the central characters in the proposed blockbuster film which had been the talk of Hollywood for some time: *The Four Horsemen Of The Apocalypse*.

Written in Spanish and first published in 1918, Vicente Blasco Ibanez's epic story recounting the horrors of the recent holocaust had been translated into English and launched on an astonished American public the following year, with the critics unanimously declaring that this was the best book about the war that anyone would ever be likely to read. Hollywood, however, had refused to even consider filming the story. Over the previous two years there had been a glut of war pictures, most of them box-office turkeys, and there was no guarantee that this one would fare better. Richard Rowland believed otherwise. The book had sold over half a million copies worldwide, with fifty reprints in the United States alone. He had therefore taken matters into his own hands, purchasing the film-rights from Ibanez for $20,000, plus ten per cent of the box-office receipts.

To a certain extent, Rowland pacified his Hollywood associates by hiring June Mathis, the most successful scriptwriter in America at that time, to adapt the story for the screen. Such was this unassuming, plain-looking, thirty-eight-year old woman's power in Hollywood that as soon as the chiefs there heard that *she* had agreed to do the script, Rowland received their full co-operation. Mathis was, in turn, given the go ahead to choose her own director, star and co-star for the film-spectacular which would employ 12,000 people in its production and cost over $1 million to make.

Mathis opted for a dashing, sophisticated young Irishman named Rex Ingram to direct, and he brought along his actress fiancée, Alice Terry – who, as Alice Taafe, had appeared alongside Rudy as an extra in *Alimony* – as part of the deal.

Ingram, would, over the next few months, employ fourteen cameramen to shoot over 500,000 feet of film, and no fewer than twelve assistant directors to handle the production's massive personnel. For the French locations he commissioned the reconstruction of an entire French village in the hills outside Los Angeles. This, according to his publicist 'used up 125,000 tons of masonry, steel, timber and other essentials', and was served by several canteens, three costume factories, a commissary and armoury, and a hospital which catered for the dozens of injuries inflicted during the battle scenes. June Mathis also insisted upon props' authenticity – a mania which Rudy would later inherit with disastrous consequences – demanding *original* paintings, curios, antiques and musical instruments. The mere *thought* of how much this particular exercise would cost filled Ingram with horror, until Mathis solved the problem she had created in the first place by personally contacting museums and private collections and persuading them to loan their exhibits to Metro. Even so, the cost of insuring them and guarding them around the clock would be exhorbitant enough to send the budget, and Ingram's blood-pressure, soaring.

Mathis had first become aware of Rudy after seeing his fleeting appearance as a co-respondent in *The Eyes Of Youth* – which had contained a virtual rape scene – and she later said that she had been so bowled over by his beauty, depth of expression and perfect timing that she had been willing to put her career on the line and risk her reputation by taking him on. Ingram, however, was not at all happy about having a little-known actor in so monumental a project – but when Mathis quietly pointed out that *she* had been the only one to *want* him as director, Ingram backed down gracefully.

Rudy's salary for *The Four Horsemen Of The Apocalypse* was fixed at $350 a week, which was less than he had received for his last two films. He did not mind this, however, as everyone connected with the production assured him that *this* one would succeed in making him a household name.

The first evidence of Rudy's star status occurred ten days later when, having completed *The Wonderful Chance*, he returned to Hollywood to be met at the railway station by several press-photographers and a liveried chauffeur who drove him to the Hollywood Hotel, where a suite had been booked in his name. The next morning, at the studio, he was shown to his own dressing-room, but instead of a promised press-conference the only person there was June Mathis, who very gently read him the riot act: as Julio, he was in a very privileged position and the envy of every actor in town, therefore he was to obey the director's every instruction and *never* question his judgement. Mathis told him that if he felt unhappy about any aspect of the film, he should report his grievances to her without delay, and not discuss them even with Ingram. Rudy was so grateful for the enormous opportunity he had been given that he would have agreed to anything. Throughout the entire shoot he became the epitome of hard work, discipline and punctuality. There were no late nights, no dancing apart from the two on-set tango sequences, no tantrums, and above all no clandestine visits to the Torch Club, though with the advent of Paul Ivano these had been curbed somewhat.

Rudy actually told June Mathis about his relationship with Ivano, and she agreed to his request that the young man be allowed to work on the production, for two reasons. Firstly, because his personal experiences in the thick of the fighting made him an ideal technical adviser ... and secondly, because as a steadying influence Mathis believed that he would prevent her 'dear boy' from straying away from the straight and narrow. The line *was* drawn, however, at Rudy's suggestion that Ivano should be allowed to move into his suite at the Hollywood Hotel. The press, anxious to report everything they could dig up about the man who was appearing in the most expensive movie ever made, were rarely away from his door, and the last thing the studio wanted was a scandal. When Mathis was made to see how much the two men loved each other, a compromise was reached – Ivano gave up his tiny bungalow, and found him and Rudy an apartment in the Formosa, at the corner of La Brea and Hollywood Boulevard.

When Rex Ingram and Richard Rowland played through the rushes of the film after just one week's shooting, they realised that June Mathis's judgement had been spot-on and that Metro indeed had the makings of a major star on their hands. Ingram's cameraman was John Seitz, a talented individual whose 'truc' was to take 'so-so' women such as Barbara LaMarr and Alice Terry and photograph them so that they looked ravishingly lovely. With Valentino, whose looks were stunning even in battle-scenes when his face was grimy and covered in a week's growth of beard, Seitz found every shot simplicity itself, and he instinctively knew even with just two scenes in the can that Rudy would run away with the picture. So too did June Mathis: in her original script, she had faithfully adhered to Ibanez's novel by keeping the part of Julio relatively small. Now, after a hasty rewrite, she turned him into the film's leading character.

4

The Incentive of Chivalry

> *'A studio, the glaring lights, the hammering of the carpenters, the noise and smell of it all – THAT is really home!'*

Running at over two hours and covering eleven reels, *The Four Horsemen Of The Apocalypse* tells the story of the descendants of a wealthy Argentinian landowner, Madariaga, who has two daughters. One is married to a Frenchman, Desnoyers, the other to Hartrott, a German. Both families tolerate living under the same roof until the old man dies without leaving a will, whereupon his fortune is divided equally between his daughters who, in the wake of the European conflict, return with their husbands – technically enemies – to the latter's respective countries. Henceforth, whilst the Hartrotts are retained in the minor key, much of the action takes place in Paris and centres around the selfish, arrogant Julio.

By day, Julio earns his living as a respectable painter in Montmartre though, having been encouraged in his wild ways by Madariaga, his real passions are seducing rich women and dancing the Argentinian tango. Julio has been openly conducting an affair with the beautiful Marguerite (Alice Terry), the wife of his best friend, Etienne Laurier (John Sainpolis). She is, however, reluctant to see him again after his antics at the Tango palace – savouring a rose she touched, burning his fingers whilst lighting a cigarette, then kissing the sugar lump before dropping it into her tea – made them the centre of attention. Julio therefore suggests a compromise

– that they should meet at his studio. 'I promise to be good,' he says, cocking one eye at the camera. Here, however, they are caught out by Laurier, who challenges Julio to a duel and tells Marguerite that he will divorce her – changing his plan of action only when he is suddenly mobilised.

At first, Julio is indifferent towards the war, and thinks only of himself. 'Just imagine what it will mean,' he tells a friend. 'No parties, no pretty clothes – women in mourning, nothing but misery!' Then, when Marguerite joins the Red Cross, he goes after her, only to find her nursing her husband, who has been blinded whilst fighting at the Front. Julio ends their affair, enlists, and on the battlefield – ironically, face to face with his German cousin – dies gallantly defending a country which is not his own.

Unforgettable, of course, was Rudy's opening scene in *The Four Horsemen Of The Apocalypse*, which takes place in an Argentinian dance-hall. He actually *materialises* on to the screen in sumptuous close-up, clenching his perfect white teeth around a cigarillo and blowing the smoke down his flared nostrils – in the words of the film historian, Alexander Walker, 'like a stud stallion on a frosty morning'. The effect of this scene, more than seventy years on, is *still* electrifying ... but there is more to come as the swaggering gaucho interrupts the dancing couple on the floor. This is no polite 'excuse-me', but a sharp tap on the man's shoulder before bringing him down with a lash from his stock-whip! Julio-Rudy then executes the most sensual dance-routine in film history, finishing the piece by planting a masochistic kiss on his partner's lips – bringing the actress (Beatrice Dominguez) towards the point of orgasm, she later confessed. An absolute masterpiece!

Whilst shooting the film, Rudy had managed to get away every now and then to spend a little time with Paul Ivano at their apartment in the Formosa, and the new star had even posed for photographs with his 'room-mate'. Rudy, however, would never be capable of sticking to one person at a time: something *all* his lovers would have to contend with, though most of them were also playing the field, and never minded sharing him. A key scene in *The Four Horsemen Of The Apocalypse* takes place in the Tango Palace, when a crowd of revellers are interrupted to be told that war has been declared. But whilst all eyes are focused on the central female oracle, poised before the French tricolour, a tall, straight-backed young man in evening dress only has eyes for Julio. This was clearly captured on one of the publicity stills. It was Rudy's second meeting with José-Ramon Samaniegos, and within an hour of finishing the scene, the pair were in bed together.

Born in Durango, Mexico, in 1899, and the eldest of thirteen children, José-Ramon (these were but two of his fourteen names) had arrived in Los Angeles in 1913 with his family, having fled the Huerta revolution. His first job had been washing dishes in a restaurant, though when the manager heard him crooning in the kitchen, he had promoted him to resident singer! There followed a variety of occupations: dancing the tango with his sister Carmen, working as a bit-player in summer stock, dancing ballet in Pavlova's chorus, and latterly working as an extra in any number of films featuring Mary Pickford, Wallace Reid and Sessue Hayakawa.

Almost as muscular and handsome as Rudy, but equally as narcissistic, José-Ramon had quickly amassed a coterie of lovers of both sexes. When Rex Ingram discovered him, he had also been working as an artists' model, posing nude for the students of the J Francis Smith Institute in Los Angeles, but soon after becoming involved with Rudy he amended his name to Ramon Samaniegos. The final transformation would come a few years later, when Ingram would baptise him Ramon Novarro, after the famous beauty-spot in the San Fernando Valley.

Ramon Novarro once confessed that Valentino had been the great love of his life, a fact which may or may not have been true: in 1933 *the* man would be the Austrian dancer, Frédéric Rey, whom he poached from Mistinguett. Ten years later, it would be the pianist, Vladimir Horowitz. For Rudy, however, Novarro appears to have been little more than a passing fancy: a passionate, loveless, purely sexual liaison. What *is* strange is the way in which Rudy thanked the young Mexican for having sex with him. Occasionally, stars of the silent era commissioned sculptures or portraits of themselves in the hope that they might be remembered long after their images on the screen had faded. Others left handprints and signatures in the cement outside Grauman's. Rudy, however, precursed the modern-day porn-star, Jeff Stryker, by presenting Novarro with a life-size replica of his manhood – a ten-inch Art Deco phallic emblem adorned with his signature, in silver ... which the actor 'loaned out' to Frédéric Rey in 1936, according to the dancer, 'To give me an idea of what it had been like, getting it from Valentino.'

The eight months separating the completion of *The Four Horsemen Of The Apocalypse* and its release were tense with expectation – wondering if all the hype would pay off, or whether life would revert to bit parts and giving dancing lessons. Paul Ivano's suddenly being called away did not help. Ivano's friend, Max Linder, the greatest French film comic of his day, was about to begin shooting his new film, *Seven Years' Bad Luck*, in Hollywood, and he had engaged Ivano as his assistant director. Then, just as suddenly, Metro contracted Rudy to play opposite Alice Lake in *Uncharted Seas* – billed as *An Arctic Adventure*.

This production allowed the Hollywood moguls to first witness the soon to be famous Valentino temper in all its terrifying glory. Alice Lake made it clear from their first day on the set that she disapproved of 'gigolos and pretty-boys', and Rudy told Wesley Ruggles, the director, that if he was expected to put up with such insults, he should at least be compensated by an increase in pay. Ruggles relayed this demand to Richard Rowland, who would not be swayed by such histrionics from his *major* stars, let alone a temperamental young Latin who was just starting out. Rudy's salary would rise *only* when he had proved his worth to the public – after the release of *The Four Horsemen Of The Apocalypse*.

Upon hearing this, Rudy threatened to tear Ruggles apart with his bare hands, called Rowland all the filthy names he could think of – in Italian, in the privacy of his office – then spat out the same expletives in English, to Alice Lake, causing her to faint on the set. This brought a severe reprimand from June Mathis, who must have felt like some monstrous wicked stepmother ticking off an errant child when Rudy suddenly burst into tears and flung himself against her shoulder! Another tantrum followed a few days later, on 17 January 1921, when he learned that Jean Acker was suing him for maintenance of $300 a month, plus all her legal fees, on the grounds that *he* had deserted *her*. The papers were tucked under his plate and wheeled into his suite at the Hollywood Hotel with his lunch, so incensing Rudy that he picked up the trolley with one hand and smashed it and its contents against the wall, whilst the waiter fled for his life. The damage he caused cost him a whole week's salary, but he was unrepentant, telling a reporter, 'I should have acted like a *real* Italian husband. In Italy, when wives are disobedient they are *thrashed*!'

It was whilst he was making *Uncharted Seas* that Rudy once more came face to face with the horrendous Nazimova, who was searching for a 'tall, dark and handsome' actor to play the part of Armand in her avant-garde production of *Camille*, an epic which would more closely resemble the contemporary London stage-version with Tallulah Bankhead and Glenn Byam-Shaw than the Greta Garbo-Robert Taylor classic of the next decade.

Rudy had never forgiven Nazimova for her earlier insults, and often referred to her as 'that Russian hag', a term which was only marginally less offensive than some of the names she was calling him. When June Mathis informed him, however, that Nazimova had paid a clandestine visit to the set to watch him working on his new film, and that she had found his acting 'most interesting', he was flattered and agreed to meet her.

The Crimean-born actress and former professional violinist, then forty-one, had made her name before the war, portraying Ibsen's heroines on Broadway and even having a 39th Street theatre named in her honour. For *War Brides*, her movie debut of 1917, Lewis Selznick had paid her a staggering $1,000 a *day*, and the critics had declared it one of the best films of the decade. The following year, she had signed a $13,000 a week contract with Metro, and relocated to Hollywood with Charles Bryant, her British common-law husband who directed many of her subsequent films.

When Nazimova returned to the set of *Unchartered Seas* to offer Rudy the part of Armand, he was still wearing the Arctic costume, and drenched in fake snow. She made no effort to apologise for upsetting him; he gave no indication that he would ever grow to like her. 'I was not impressed,' Nazimova recalled some years later. 'Valentino was fat and far too swarthy. His bushy black eyebrows were grotesque!' Rudy had warned June Mathis what would happen if this grossly overbearing woman ever tried to boss him around, and he had sworn *never* to address her as 'Madame', as even her very closest friends were instructed to do. He also declared that he would put her over his knee should she insult him again. This, of course, was typical Valentino – afraid of absolutely no man, yet putty in the hands of strong-willed women. When Nazimova ordered him to wash the 'shit' out of his hair and pluck his eyebrows before submitting to a screen test, something he would not have done for an Ingram or a Selznick, he complied without argument ... passing the test and receiving what was in those days a privileged invitation to join the Nazimova clique.

Despite the presence of Charles Bryant, Nazimova's love-interests were centred around The Garden of Alla, her three and a half acre bungalow complex at 8080 Sunset Boulevard, with its miniature forest of fruit trees and Black Sea-shaped swimming pool – or at Mary's, her 'girls only' bar on Sunset Strip, opposite the Café Gala gay bar. Here, the undisputed doyenne of Hollywood's lesbian set, she ruled over her infamous 'Sewing Circle' like a warrior queen. Nazimova's 'intellectual conquests' included the film director Dorothy Arzner, Dolly Wilde – Oscar's niece, hailed as 'the only Wilde who liked sleeping with women' – Mildred Harris, the former nymphette bride of Charlie Chaplin, Jean Acker, and her most recent and cherished protegée, Natacha Rambova. 'Most of my friends are young girls,' Nazimova confessed to Motion Picture magazine, a decade before Tallulah Bankhead re-adopted the phrase as her own.

Jean Acker's presence at the Nazimova court must have been very unsettling for Rudy, who perhaps unwisely visited The Garden of Alla for the first time with Paul Ivano tagging along for moral support. Nazimova, who of course knew that he was Rudy's lover, had hired him as technical adviser for *Camille*, hoping that the proceedings might be enlivened should a few sparks start flying. Throughout the production she would constantly mock the way he pronounced his lover's name – 'Wewdy' – and refer to him as 'Paul Ivanofuckingawfulbitch'.

The wily Russian's *ulterior* motive for offering Rudy the part of Armand, however, was entirely selfish: the elevation of Natacha Rambova, a somewhat exotic name for Winifred Shaughnessy, the step-daughter of the Salt Lake City cosmetics tycoon, Richard Hudnutt. Rudy's star was now quite obviously in its ascendancy, and Nazimova convinced Rambova that if, between them, they could transform him into Hollywood's top male star, then Rambova would reap the rewards and become one of the most powerful managers in America. Nazimova also knew enough about Rudy's reputation for narcissism and vanity to be aware of the fact that he would never be able to resist falling for anyone, particularly an attractive woman, who plied him with compliments about his own beauty and talent. The Russian was right: Rudy fell under Rambova's spell at once, declaring her to be the most intoxicating creature he had ever seen.

A few years later, Rambova told *Photoplay*'s Ruth Waterbury, 'It wasn't love at first sight. I think it was good comradeship more than anything else. We were both very lonely but we had known each other more than six months before we became at all interested in each other.' In fact, the truth is that when Rambova had *first* gone out on a date with Rudy, she had been appalled by some of his mannerisms, reporting back to Nazimova, 'Valentino certainly has some star quality, but he is still a stupid, greasy Italian peasant with the table manners of a pig, who makes me want to throw up!'

Arguably no other woman in movie history has manipulated a man so calculatingly and cruelly as Rambova did Valentino, and though he was warned to steer clear of this grasping egomaniac by close, caring friends such as June Mathis, mentally he was too weak to drag himself away from her spell, and only realised just how truly evil this woman could be when it was too late.

Born on 19 January 1897, Winifred Shaughnessy had spent much of her childhood being cared for by her maternal aunt, Teresa Werner, of whom Rudy would later become very fond. She had then been sent to Leatherhead Court, a boarding school in Surrey, England, where she had discovered a passion for ballet. In

1910 she had visited London to see the legendary Anna Pavlova, though no one had inspired her more than Theodore Kosloff, Pavlova's contemporary whom she had met several times in the British capital.

In 1914, Kosloff – an unsavoury character who frequently found himself on the wrong side of the law because of his penchant for under-aged girls – had defected to New York to open a dance-school on 42nd Street, and when Winifred had returned to America not long afterwards, she had persuaded Aunt Teresa to enrol her there as a student. Within weeks she and Kosloff – sixteen years her senior and married with an invalid child – had become lovers, and it was he who had advised her to change her name to Natacha Rambova. In order to 'complete' the transformation, she had begun speaking with a heavy Russian accent.

For several years, Rambova had toured the United States as a member of Kosloff's Imperial Russian Ballet, soon extending her talents to costume and set design, becoming so fanatical about this aspect of her work that her ardour for Kosloff had quickly cooled. In 1917 Cecil B DeMille had commissioned her to design the Aztec costumes for his epic, *The Woman God Forgot*, starring Kosloff and Wallace Reid ... but then had come the Russian Revolution, and with it the collapse of Kosloff's holdings, which had all been ploughed into a Moscow apartment-block, an event which had brought about the dissolution of his ballet company. Not to be outdone, the dancer had appeared in several more DeMille films, including *Why Change Your Wife?* and *Forbidden Fruit*, both with costume designs by Rambova – in the latter she had created a stunning ballgown for Agnes Ayres. Then, in the autumn of 1920, Kosloff and Rambova had been summoned to The Garden of Alla with a view to working on Nazimova's new picture, *Billions*, which had truly spelled the beginning of the end for the couple. Rambova had spent the night in Nazimova's boudoir, explaining to Kosloff the next morning that she had needed a shoulder to cry on because someone had informed her that he had recently had sex with two ten-year old girls. A furious row had ensued: grabbing his hunting-rifle, he had intended to kill her, but a friend had grabbed the weapon as it had gone off, and

Rambova had only received a flesh wound to the leg. Nevertheless, she had fled to Nazimova, and the actress had taken her under her wing ... as art-director and lover.

Rambova and Nazimova were now eager to begin shooting *Camille* but Rudy was contractually obliged to complete a film for Metro. *The Conquering Power* was June Mathis's adaptation of Balzac's *Eugenie Grandet*: Rex Ingram and Alice Terry were once more to be director and co-star. Rambova's unsettling influence on Rudy, so early in their relationship, caused him great problems with the studio even before shooting began. He had once more asked Richard Rowland for a $100 a week increase in salary, which in all honesty he now deserved, and once again he had been turned down. Rambova, gently at first, rebuked him for not standing up for himself, and the next day he had *demanded* the money. Rowland begrudgingly awarded him another $50 a week, explaining that the company was on the verge of bankruptcy and could not *afford* to pay him any more, adding that if he could be just a little more patient until after the release of *The Four Horsemen Of The Apocalypse*, the future rewards might be considerable for everyone. Patience, however, would never be one of Valentino's finer virtues, and when he began arriving on set looking a mess after the all-night parties at The Garden of Alla, and criticising not just the other players, but Rex Ingram for showing too much favouritism to Alice Terry, the equally fiery director turned on him in front of the entire cast and accused him of acting 'like a prima donna virgin'. This comment was interpreted by Rudy as a slight on his manhood, and resulted in a violent outburst, peppered with expletives, which would have turned into a fist-fight had it not been for June Mathis, who threatened to have *both* men fired from the production if they did not behave.

The film was completed, with Rudy and Ingram barely on speaking terms, and with the latter exacting his revenge by cutting Rudy's part to such an extent that he ended up little more than an accessory to the already fading Alice Terry. Declaring that he would never work with this 'hot-headed Eye-Tie' again, he told a press-conference, 'I can take any good-looking extra and turn him into a star. Valentino isn't the only one.' Ingram seems to have been aware that Rudy and Ramon Samaniegos (as he was still known) had become lovers during *The Four Horsemen Of The Apocalypse*. If this is so, then the director's subsequent action proved that he too could 'play the bitch' ... by hiring the young Mexican to play opposite Alice Terry in *The Prisoner of Zenda*. And of course, he *did* make him a star.

Twenty-five years on, Rex Ingram had *still* not forgiven Rudy. When asked by a reporter what had made the actor so special to so many people, all he could say was, 'Valentino was just another lucky, good-looking guy who copped a sensational role because of a good cameraman. Cast properly, Julio would have made *anybody*.'

On 6 March 1921, coinciding with the dedication of the Tomb of the Unknown Soldier in Arlington National Cemetery, *The Four Horsemen Of The Apocalypse* opened simultaneously in New York, Boston, Chicago, Philadelphia – and Los Angeles, where Rambova was Rudy's date for the première. The critics unanimously declared it a triumph, and Rudolph Valentino was officially declared a living legend.

The film's special effects were proclaimed equally innovative – these and the behind-screen sound-effects added a harsh touch of realism which some cinemagoers found *too* disturbing. Studio technicians banged drums, fired revolver shots, clashed cymbals and set off magnesium flares during the battle scenes. Huge billows of artificial steam preceded the appearance of the terrifying, mythical beast from whose jaws rode the Four Horsemen of the Apocalypse: Conquest, War, Pestilence and Death.

The film was a smash hit all over the world, challenging the general opinion by declaring that war was *not* the answer to the problems which society had brought upon itself. Heralding the conflict, the words of Ibanez, the pacifist, filled the screen: 'In the enemy's land, they too are singing and shouting as they wave *their* flag – believing *they* are also right and that God rules for *them*!' It was precisely because of its anti-war values that the film was championed by the League of Nations and distributed to each of the fifty countries represented by the organisation – even the ones who had played no part in the fighting. Only the Germans voiced their

disapproval, for obvious reasons. June Mathis had incorporated a scene where a German officer nonchalantly munches an apple whilst French patriots are being executed, and the German government, denouncing the film as 'corrupt, inaccurate and immoral' not only banned it in their own country – the German Ambassador to Italy also tried to prevent it from being screened there, but without success, particularly as its star had come from Italy in the first place! And, most importantly for Metro, in grossing an unprecedented $5 million at the box-office, it saved the company from the receiver.

Rudy was justifiably proud of his achievement, but he told June Mathis that in no way would he continue working for a studio which clearly did not have his interests at heart, with or without Rex Ingram. Mathis had been hired by Nazimova to write the script for *Camille* so she hoped that by still working with him she might get him to see sense. After seeing photographs of Rudy and Rambova in the newspapers, dancing the tango at the Alexandria Hotel, the whole of Hollywood was aware that Mathis's 'dear, dear boy' was completely under Rambova's spell. Nevertheless the scriptwriter was optimistic that once he had suffered the rigours of making a film with Nazimova, he would soon return to the real world.

Today, Nazimova would be regarded by the critics as little more than a camp joke. Her hammy, over-the-top posturing, together with her dropped heavy-lidded eyes, wildly extravagant gestures and an ability to authentically faint on cue whenever she felt emotional – which was most of the time – only appear ridiculous, yet in her day she had the same effect on female admirers as Omar Shariff and other exotic-looking stars would have, forty years later.

Most film buffs would agree that Nazimova's finest moment was in the 1940 film, *Escape*, when as a no-longer beautiful sixty-two-year old she played a widow who is rescued from a concentration camp by Robert Taylor. In 1977 she was portrayed in Ken Russell's biopic, *Valentino*, with astonishing verve and accuracy by French star Leslie Caron. Her entrance into Campbell's Funeral Home – attended by eight veiled lesbian slaves, she wears a voluminous black train covered with hundreds of camellias and pronounces in a staged, high-pitched voice, 'Where is he? Where is my sweet Armand?', before promptly fainting for the benefit of the press photographers – remains one of the greatest moments of camp ever captured on celluloid.

Camille was to be Nazimova's final film for Metro. Tired of her aggressive, domineering ways, the company had decided to terminate her contract, though she told the press that she was *glad* this had happened, adding, 'From now on, Nazimova will direct her own productions of the great classics – and what is more, she will do them the way they *should* be done!' She was, of course, a little too old to be playing Dumas's doomed heroine, Marguerite Gauthier, and *Camille* was and will remain *her* film, never Rudy's. She herself had written the script, under the pseudonym Peter M Winters, and although she had hired Ray C Smallwood to direct, and Paul Ivano was listed in the credits as technical adviser, it was *she* alone who ordered them how to direct and advise. Only Rambova had free rein over the sets which, though they *were* bizarre, were nevertheless fascinating and way ahead of their time.

Nazimova had brought her Marguerite forward to the modern day, claiming that she did not want it to be confused with the two disastrous film versions of 1917, and Rambova really did allow her imagination to run wild. She used as her inspiration the contemporary works of the Parisian designer, Emile-Jacques Ruhlmann, and those of the German Expressionist architect, Hans Poelzig, who had recently remodelled Max Reinhardt's *Grosses Schauspielhaus*, in Berlin ... enabling this particular Camille to party and eventually expire in a setting embellished with semicircular onyx and glass doors, bare walls, pendulous electric lights, circular windows which looked out on a perennial snowstorm, and a wealth of Art Deco furniture, including a circular, lace-draped bed. The film also included a 'dream sequence' from *Manon Lescaut* during which the leading players donned 18th-century costumes and powdered wigs.

The critics, however, did not know what to make of the film or its leading lady, upon its release in September 1921. Some raved about her 'dazzling but baffling beauty'; others merely pondered why she spent so much time wandering about the set in her curious, lizard-tailed dress, 'looking like an over-painted doll'. A childhood attack of chickenpox had left Nazimova with the most dreadful complexion, and in some scenes she is wearing so much rice-powder on her face that she resembles a walking corpse. In addition, her massive bubble-perm gives the impression that her ridiculously slender neck is about to snap at any moment.

Nazimova was hammered mercilessly for her decision to rewrite Dumas by not having Armand present at Marguerite's deathbed scene. Indeed, in this film her goal appears to have been to transfer the characteristics of the leading two players on to the screen, as opposed to what June Mathis had intended. Nazimova's Marguerite is arrogant, cold and overbearing, whilst her lover presents himself as weak and subservient – exactly the image Rudy would project, once he had fallen into Rambova's clutches. Many times in the near future he would be reminded of his plum line in *Camille*, when he tells Marguerite, 'I wish I were a dog, so that I might care for you!'

Rambova continued working with her mentor, and shortly after *Camille* was released, Nazimova commissioned her to design the sets and costumes for the first of her promised self-financed 'classics' – Oscar Wilde's *Salome* which, she declared, would be an all-gay production as an ultimate tribute to the great man's genius. Rudy was offered the role of John the Baptist, but for obvious reasons turned this down. Far from being ashamed of his sexuality, he nevertheless recognised the dangers to his career should he share his amorous preferences with the world. Needless to say, the film would be hit by the censor, and when it was eventually released at the end of 1923, despite several quite beautifully filmed and acted sequences, it flopped, losing Nazimova a fortune.

5
The Symbol of Devotion

'In my country, men are always the masters and women are happier for it.'

Metro did not stick to their promise to raise Rudy's salary, despite the phenomenal success of *The Four Horsemen Of The Apocalypse*, and he complained bitterly to June Mathis, begging her to help him. His expenditure far outweighed his income, even this early in his career, and he and Paul Ivano had been compelled to give up their apartment at the Formosa. Both men had moved into Rambova's small duplex at 6612 Sunset Boulevard which she already shared with two dogs, any number of cats, and a lion cub given to her by Ivano, which she had baptised Zeta. Much of the time, however, Rambova's animals were looked after by a friend whilst the trio spent most evenings at the nearby Garden of Alla, living off Nazimova's generosity. All four were heavily into spiritualism and frequently held seances, inviting fellow enthusiasts such as June Mathis, and the actresses Viola Dana and Nita Naldi. Before making any major decision, Rambova would always 'consult' with her guide, a long-dead Egyptian named Mesalope. Similarly, Rudy would risk ridicule by confessing that he too had a familiar, a Redskin brave named Black Feather, to whom he turned whenever he was in need of spiritual comfort. In his autobiography, Rudy declared that in his opinion, no child inherited characteristics from its own family but from the 'commingled blood' of its ancestors. 'Aliens from their immediate families, they claim kinship with some old buccaneer, some dreaming poet, some isolated lady or some cavalier knight of whom they have probably never heard, but whose long-ago story they are reliving, none the less.' Nita Naldi, however, who always made fun of Rudy's 'spook-chats', once told an astonished reporter, 'It was a good thing for Natacha and Rudy that they had *spiritual* intercourse, because they sure as hell never had the normal kind, least not with each other!'

Rudy would always maintain that *he* had barged into the office of Jesse Lasky, the head of Famous Players-Lasky (later Paramount), boasting of how, once he had rattled off a long list of grievances against Metro, Lasky had immediately offered him a $500 a week contract. This is not true. The one-picture deal, which included an option for the company to retain Rudy on their payroll only if they saw fit, was in fact negotiated by June Mathis, who was also in search of advancement – she was contracted by Lasky on the same day as Rudy, and made sure when he signed his part of the deal that Rambova was not present. Rambova hit the roof when he informed her what he had done, declaring that he had been a fool to submit to any contract worth less than $1,000 a week.

What infuriated Rambova most of all, however, was Jesse Lasky's choice of Rudy's first role for Famous Players-Lasky: a swarthy Arab seducer in an erotic film about desert sex and machismo, entitled *The Sheik*, which she virtually *ordered* him to reject!

Just about the only thing Rudy and Rambova had in common, apart from their love of animals, was a passion for European culture, an interest which was shared by fellow 'exiles' Paul Ivano and Nazimova, so Rambova tried to get them on her side to prove to Rudy that in persisting with these 'trashy' romantic parts, he was only wasting his *true* talents as a dramatic actor. Nazimova and Ivano, however, who also shared Rudy's love of escapism, having both fled to Hollywood *away* from oppression, could not agree, though both suggested that he should ask for more money. This he did, and Lasky upped his salary to $750 a week. This placated Rambova somewhat, so Lasky decided to keep her sweet by paying her and Ivano the customary $10 a day to appear in the film as extras, playing a pair of socialites. Another extra, playing an Arab child in her screen debut, was eight-year old Loretta Young.

Rudy became briefly involved with Richard Arlen, a twenty-year old bit-player who also starred in *The Sheik*. A former pilot with the Royal Canadian Flying Corps, Arlen had been 'spotted' by Jesse Lasky whilst working as a studio messenger-boy, though Rudy knew him already – a boxing enthusiast, Arlen had sparred with him several times at the Los Angeles Athletic Club. 'He had the most electrifying charisma that I've ever known,' Arlen said many years later. 'He was gentle and kind – and more than a little paranoid about losing his beautiful black hair. And *what* a physique! Much, much better in the flesh than in his photographs! There's *never* been anybody in my life quite like Rudy!'

Arlen himself would become an overnight sensation in 1927 when cast opposite Charles 'Buddy' Rogers in *Wings*, arguably the best film ever made about World War I, and the first to feature a man kissing another man openly on the mouth – and to attract no criticism – during Arlen's death scene, after his aviator pal Rogers has shot him down accidentally.

The Sheik was based on the novel by E M Hull, parts of which were deemed near-pornographic in those days. It had first been published in Great Britain in 1919, and though the critics had generally hated it, the more they had denounced it, the more it had captured the public's imagination, selling over 50,000 copies. And then a newspaper had dropped the bombshell: the book's 'perverted man-of-the-world' author was actually Edith Maude Winstanley, the genteel, middle-aged wife of a Derbyshire pig-farmer!

The book told the story of the beautiful but liberated English rose, Lady Diana Mayo, who is abducted by the dusky savage who neither knows nor cares about etiquette and the finer points of courtship. Scooping her up into the saddle as if she weighs nothing, and all but crushing the life out of her with his massive arms, off he rides with her to his desert tent, where he forces her to submit to his masochistic sexual desires. And what shocked, of course, was the fact that the heroine actually *enjoyed* being told,

'Lie still, you little fool!' before being virtually raped by this fearless, virile animal whose only 'apology' is, 'Better that it is me than my men!'

The Sheik would seal Valentino's fame as the World's Greatest Lover, as in cinemas across the globe women fainted in droves and Rudy's gay admirers battled with their emotions, attempting to conceal the effect he was having on them. Moralists and Bible-bashers would proclaim some scenes lewd, particularly where he leered and popped his eyes, flared his nostrils, bared his chest and generally looked drop-dead gorgeous. When Sheik Ahmed Ben Hassam (aka the Scots Earl of Glencarryl, who we learn was abandoned in the Sahara as a baby) menaces Agnes Ayres with what could well be a fate worse than death – 'Why have you brought me here?' she asks, to which comes the response, 'Are you not WOMAN enough to know?' – thousands of women, and men, of all ages wished for but one thing, to have been in her place!

Characters such as Ahmed Ben Hassan were alien to the American public, who for years had been accustomed to seeing their villains meet a sticky end, more often than not at the hands of some handsome, rugged all-American, Wallace Reid-type hero. And yet, not only was this hellish man better looking than every single one of his contemporaries, his story also had a happy ending, for before the credits roll the lovers are married.

The title of the World's Greatest Lover, however, was not carried over into Rudy's private life. Although head-over-heels in love with Rambova, and seemingly terrified of displeasing her, *she* was only ever passionate about her work, and persisted in moaning to all and sundry that, as Hollywood's Number One Star, Rudy was selling himself short when 'lowly' types such as John Barrymore and Douglas Fairbanks were commanding massive salaries by making films which were even worse than *The Sheik*. This was, of course, only *her* opinion. From Jesse Lasky's point of view, and speaking with the experience of a man who had seen countless five-minute wonders, Rudy still had a long way to go before he could consider himself amongst the Hollywood elite.

A year or so later, Natacha Rambova would define the difference between Latin lovers and their American counterparts to

Photoplay's Ruth Waterbury, saying, 'With American men, lovemaking is merely an annoying preliminary. With a Latin it is like the obligato of a delicate musical motif. It runs softly in and about the creative melody. Beauty like that should not be destroyed.' This was florid phrasing indeed, coming from a woman who is widely reputed never to have had a sexual relationship with *any* man, although Rudy is said to have *attempted* to have sex with her on at least one occasion. Some sixty years after his friend's death, Paul Ivano spoke of Valentino's apparent priapism, recounting an episode where his lovemaking to Rambova had been *so* wild that she had gone into a cataleptic fit. Rudy had rushed into Ivano's room, sporting an erection which would not subside, and screaming that he had killed her. Ivano had added how he had revived the 'corpse' by sponging it down, but whether this story was but an attempt on Ivano's part to draw attention away from what had *actually* transpired between himself and Rudy, or merely to hammer home the point that to be a good lover one *must* be blatantly heterosexual and capable of sending a woman way beyond the normal realms of ecstasy, is a matter for conjecture.

In the year of his death, Rudy confessed to Jacques Hébertot, of whom more later, that since finishing *The Four Horsemen Of The Apocalypse* he had slept only with Paul Ivano and a select handful of close male friends. Rudy himself, when questioned about his on-screen seduction techniques in *The Sheik*, buffed up his macho image by telling the press, 'In Castellaneta, where I come from, it has always been traditional for a man to beat his wife if she steps out of line!' And quoting from an 'Arab medical textbook', his friend Chaw Mank almost advocated rape some years later, by reiterating, 'Breaking a maiden's seal is one of the best antidotes for one's ills. Cudgelling her unceasingly, until she swoons away, is a mighty remedy for a man's depression.' But if many were prepared to believe stories that Rudy might have enjoyed roughing up his lovers, off the screen, nothing could have been further from the truth. Both Jacques Hébertot and Richard Arlen later declared that Rudy had been the tenderest, most considerate of lovers, and that he had never once revealed the slightest sign of this alleged abrasiveness.

In August 1921, Rudy and Paul Ivano left for a secret location on the Barbary Coast to begin shooting *Moran Of The* Lady Letty. Ivano had been hired as the film's stills photographer, as had happened with *The Sheik*, though within days he would be appointed assistant cameraman to William Marshall ... indeed, some of the key scenes were actually filmed by Ivano when, on the third day of shooting, Marshall succumbed to seasickness.

As Rambova was still working on *Salome*, Rudy and Ivano were afforded more freedom than over the preceding few months, and wishing to recapture their former bohemian spirit they rented a simple, one-bed room at San Francisco's St Francis Hotel. Then, to curb the gossips, over the next few weeks they dated a succession of starlets who were, of course, always dispatched to their own rooms before Rudy and Ivano turned in for the night.

After the comic strip escapism of his previous film, yet to be seen by the public, Rudy had demanded a 'return to reality', in anticipation of having to placate the so-called machismo of Americans who, he was sure, would only berate him for camping it up as an Arab stud. Directed again by George Melford, *Moran Of The* Lady Letty was based on the 1898 novel by Frank Norris, the Chicago-born former journalist and author of rugged adventure books who had taken part in the 'Jameson Raid' which had preceded the Boer War. Rudy played Ramon Laredo, a young socialite who shortly before his wedding is press-ganged into sailing on a pirate ship by its evil captain, 'Frisco' Kitchell (Walter Long).

Off the coast of Mexico, the pirates come across the *Lady Letty*, whose crew have been asphyxiated by its cargo of burning coal, and rescue its only survivor, the skipper's daughter Letty Sternersen, also known as 'Moran' (Dorothy Dalton). Ramon immediately falls in love with her – forgetting about his rich fiancée, whose huge yacht cruises by whilst he and Moran are kissing – and when he learns how Kitchell is planning to sell her as a slave to a band of outlaws, he incites the crew to mutiny. After the two sides have battled it out, a lengthy fist-fight erupts between Ramon and the captain – beginning in the cabin, it extends along the deck, up the mast and into the rigging, and finally out on to the yard-arm, where the hero knocks his adversary to his death, sixty feet below.

Rudy's Ramon Laredo was a meaty, double-fisted role which would earn him a lot of male fans who were *not* gay, though these might not have approved had they been aware of his ongoing involvements with Paul Ivano and the musclebound George O'Brien, who appeared in the film as a deckhand, and who was not averse to sharing a bed with Rudy and Ivano after a hard day on the lot.

Rudy was not happy, however, to be working again with Dorothy Dalton, a butch-looking prima donna who never stopped reminding him that it was *her* film, and that most of his scenes from their first film, *The Homebreaker*, had ended up on the cutting-room floor. History, of course, would exact its revenge. In 1924, the actress gave up her screen career to marry Oscar Hammerstein's Broadway producer son, Arthur, and though Dorothy Dalton's name *does* head the credits for *Moran of the Lady Letty*, the film is only remembered today because of Valentino's presence.

Although Rambova seems to have been willing to turn a blind eye on Rudy sleeping with other men she saw red when a photograph of him dancing with the actress Aileen Pringle appeared in a newspaper and, aware that he had a very tight schedule to adhere to, she set off for San Francisco where the pair were summoned, like naughty schoolboys, to her mother's apartment on Nob Hill. Once he had adequately explained himself, Rudy had been shown around the luxurious, antique-filled apartment – the Hudnutts were in Europe, on vacation. For the first time Rudy became aware of how fantastically wealthy Rambova's family were, which was, of course, part of the first stage of her plan to get him to marry her.

According to Paul Ivano, until that day Rudy had known little of Rambova's background. The fact that most of the furniture in her duplex was second-hand, and chairs and tables were made from old packing-crates which the pair had spent hours Chinese-lacquering, had given him the impression that, like himself, she too had been compelled to live hand-to-mouth much of the time. That she could have quite easily asked her family for money when times had been lean, but that she had opted for independence instead, impressed him no end, and he decided there and then that he could do no worse than put his future into her hands.

An example of Rambova's ability to get Rudy to do virtually anything occurred a few days after shooting had finished on *Moran Of The Lady Letty*. Posing for so-called 'French postcards' was nothing new in twenties Hollywood. Richard Barthelmess had already flaunted his considerable assets, and George O'Brien, struggling then to make a name for himself as Rudy had a few years earlier, had supplemented his meagre extra's income by visiting a photographic studio in San Francisco and posing for a series of 'health and strength' shots. In these pictures the actor is totally nude and tastefully emulates a number of famous Greek and Roman statues: Cupid, the Discus Thrower and Michelangelo's David all circulated amongst the Hollywood underground during the early 1920s, but Rudy received his set of prints long before anyone else saw them, and kept one in a frame on his bedroom wall. Therefore, when Rambova informed Rudy that *she* had arranged a photographic session at MacGregor's studio, in the city's Post Street – thought to have been the studio used by O'Brien – he was not in the least nervous at the prospect of baring all for the camera.

Rudy was surprised to find that Helen MacGregor, the owner of the studio, was a plain-looking, middle-aged spinster who was not in the least impressed by his celebrity status. Neither was Rambova expecting him to pose in the nude – at least, not quite. She had decided that he would emulate Nijinsky's most celebrated role, *L'après-midi d'un faune*, which she had seen the greatest dancer of his day perform in New York in 1916. The results, in fact, were almost as provocative as the O'Brien and Barthelmess photographs. Wearing nothing but a fig-leaf-covered posing pouch, pointed ears and a bushy tail, Rudy allowed Rambova to paint his torso, arms and legs in black and white segments, and when this was dry she coated his entire body in petroleum jelly until it shone. Thrusting his pelvis audaciously towards the camera and occasionally using a flute, stone pillar or a bunch of grapes as a prop, he looks superbly muscular and, in some shots, even more convincing than the Russian had done.

On 30 October 1921, *The Sheik* opened to scenes of sheer madness in cinemas across America; in its first season, over 100 million people, most of them women, flocked to see it. This was of course the onset of The Roaring Twenties, the age of the 'new woman', the sexually-liberated 'flapper' who smoked cigarettes, sipped illicit whisky and threw away her corsets before rushing off to find some beau with whom to have an affair. Valentino's on-screen machismo also appealed to another type of woman: the type who had been raised with the notion that sex was purely for procreation, a husband's connubial right which was deemed a sin to take pleasure from, let alone fantasise about. Yet in darkened auditoria all across the country, before words began getting in the way, a woman could stare at Valentino's image on the flickering screen and imagine that this quintessence of virility and physical beauty was mouthing absolutely *anything* to her alone ... and so could many of the men, who fought for seats 'out of curiosity', or 'to see what all the fuss was about'. Although Rambova came to like the film, and during its production executed an exquisite portrait of Rudy in his most celebrated role, he himself often confessed to hating it, partly because he was unfamiliar with the director, George Melford, but largely because June Mathis had not been on the set to guide him through his paces, as she had with *The Four Horsemen Of The Apocalypse*.

Just as Julio's bolero had suddenly become one of the country's top-selling women's fashion accessories, so the new film resulted in a massive *Sheik* explosion, though until the end of 1921, incredibly, most Americans did not even know what a sheik *was*. Jesse Lasky put this to rights by commissioning publicity posters explaining not just this, but how to *pronounce* the word: SHRIEK ... FOR THE SHEIK WILL SEEK YOU TOO!

Now, Americans were provided with *Sheik* hair-tonic, bell-bottomed trousers for women *and* men, and even *Sheik* toothpaste, whilst the nation listened to Rudy Vallee crooning 'The Sheik of Araby'. *Sheik* vaseline was purchased discreetly by Rudy's gay fans, many of whom started shaving their chests the way he did ... and Joseph Schmidd Inc., one of the country's leading pharmaceutical companies, began a massive publicity campaign for their 'longer-length' (naturally!) condoms, which were sold in commemorative 'beaut-boxes' with Rudy's picture on the lid. Indeed, everything Rudy did was turned into a publicity gimmick ... if he went into a restaurant and ordered an omelette for breakfast, the next morning the establishment would have *Sheik* omelettes on the menu!

At around this time, Paul Ivano, assisted by two secretaries provided by Paramount, set up the first Rudolph Valentino Fan Club, primarily to stave off the five sacks of mail which were being delivered to the studio every day. Initially, Rudy failed to comprehend why so many people should have wanted to write to him, particularly as at best he could only scribble a handful of replies every now and then. Then June Mathis pointed out to him that, just as she had become a kind of surrogate mother figure for him, so these fans – most of them women – had derived comfort from him after losing sweethearts, husbands and loved ones during the war. He was however surprised – shocked, even – by the contents of some of these letters ... the fact that so-called ladies could request clippings from his fingers and toenails and his *pubic hair*, or that male fans should have the *courage* to include their names and addresses with packages of underwear, which he was expected to wear and even ejaculate into before returning!

It is extremely unlikely that Rudy complied with *such* requests, though in the formative weeks of his fan-club he did sign 500 photographs every day, and over the next few years he wrote a series of lengthy, sometimes highly personal missives to some of his less-obsessive admirers – including Chaw Mank, the young bandleader who became a close friend and who, in 1922, began editing the bi-monthly *Movie Fan News*, one of the first such publications in the United States.

The Sheik also brought Rudy his first public attack. Henry L Meyers, a senator from the Bible-Belt, quoted the film as *the* example as to why there should be an immediate enforcement of a motion picture censorship law:

> Pictures are largely furnished by characters such as one Valentino, now figuring as the star character in rape and

> divorce sensations ... And in Hollywood, California, there's a *colony* of these people, within which debauchery, riotous living, drunkenness, ribaldry and free love where former bartenders, butcher-boys and variety actors who once were paid $10 and $20 a week are now earning salaries of $5,000 a month and do not know what to do with their wealth, extracted largely from poor people who part with their 25 or 50 cent admission fees so that *they* can spend it on 'high-rolling' and dissipation. It is from these sources that our young people are deriving a large part of their inspiration, education and views of life. Looks like there *is* some need for censorship, huh?

Meyers' report, for the Congressional Record, would not be made public until 29 June 1922, but it was handed to Will H Hays, President Harding's former Postmaster General, who in the wake of the Arbuckle trial – the actor was finally acquitted, and received an unprecedented public apology from the jury for the unnecessary agony he had been forced to endure – had resigned his post to take up a $100,000 a year position as president of the newly-founded Motion Picture Code. This organisation's job was to pull together with the Catholic Church and the Bank of America to 'clean up' the movie industry, in the same way as Prohibition was supposed to be protecting the country from the 'evils' of alcohol.

Described by Kenneth Anger in his *Hollywood Babylon* as a 'prim-faced, bat-eared, mealy-mouthed political chiseler', and a man who knew absolutely nothing about the film world, Hays very quickly compiled a 'Doom Book' containing 117 names of Hollywood stars and their associates who were guilty of 'moral turpitude' – in other words, of corrupting the public by the manner in which they were conducting their lives. Wallace Reid, who had become addicted to morphine after being injected with the drug following an injury on the set – in effect, so that he could continue working and save the studio from closing down for the day and everyone being sent home on full pay – was declared 'diseased' by Hays, shoved into a padded cell, and allowed to die. Charlie Chaplin was accused of sleeping with under-aged girls, but allowed to continue working; Mae West, Jean Harlow and Tallulah Bankhead were later denounced as 'prurient filth'.

One of the upholders of the Motion Picture Code was Alice Hall, an acid-tongued reporter from *The Picturegoer* who arranged an interview with Rudy in a tiny Italian restaurant not far from Hollywood Boulevard. When he discovered that Hall's intention was to reveal to her readers that Valentino was effeminate, and a 'pig' at the dinner table, he was understandably reluctant to keep the appointment. Then he decided that he *would* go, and put on a display of charm and manners which would knock the tetchy scribe sideways – or give her a piece of his mind, which of course would have done little to change her seemingly preconceived opinion of him. Hall was deliberately kept waiting for over half an hour, whilst Rudy ate elsewhere, and she was about to leave the restaurant when he showed up, looking convincingly sorry. 'The melancholy face brightened with a magnetic smile,' she recalled, 'and the black eyes flashed greeting as Rudolph Valentino, the culprit, came forward, walking with a sort of undulating motion that spoke of grace – and yet gave not a single hint of effeminacy.'

Rudy then decided to 'get even' with his interviewer, before giving her the opportunity to offend him, by ordering strong black Turkish coffee and honey cakes – his highly-recommended laxative and a trick he often played on people he disliked – before asking her, very loudly, 'And what about *you*, my dear? Do *you* think that women like cavemen?' Hall could only stare open-mouthed as he continued, 'Well, I'm *sure* they do. They may *pretend* that they don't, but it's never any more than pretence. Women *love* to be conquered, Miss Hall. They *love* finding self-expression in submission!'

Once Hall had recovered from the shock – she later claimed that Valentino had also asked her if she had ever masturbated whilst watching him on the screen – she levelled at him, 'And what about *you*, Mr Valentino? Are *you* an authority on cavemen?' To which he responded, with a saucy wink, 'My chief interests away from the studio, Miss Hall, are my dogs and my horses. I have two prize-winning Great Danes – and I like to *ride* every day of the week!'

Surprisingly, Rudy's sexuality and that of his male friends was never investigated by the Hays Office. Indeed, one may only begin to imagine what Hays' assistants would have made of the goings on at the Torch Club or the wealth of gay bars on Sunset Strip, though some sources maintain that these were 'overlooked' owing to Hays' own alleged sexual orientation.

Under the Hays regime bad language, open-lipped kissing, murder, overt violence, substance abuse, drinking and even hirsute chests were outlawed on the screen. Yet, aside from Henry L Meyer's diatribe, Rudy – like Garbo, a few years later – was able to pursue his career unhindered by these absurd censorship laws because, though he bared his chest in almost every one of his films, he did not have to do much, physically, to incite eroticism on the screen – other than lear, flash his eyes or flare his nostrils – and he could not, he declared, be censored for doing what only came naturally! His acting, of course, amounted to considerably more than this.

Smack in the midst of the tremendous excitement which greeted *The Sheik* came Rudy's divorce from Jean Acker, an event which, the press promised, would become the media sensation of the year and offer an amusing antidote to the 'salacious' Arbuckle scandal which was currently monopolising the gossip columns. And, unlike this dreadful business which had ended Arbuckle's career, Rudy's court appearances would do his reputation no harm at all.

The proceedings opened in Los Angeles on 23 November 1921, with Judge Thomas Toland presiding, and whilst both parties vied for the best newspaper headlines over the next few weeks, Rudy's fans clung to every word which was said about this sham marriage which had obviously caused their idol much pain. Jean Acker was the first to take the stand, telling the jury that marriage to Valentino had been humiliating because, whilst she had been earning upwards of $200 a week making films for Metro, he had been persistently broke. She had, however, tried to help him in his career by supplying him with money, clothes and underwear – placing enough emphasis on this last word to give the impression that Rudy had been in the habit of borrowing *her* underwear. There were guffaws from the gallery when Acker divulged that

Rudy had also purloined large quantities of her favourite, very expensive French perfume.

Acker than produced as evidence one of Helen MacGregor's photographs – the one of Rudy's faun, crouching submissively at Rambova's feet – and rattled off a lengthy spiel of how, whilst he had failed to support his wife, he had clearly not been averse to providing for his mistress. Then, suddenly touching her forehead as if about to faint, she requested a glass of water before continuing. Not only had their union never been consummated, in January 1920, the court learned, Rudy had barged into her bathroom whilst she had been sitting naked in the tub, and thumped her!

When the time came for Rudy to take the stand, the courtroom was packed to the rafters. Hardly any of the general public had heard him speak, and when his voice was revealed to be as dark, sexy and alluring as the rest of him, several female fans passed out cold and the proceedings were halted whilst they were carried out or revived. Having explained to the jury how he had pleaded with his wife to admit him to the bridal chamber, Rudy confessed that he *had* hit her, but only out of extreme provocation because she had insulted him. This brought a sharp intake of breath from the public gallery – again, many fans wished that they too could have been on the receiving end of such sex-orientated violence. Rudy also raised a few laughs when he added that he had wanted to marry Jean Acker because he had believed her to be a 'normal' woman. His reaction to the MacGregor photograph – which, as there is no evidence supporting the statement, appears to have been an outright lie – was that the picture was but one of a series supporting a film project he and Rambova were working on, entitled *A Faun Through The Ages*. As for the matter of his finances at the time of his marriage, he pointed accusingly at his wife and pronounced loudly and clearly, 'I took her to be my lawful wedded wife, for better or for worse, for richer or for poorer. What more can I say?' He then produced *his* evidence – a letter which he had written, in broken English, to Jean Acker on 22 November 1919, just over two weeks after their wedding. Judge Toland read it out to the court, his voice getting progressively louder on account of the sniffling from Rudy's fans – if this dreadful woman had wronged *him*, then they too had been wronged. The letter concluded,

> I am at a complete loss to understand your conduct to me ... Since I cannot enforce my presence on you, I guess I better give up. I am always ready to furnish you a home and all the comfort to the best of my moderate means and ability. Please dear Jean, darling, come to your senses and give me an opportunity to prove my sincere love and eternal devotion to you.
>
> Your unhappy, loving husband. Rudolpho.

It was probably inevitable, given the wealth of public support for this man, that in his summing up on 10 January 1922, Judge Toland should declare that in his opinion, Rudy *had* been deserted by his wife, and he granted him an interlocutory decree, with the divorce to be made final on 4 March 1923. Jean Acker was awarded a one-off alimony payment of $12,000 – money which Rudy borrowed from Paramount, a smart move on the part of Jesse Lasky who, until the loan was repaid, would have total control over Valentino's career ... or so he believed. His legal fees, Lasky declared, Rudy would have to sort out himself.

That same evening, celebrating his victory in a Los Angeles speakeasy, Rudy proposed to Rambova, who there and then rang Nazimova to inform her than their plan had borne fruit.

6
The Caress of Romance

'Does one EVER know women?'

Exactly *why* Rudy should have wanted to marry Natacha Rambova in the first place baffled his friends and colleagues. Jesse Lasky detested her, and had already publicly declared that if Valentino persisted in allowing her to meddle in his affairs, she would pose a very serious threat to his career. June Mathis, who had done her utmost to prevent him from being 'shanghaied' into making *Camille*, and who, of course, was well aware of Rudy's sexual preferences, was terrified of him making the mistake of marrying another lesbian. Other close friends, like George O'Brien and Charles Farrell, who themselves were, or soon would be, partners in so-called 'twilight-tandems' quickly pointed out the benefits of such unions – providing, of course, that he and Rambova intended their marriage to be used *only* as a cover-up. From Rambova's point of view, this certainly was the case – as for Rudy, he really was in love with the woman, albeit that his kind of love did not lean towards the physical, and his prime concern after the divorce hearing was to find them a place to live, in a style which befitted Hollywood's new, self-styled 'royal' couple.

Although the success of *The Sheik* had resulted in Rudy's salary being upped to $1,250 a week, financially he was far from secure because he was still spending extravagantly and living way beyond his means – encouraged to do so, of course, by Rambova. Even so, this did not deter him, and he shopped around for several weeks before settling on an empty, Spanish-style property at 6670 Wedgewood Place, in the Whitley Heights district, within easy walking distance of Hollywood Boulevard. Exactly how much the house had been on the market for is not known, though Jesse Lasky – who on behalf of Paramount was loaning Rudy the money for the deposit – was able to get the vendor to drop the price considerably because it was in such a state of disrepair: the gardens were knee-high in weeds and rubbish, there was no electricity, gas or hot water, most of the doors and window-frames needed replacing, and the roof leaked. Fortunately, in those days when labour came very cheap, even in Hollywood, Rudy was able to afford to hire a small team who moved in at once to begin renovations. Nothing would have pleased him more than to have personally supervised the landscaping of his gardens – this had been a dream of his, ever since he arrived in New York clutching his agricultural diploma – but at the end of January 1922, Jesse Lesky summoned him to begin working on his next film.

Elinor Glyn was a British socialite who had rocketed to fame in 1907 with the risqué novel, *Three Weeks*, and a few years into her Hollywood career she would achieve infamy – and a fee of $50,000 – by coining the ridiculously simple term 'It' for sex-appeal. Glyn, a fifty-seven-year old matron and self-styled 'arch-duchess of etiquette, manners and lovemaking', really had looked the part when she arrived in Hollywood at the end of 1921. A heavily-built woman with piercing green eyes and a shock of red hair, she had barged into Jesse Lasky's office wearing a floor-length leopardskin gown, and $250,000 worth of diamonds. Lasky, who had failed to obtain the screen-rights to *Three Weeks*, had simply plucked a title out of thin air – *The Great Moment* – and hired Glyn to write a story around this as a vehicle for Gloria Swanson, the former Mack Sennett bathing-belle, already a massive star in Hollywood. Glyn had obliged, but before signing the contract she had ensured that a clause be inserted giving her final approval of Swanson's leading man. Lasky had sanctioned this, and Glyn had 'perused' dozens of young hopefuls, including Richard Arlen and Thomas Meighan, before being introduced to Rudy at a party. Here, surrounded by a sea of reporters, he had kissed her hand and she had loudly pronounced, 'My dear Mr Valentino, you are far and away quite the greatest lover the screen has ever known. Please say you will appear in *my* film!' But before Rudy had been able to answer, Rambova had chimed in, 'No, he will *not*!', and Lasky had subsequently engaged Milton Sills.

Now, however, Elinor Glyn would not take no for an answer, and she asked Lasky to arrange a meeting with Rudy so that she could tell him about her latest project, *Beyond The Rocks*, which was being adapted for the screen – again with Gloria Swanson as leading lady. Lasky arranged for himself, Glyn and Rudy to lunch at the Ship's Café in Santa Monica. Neither Rambova nor the press were informed, and before the first course had been served, Rudy had consented to play the young English aristocrat, Lord Bracondale, described by Glyn as 'a model of sartorial elegance', though by the end of the meal she was not of the same opinion of the actor, whose table-manners left much to be desired. Rudy burped his way through five courses, ate all the leftovers from Lasky's and Glyn's plates, drank the gravy from his own, and picked his nose with his teaspoon.

Encouraged by Elinor Glyn, Rudy submitted an article to *Photoplay* entitled 'Women And Love' – though much of its content had in fact been penned by Glyn herself. For the thousands of Valentino fans who snapped up every copy of the magazine within hours of it hitting the news-stands, however, *only* he could have made a statement such as, 'One can always be kind to a woman one cares nothing about ... and cruel to a woman one loves!'

Once more, Rambova criticised Rudy for agreeing to appear in 'costume-drama trash', particularly when she learned that Elinor Glyn's book had been given the thumbs-down by British critics – some had denounced it as both illiterate and ungrammatical. And when Rudy explained that he would be working with Gloria Swanson, at twenty-four already enjoying the reputation of a voracious maneater, Rambova declared that if he *was* going to do the film, then she would be present every moment he was on the set!

Over the next four weeks, the director of *Beyond The Rocks*, Sam Wood – who had also directed *The Great Moment* – and the rest of the cast lived off their shattered nerves. Much to Rudy's surprise, Gloria Swanson could not stand him – this probably had a lot to do with Rambova, who never missed out on an opportunity to tell her how fortunate she was to be working with an actor of the Great Valentino's ability. There were also fireworks between the director and his leading man when Rudy ignored Wood's instructions, playing every scene the way Rambova *ordered* him to ... which brought the scoff from Swanson, 'And they call this dago the World's Greatest Lover? I'd prefer to call him the World's Biggest Wanker!' Rudy reacted to this by ensuring that he always had his mouth full of crushed garlic whenever he had to kiss her.

There were further screaming matches between Rambova and some of the other actors, whom she accused of over-playing the best scenes at Rudy's expense – and between Rudy and the cameraman, Alfred Gilks, whom he yelled at, accusing Gilks of not filming him from his best angles ... a silly dispute, for Valentino was so dazzlingly photogenic that there *were* no bad angles. Then, halfway through shooting, when Rambova spat at Gloria Swanson for missing a cue, the entire cast and crew walked off the set. This prompted a personal appearance from Jesse Lasky, who appealed for calm – and for Rudy's feelings to be taken into account following his 'harrowing' ordeal in the divorce court. The picture was finished on time, with Wood and Swanson both telling Rudy to his face that they never wanted to *speak* to him again, let alone work with him.

At the end of January 1922, a somewhat tremulous Rudy met his prospective in-laws for the first time. 'My people were furious,' Rambova told Ruth Waterbury. 'The thought of my being married to an actor seemed terrible to them. All that publicity was quite the last straw with them.' She had wanted her parents to be 'received' at Whitley Heights, but as the house was still being renovated they had to make do with her duplex which, she told them, she was renting 'between homes'.

The Hudnutts were met at the railway station by a hired liveried chauffeur, and several 'maids' – hoofers supplied by the studio – fussed over them during their first day in Hollywood ... until Rudy, unable to stand the pretence any longer, told them the truth.

This made for better relations all around. Rudy later said that from the first firm handshake he had found his new family wholly unpretentious, friendly, and suitably but not over sophisticated, and nowhere near as snobbish as their daughter had made out. They too were impressed by his easy-going charm, though like Elinor Glyn they had more than a little to say about his at-table 'sound-effects'. Mrs Hudnutt, however, was the one with whom he would forge the closest attachment, forcing the conclusion from Rambova, '*All* women love the man who appeals to their maternity. Rudy does that instinctively and it is devastating in its effects on feminine resistance.'

Mrs Hudnutt even insisted that Rudy would soon have to begin calling her 'mother', though this would of course have been expecting *too* much. The evening also produced an amusing moment, when Mrs Hudnutt asked after dinner if she might use the bathroom; she was sitting on the toilet when the lion-cub, Zela, suddenly leapt out from behind the shower curtain, planted her paws on her shoulders and began licking her face!

A few days after the Hudnutts had returned to San Francisco, June Mathis collected Rudy from the duplex – having made sure that the troublesome Rambova was not at home – and drove him to Jesse Lasky's office, where he was offered the coveted role of the young bullfighter, Juan Gallardo, in Mathis's adaptation of another Ibanez blockbuster, *Blood And Sand*. Rudy could not have been more delighted: Bebe Daniels was to be his co-star, George Fitzmaurice would direct, June Mathis would be with him all the time he was working, and, most important of all, the locations would be authentic because Lasky had arranged for the film to be shot in Spain.

For once, Rambova was on Rudy's side. The reviews for *Moran Of The Lady Letty* had not been unflattering, but they had scarcely matched those for *The Sheik*, which proved but one thing – Valentino's public preferred to see him in costume dramas as opposed to contemporary ones. Within the week, however, Jesse Lasky had been compelled to revise his plans regarding the new film, though he was so fearful of Rudy's reaction that he sent June Mathis to the duplex, knowing that the actor would never throw a tantrum with her, no matter *how* grim the tidings. Again, the scriptwriter waited until Rambova was not around before informing him that both George Fitzmaurice and Bebe Daniels had dropped out of the production on account of 'work commitments' – Mathis did not have the heart to tell Rudy that neither of them were willing to tolerate Rambova's meddling – and that, after a more detailed analysis of the film's projected costs, *Blood And Sand* would now be shot on a Hollywood back-lot, though he was assured that the sets would be so authentic that the public would never know the difference.

Rudy was bitterly disappointed. Since his mother's death he had worried constantly about his brother and sister and had hoped that he might see them during his trip to Europe. Mathis explained to him that the studio had changed their minds purely for financial reasons, maintaining that it would be cheaper incorporating actual footage of bullfights shot in Madrid and Seville. Rudy therefore suggested a compromise: if Lasky could find him someone to teach him the rudimentaries of bullfighting so that he could master some of his own stunts, there would be no arguments from him concerning the change of director and co-star! Lasky kept his side of the bargain by providing him with the services of a former professional matador, and a portable arena. During training sessions, however, Paramount's insurers insisted that Rudy be restricted to fighting only horned cows, and always with a marksman close at hand.

For Rudy, authenticity was what movie making was all about. 'From the start I disassociate myself from the character I am to portray, and live and love as I imagine *he* would,' he wrote in *Movie Weekly* after the film's release. 'While I am making a picture, I cease to be Valentino and become the character I am playing until the picture is finished.' He even went to the trouble of pronouncing all of his lines in Spanish – though his voice would not of course be heard – afraid that lip-readers would accuse him of being a phoney if he delivered them in English! He was apparently *so* convincing, Rambova recorded in her memoirs, that throughout shooting he was often mistaken for a *real* Spaniard! She told Ruth Waterbury,

He would stop by every evening on his way home to see me, but he might as well have been bound up in the covers of a book for all the humanness he possessed. He was that bullfighter *all* the time. He would swagger in and be very loudmouthed and dictatorial, or else I would see him leering at me the way he looked at Dona Sol, or gazing at me with the great beseeching eyes he used in the film towards his little wife, and of course the amusing part of it was that he was supremely aware of it. He never dropped the part for a moment!

Paul Ivano also spoke of how Rudy would wear his Juan Gallardo get-up in the bedroom, re-enacting some of his bullfighting scenes as a prelude to sex. He concluded, 'At first it was quite exciting, but after a while even that grew boring. We had a real-life toreador in the house and he was a goddamned nuisance!'

Rudy was introduced to his replacement director, Fred Niblo, who would later direct Ramon Novarro's infamous *Ben Hur* and Garbo's *The Temptress*. With Niblo was Dorothy Arzner, a member of Nazimova's 'sewing circle' who would edit this and many more classic silent pictures before achieving recognition as one of the most innovative directors of the Thirties. Nothing, however, could have prepared the usually unshockable Rudy for his meeting with his new co-star ... the flamboyant, grossly outspoken Nita Naldi.

Few Hollywood actresses have been able to out-vulgar Nita Naldi – born Donna Dooley in New York City in (she claimed) 1900, forced into a convent education simply because her great-aunt happened to be the Mother Superior, and kicked out again because she had proved thoroughly uncontrollable ... leaving the cloisters on the Friday and by Monday dancing topless in a New York burlesque. Soon afterwards she had been discovered by Hollywood's most notorious womaniser, John Barrymore, and having passed the test on the obligatory casting couch, she had been offered a part in his *Dr Jekyll And Mr Hyde*. More famous in the film world for her large breasts than for any acting talents, Nita Naldi's very first words to Rudy, in Jesse Lasky's office, after he had executed a polite little bow before kissing the *palm* of her hand – as Elinor Glyn had taught him to do in *Beyond The Rocks* – were, 'Howdy, Rudy! Wanna feel my tits?'

Naldi's obsession with her breasts would continue throughout her life. Even as an old woman she would expose them to reporters to show how firm they still were, and the first time she revealed them to Rudy, in front of everyone on the set of *Blood And Sand*, Fred Niblo blew his top and threatened to fire her for 'humiliating' his star ... until Rudy quipped, in a rare outburst of humour, 'For one awful moment I thought I was back in Castallaneta, amongst my father's milk cows!'

Unfortunately, this was the only jollity that Niblo experienced from Rudy, for once Rambova began visiting the set – encouraged to do so in a moment's weakness by Jesse Lasky, who had never forgiven himself for sending June Mathis to do his dirty work – he began to regret his change of heart. 'The part of Juan Gallardo meant so much to him that he ignored the way the company were treating him,' Rambova told Ruth Waterbury, 'And they couldn't have treated him worse. They gave him a dressing-room that was really a little hole. On location they gave him a scrap of mirror just big enough for him to see his face in, rather than the full-length one they furnish every other star with. He had to dress and undress before the whole lot.'

Stripping off in public did not of course overtly perturb Rudy, who was so proud of his physique that he would peel off his shirt or vest and flex his muscles at whoever happened to be passing ... although in this instance, Rambova was absolutely right: compared to some of the stars then regarded by the media as Valentino's equals – Barthelmess, Meighan and the Talmadge sisters – the studio *were* treating him shabbily. Shooting was therefore held up until Rudy had been supplied with an en-suite dressing-room, built and decorated to Rambova's specification.

Rambova next delivered a list of grievances concerning the technicians, the cameraman, and the other actors apart from Nita Naldi – astonishingly, the only one of Rudy's leading ladies she not only approved of, but befriended – and Niblo himself, before dismissing June Mathis's script as 'artless tripe'. For Niblo, this was the last straw: he told Jesse Lasky that unless this 'she-devil' was removed from the lot, he would not be responsible for her safety. At this, Rudy let off a little steam by putting his fist through one of the sets, declaring that if Rambova *was* asked to leave, then he would go with her. Shooting was resumed, but in an atmosphere described by Fred Niblo – yet another director who swore never to work with Valentino again – as, 'Like sitting on top of a volcano, never knowing when the goddamned thing's going to blow!'

Rudy's sexual potency, coupled with his acute sensitivity and a knack of knowing when and how to express emotion without becoming over-sentimental – a taboo amongst American males – enabled *Blood And Sand* to become one of his most popular films. It was certainly his personal favourite.

Juan Gallardo, the good-for-nothing cobbler's son from the de la Feria suburb of Seville, is obsessed by the *corrida*. We first see him as a wide-eyed, grinning youth, with a shock of un-Valentino-like unruly hair sticking out from under his cap, entertaining the locals in a makeshift bullring with a group of ragamuffin friends. When one of them is killed by the bull, he dispatches the beast, then rushes off to tell his mother (Rose Rosanova) of his aspirations. 'Some day I'll build you a big house, and you'll have a fine carriage and all the silk dresses and shawls you want,' he promises, whilst she patches a hole in his trousers. Rudy particularly liked working with Rosanova, declaring that in some ways she reminded him of his own mother – their scenes together are quite touching, and one can almost imagine that it is Gabrielle Guglielmi who is chasing her wayward son around the kitchen with a broom!

In next to no time, Gallardo is the idol of Seville, and women who have thus far in his life only scoffed at his machismo begin pursuing him, even though he is promised to Carmen, his childhood sweetheart (Lila Lee). 'I hate all women, save one!' he tells a bistro strumpet who proffers her lips after they have danced, flinging her to the floor. Then off he goes to serenade Carmen under her bedroom window, proclaiming, 'By the figure of Faith on the Girala tower, I swear I love no one but you!'

Gallardo and Carmen are married,, but she stays at home when he leaves for the *corrida* in Madrid. Here, there is a titillating little scene where he is being dressed in his embroidered, multi-coloured 'suit of lights': his nearly-nude form is seen through a frosted screen, behind which he dresses suggestively, at one point sticking out a perfectly pedicured foot for his dresser to massage and shod. Then he suddenly springs into view, pirouetting like a ballet dancer whilst the seemingly endless cummerbund is wound tightly about his waist. 'The bull that can kill me is not yet born!' he boasts. Then, after the fight, temptation comes his way in the shape of the luscious Dona Sol (Nita Naldi) the ambassador's widow who is most certainly a tart *without* a heart. 'What wonderful arms you have,' she tells him. 'Your muscles are like iron!'

Initially, Gallardo is terrified of the vamp, but after a tremendous fight with his conscience he gives in to her demands, as the camera transfers to the almost saintly face of the spurned wife. Then follows the obligatory display of Valentino sado-masochism. Gallardo, tortured by loving two women, yet powerless to let Dona Sol go, though he wants to, reacts badly when she confesses that she dreams only of the day when his strong hands will beat her – wrecking the room, he towers over her prostrate form and levels, 'Snake! One moment I love you, the other I hate you! Serpent from hell!'

Gallardo's fate is now sealed. Dona Sol arranges for her car to break down outside his home, and when Carmen walks in on the scene there, she realises what her husband has been up to. The toreador is then introduced to the notorious bandit, Plumitas (Walter Long), the subject of the film's subplot who is being hunted by the police. The bandit explains that in their respective careers they have a great deal in common: 'If God deserts us, you will be carried out of the theatre feet foremost, and I will be shot down like a dog.' His spirit broken, Gallardo begs Carmen's forgiveness, discovers that Dona Sol has only been using him, and – moments after Plumitas has been gunned down in the crowd – he allows himself to be gored by the bull, and subsequently dies in his wife's arms in what remains one of the most moving scenes in any silent movie.

Meanwhile, on 7 May 1922, the day after Rudy's twenty-seventh birthday, *Beyond The Rocks* was premiered, disappointing some fans because Rudy's Lord Bracondale did not turn out to be some menacing, musclebound, dark-skinned seducer, but a shifty English aristocrat. He also received the most scathing attack from *Photoplay*'s Dick Dorgan, who having witnessed one of his tantrums on the set of *Blood And Sand*, felt qualified to offer the magazine's readers his 'A Song Of Hate' – a list of reasons why he, like most 'normal' American males, loathed this 'arrogant European he-vamp pretender to the Hollywood Crown':

> I hate Valentino! ALL men hate Valentino!
> I hate his oriental optics! I hate his classic nose!
> I hate his Roman face! I hate his smile!
> I hate his glistening teeth! I hate his patent-leather hair!
> I hate his Svengali glare!
> I hate him because he dances too well!
> I hate him because he's a slicker!
> I hate him because he's the Great Lover of the Screen!
> I hate him because he's an Embezzler of Hearts!
> I hate him because he's too apt in the art of osculation!
> I hate him because he's leading MAN for Gloria Swanson!
> I hate him because he's TOO GOOD-LOOKING!

Dorgan had seen a clip of newsreel film within which, during a break in the shooting of *The Sheik*, Rudy had personally fixed Agnes Ayres' makeup, with apparent consummate expertise. Such a diatribe could have been interpreted and dismissed as the ramblings of a jealous man, and Rudy almost certainly would not have risen to the occasion had it not been for the caricatures preceding the piece. The first drawing, entitled, 'As The Women See Him', depicted Rudy as suave, handsome and sophisticated ... whereas the second, 'As The Men See Him', portrayed him as a balding queen with a huge mouth, sparkling teeth, and wearing lipstick and an earring. Rudy vowed that if he ever came face-to-face with this 'toad's turd' – who in an earlier edition of *Photoplay* had referred to the sheik's mother as 'some wop or other', a slur directly aimed at Rudy's own mother – he would make him choke on his words.

Many years later, Rudy's friend, Adela Rogers St Johns – whose defence of his 'manliness' was so over the top that many people who would not normally have doubted Rudy's masculinity began doing so *because* of it – compared Rudy's cult status with that of another sexually closeted actor, Clark Gable, saying, 'Every American man was perfectly willing that his wife should be in love with Gable, because Gable is what *he'd* liked to have been. But they were not willing that their wives should have been in love with this dago.'

Immediately after the premiere of *Beyond The Rocks*, Rudy and Rambova officially announced their engagement. Both had allegedly consulted their lawyers and been told that, although California law decreed that they could not marry until the spring of 1923, there was nothing to prevent them from marrying in another state, as many other showbusiness couples had done. Rambova told Ruth Waterbury, 'When we did discover we were in love, we had it all planned that we would wait a year until Rudy's divorce was final. But I knew nothing about divorces, and neither did he. They are so different everywhere and we really thought he was divorced and thought that it was only some state law that kept us from marrying.' Rudy had already discussed the matter with Jesse Lasky, who also seems to have been of the same opinion – it was he who innocuously suggested that the ceremony should take place south of the border, in Mexico. Had Lasky been consulted one week later, however, *after* his meeting with Will Hays, the outcome of the next few days would have been vastly different.

On Friday 12 May, Rudy, Rambova, Paul Ivano, Douglas Gerrard and Nazimova drove to Palm Springs, where they spent the night at the home of Dr Floretta White, a friend of the Russian star. The next morning – it was Ivano's twenty-second birthday – the party set off for the then small town of Mexicali, where they hoped they might marry quickly and with a minimum of fuss. They had not, however, reckoned on the enthusiasm of the Mayor, Otto Moller, whose deputation met them at the border, heralded by the local brass band. In Mexicali itself, the streets were lined with several thousand wellwishers who had poured in from neighbouring communities.

Only hours later, every newspaper office in America was preparing its most exciting headline in years: Rudolph Valentino, the world's greatest lover, had committed bigamy and if found guilty could face a monumental fine and several years in jail! The *Los Angeles Record* even printed the instruction in huge letters across its front page: ARREST VALENTINO!

By this time, however, the newlyweds were on their way to the town of El Centro, where the bride spent the night with Nazimova at the Barbara Worth Hotel ... and Rudy slept with his two friends. 'Well, it *was* Paul's birthday,' he later told Jacques Hébertot. Then, the next day the party drove back to Palm Springs, where they had planned to spend a month's 'honeymoon'. They had barely unpacked their bags when Rudy received a call from his lawyer, W I Gilbert: the Los Angeles District Attorney, Thomas Lee Woolwine, had laid charges of bigamy against him and he was urged to return to Hollywood at once. The authorities, Gilbert promised, would review his case more favourably if he faced the music and convinced the DA that it had never been his intention to do anything immoral.

Because the press – and quite possibly the police – were watching Rambova's duplex, the party drove straight to the empty house at Whitley Heights, where an 'emergency' meeting had been convened between the Valentinos, their lawyers, Jesse Lasky and a representative of the Hays Office. Rambova's initial reaction was to declare that she had been taken aback by the events of the last few days: when the party had arrived in Palm Springs, she said, such thoughts had never crossed her or Rudy's minds, and it was one of their friends – she could not remember which one – who had suggested their marrying in Mexico. 'It was all fearfully respectable,' she told Jesse Lasky, a statement she would repeat many times over the coming months. And when Lasky replied that he had been told of Rudy's plans beforehand, by Rudy himself, she went completely out of control, screaming that she would exact the most terrible revenge on whoever had shopped them to the press, and threatening Will Hays with a fate worse than death. It was ultimately decided she should be removed from the scene, and that same afternoon she left for New York, where she spent the night in hiding before travelling on to the Hudnutts' Foxlair estate in the Adirondacks.

As Thomas Lee Woolwine had become inexplicably indisposed, Rudy was forced to wait until the next morning – Sunday 21 May – before driving with his lawyer and Paul Ivano to the District Attorney's office, where a very smug Woolwine charged him on two counts of bigamy: firstly, 'for marrying one Winifred Shaughnessy whilst still legally married to one Mrs Jean Acker Guglielmi', and secondly, 'for cohabiting with the aforesaid Winifred Shaughnessy in Palm Springs, California.' Bail was set at $10,000, to be paid in cash before midnight.

Rudy was faced with a massive predicament. Woolwine knew that it would be virtually impossible for him to come up with such a large sum of money at such short notice, particularly as the banks were closed – it was precisely for this reason that he had stayed away from his office on the Saturday. Rudy therefore called Jesse Lasky, drawing a blank when Lasky explained that he did not have that much cash on him, either, and neither would any of the other Paramount executives in case Rudy was thinking about calling them ... and in any case, had not the studio advanced him enough money already for his divorce settlement and for the deposit on his house?

In fact, Will Hays had *ordered* Paramount *not* to save their biggest star from going to jail: the 'foreign upstart', he declared, had foisted his corrupt European morals on American society, and needed to be taught a lesson. And, Hays added, with several of Valentino's films on general release, would not the resulting publicity be good for the box-office? Woolwine, too, had good cause to adhere to Hays' instructions. His term of office was drawing to a close, and the only obstacle standing between him and re-election was an accusation of sexual abuse from a young female typist. Therefore, whilst he *could* have given Rudy until midnight on the *Monday* to pay his bail, Woolwine was 'persuaded' not to do so by Hays – resulting in the typist being paid several thousand dollars to drop her case against Woolwine, whilst Rudy was unceremoniously thrown into jail.

For twelve hours, Douglas Gerrard and Paul Ivano contacted their friends, desperately trying to raise the money to get Rudy freed. Nazimova was out of town and Jesse Lasky, since receiving the call that Rudy had been arrested, had suddenly decided to take a vacation. June Mathis gave the two young men all the cash she had on her, but even when the trio had pooled their resources, they had nowhere near enough to get Rudy out.

A solution was found when Douglas Gerrard called George O'Brien. The actor's father, Dan – San Francisco's Chief of Police – was visiting for the weekend, and Gerrard asked him if he could pull a few strings to at least get Rudy a cell of his own until this mess had been sorted out. It may well be that Dan had already suspected that his son and Rudy had been more than just good friends – he certainly knew that George was currently the lover of the actor Thomas Meighan. Before the Chief of Police could even think of what to do, however, George called Meighan, who in the past had experienced at least one one-night stand with Rudy when they had met at the Torch Club. The money was delivered to Douglas Gerrard within the hour, and Rudy was released ... having spent a tortuous night in an open cell with a dozen of the most despicable human beings he had ever seen in his life. He is also thought to have been raped by his sadistic warder.

Thomas Meighan, then aged forty-three, still dashing and at the peak of his career, also had a good enough reason to hate Will Hays and the Los Angeles District Attorney. Only recently, Hays had begun an investigation into Meighan's private life after Thomas Lee Woolwine had informed him that the actor had allegedly importuned for sex outside a public lavatory on Hollywood Boulevard. The case had amounted to nothing, however, though when Meighan explained to Cecil B DeMille what *could* have happened because of the machinations of these detestable men, revenge came in the form of a film. DeMille's *Manslaughter*, which began shooting a few weeks after Rudy's release from jail, cynically by-passed the censor with its scenes of open-mouthed kissing, sex, nudity, hirsute bodies and gratuitous violence with the District Attorney (Meighan) comparing the revelry he had witnessed in Hollywood with the orgies that had taken place in ancient Rome ... turning his alter-ego into Attila the Hun, whose marauders, at the end of the film, wipe out the so-called 'filth' which the Hays Office so obviously despised.

Meighan and Douglas Gerrard were waiting for Rudy at the Los Angeles police headquarters, and so were an army of reporters, photographers and fans. Aided by his lawyer, Rudy had prepared a statement before leaving the Tombs Prison, part of which read:

> I loved deeply, but in loving, prompted by the noblest intentions a man could have, I have erred and if so I deeply regret that I should have done anything which might lower me in the estimation of all those American people who have been so kind to me. I was advised that a marriage under Mexican laws would be valid, and upon my arrival in Mexicali the question of this validity arose again – and again I was told by Mexican officials that my marriage would be legal. Then, upon my return to California I was advised by my lawyer that the validity of my marriage here might be questioned. It was therefore determined that we should separate, that Mrs Valentino should return to her parents in New York, and that I should remain here and continue with my work ... I have no intention, and have *had* no intention, of violating the California law, and neither had Mrs Valentino. As soon as one year has transpired, I swear that we will remarry.

Jesse Lasky, who had ignored Rudy's plight, now ordered him – again for the sake of his career, and the effect any adverse publicity might have on it – to get his bigamy trial over and done with before shooting started on his next (unnamed) film at the end of June. Again, the newspapers had a field-day, initially at Rambova's expense. Until now the media had been hoodwinked into believing that she was Russian, and when it was revealed that this exotic-looking creature was none other than plain Winifred Shaughnessy from Salt Lake City, albeit the daughter of a millionaire, she was hounded by the press at every stop along the long train journey back to New York.

When Nazimova learned how her beloved 'babushka' was being lampooned and humiliated by the press, she threatened to sue several newspapers, until her lawyer advised her that such action would be *most* imprudent: both of Rudy's wives had, after all, spent their respective wedding-nights with her. Terrified of being cross-examined in a courtroom, and a sworn enemy of the Hays Office on account of the advance publicity for *Salome*, Nazimova decided that the wisest course of action might be to flee Hollywood until the scandal had died down. She was backing her car out of the driveway at the Garden of Alla when a court official apprehended her and served her with a subpoena. Douglas Gerrard, Paul Ivano and several independent witnesses from Mexicali and Palm Springs were also summoned to the hearing.

The proceedings went smoothly enough. Jesse Lasky had given Ivano and Gerrard an ultimatum: either they perjure themselves by demonstrating to the court that the marriage had not been consummated, or they would never find work in Hollywood again. Nazimova, of course, was a law unto herself, and Lasky kept his fingers crossed that she would not go over the top when called to give evidence. Ivano and Gerrard had no need to commit perjury. Both men informed the judge, J Walter Hanby, that because Rambova had complained of feeling unwell – which *may* have been true – Rudy had spent his wedding-night in their room, which was certainly true. Much to Lasky's relief, Nazimova told exactly the same story, as did Floretta White, who added that she could personally vouch for the fact that the Valentinos had not been alone for a single moment during their stay in Palm Springs, which in her professional opinion as a well-respected doctor meant only one thing – the marriage had not been consummated, therefore they were not legally married!

In his summing up on 5 June, Judge Hanby had no alternative but to exonerate Rudy of bigamy due to insufficient evidence against him. Rudy, however, no doubt acutely embarrassed that his virility would be questioned more than ever now that the press were aware that he had failed to 'make it' on *two* consecutive wedding-nights, only made a rod for his own back by repeating to the packed courtroom the public apology he had made earlier to the press, concluding, 'And I give you my word, at the end of the year's waiting, Natacha and I *will* remarry!' Until this time, Rambova had agreed to stay with her parents, though as a cautionary measure, Judge Hanby issued a decree forbidding the couple from sharing a hotel room, or spending any time unchaperoned under the same roof.

7
The Sympathy of Understanding

'If a man has one friend upon whom he can rely, or at best two or three, he is indeed blessed among men.'

Now that he was officially single again, Rudy's friends begged him to reconsider very seriously before getting hitched – particularly to Natacha Rambova, whom they hoped they had seen the last of. Jesse Lasky even offered to fix him up with studio dates, as a means of convincing his colleagues and the increasing number of actors, directors and technicians who were refusing to have anything to do with a Valentino picture whilst she was around, that the 'she-devil' had gone for good. This only made matters worse. Rudy angrily declared that such women were but whores, and in all his adult life he had never resorted to paying for sex – quite the reverse. Jesse Lasky, a man who disliked being told to mind his own business, even though like many of the Hollywood moguls he had fashioned a career out of organising the lives of his stars, lost his temper and threatened to fire Rudy unless he obeyed orders, to which the actor responded caustically: '*Dogs* and *servants* obey orders. I am neither!'

Over the next few weeks only June Mathis, Paul Ivano and Douglas Gerrard were allowed anywhere near Rudy as he flung himself into the restoration programme at Whitley Heights, helping the workmen to dig drains, tear up weeds and mend the roof. Occasionally, of an evening he would spar at the local gym with Richard Arlen or George O'Brien, and most days would be rounded off by a visit to the Torch Club, where he would 'cool-off' in one of the bareback pools.

Working out of doors did Rudy no harm at all. Over the previous few months he had coped with his frustrations by over-eating: Hollywood had a wealth of Italian restaurants, and being a pasta addict, he had not been averse to consuming three meals in a single sitting. He had also been getting through three packs of cigarettes a day – indeed, there are virtually no off-set photographs taken at this time when Rudy is *not* smoking. Now, however, by 'consulting' his familiar, Black Feather, he was convinced that he would kick the latter habit completely ... until the young brave informed him that maybe *two* packs a day would not prove *too* harmful. His food intake he managed to control without any difficulty, and after several weeks' rigorous exercise and weight-training he managed to get himself back into his usual tremendous physical shape. In August 1922, a middle-aged female journalist reported how she had almost died of heart-failure when Valentino – posing for a series of 'Rudy the Redskin' photographs, wearing pigtails and a skimpy loincloth and in some shots holding his quiver *most* provocatively – invited her to weigh and measure him! She wrote in her column:

> Five-eleven, 180 pounds, 44-32-38 – and will someone *please* pass me the smelling salts?

Rudy was up on the roof of his house, helping to fix some loose slates, when June Mathis dropped by with the script she had just finished working on. At first she did not recognise him: he was stripped to the waist, dirty and perspiring, and he had not shaved for more than a week – hardly the Valentino she had had in mind for *The Young Rajah*, based on John Ames Mitchell's novel, *Amos Judd*. Mathis told him this, albeit jokingly, but Rudy was not in the least amused. After flicking through the script, which called for him to pose near-nude in some scenes, he told his friend – with a few choice expletives – that although he had transformed himself into a very convincing sheik, he would never get away with playing a Hindu, and neither would he try! Mathis then accused him of doubting her professional judgement, and reminded him rather too sharply that if it had not been for *her* insistence that the part of Julio in *The Four Horsemen Of The Apocalypse* be given to him, there would *be* no Valentino. Rudy's reaction to such a rash scolding from the woman he cherished almost as a surrogate mother was to suddenly burst into tears, then get down on his knees to beg her forgiveness, swearing that he would never speak to her in such a way again. He then pleaded with her to 'set him any task' to prove how much he loved her ... hardly expecting that this would be quite so Herculean as trying to convince Jesse Lasky to take on a film he had known absolutely nothing about!

The Young Rajah tells the story of Amos Judd, a Harvard student who discovers that he is not only the long-lost son of the Maharajah of Dharmagar, but also a psychic who feels a burning spot on his temple each time he is about to see a vision of the future. Lasky read the script – then informed Rudy that the only fit place for it was the waste-bin, before berating him with the ill-chosen remark, *I'm* the boss around here, Mr Valentino. You're only the *actor*!' This time there was no blubbering from the actor, just a torrent of abuse which left the mogul shocked to the core. Lasky later said that each time Valentino lost his temper he imagined that it could never get any worse, only to realise during the next outburst that it could. This time, however, Rudy was speaking in defence of someone else, though he did not divulge his one-off tiff with June Mathis. He screamed that unless Paramount allowed him to do *The Young Rajah*, he would tear up his contract and find himself a studio who would. Such a remark, coming from anyone else in these days of the studio system, would almost certainly have resulted in instant dismissal. Lasky, however, was shrewd enough to realise that a star of Valentino's magnitude would have been able to command from *any* studio considerably more than the $1250 a week pittance he was being paid by Paramount and, grateful at least that Rambova was three thousand miles away and incapable of disrupting *this* film, he backed down. He was also worried about the $40,000 which Rudy owed the studio.

What Lasky had not reckoned on was the power of the telephone. Each evening after leaving the lot, Rudy called Rambova, usually from Lasky's secretary's office, to explain what had happened that day on the set, and to receive a list of instructions from her to be incorporated into the next day's schedule. Each week she sent him an envelope containing the latest amendments and additions to the film's set and costumes designs which, she declared, had come about as the result of her 'collaboration' with a friend from the spirit world. This only amused Lasky, who did not care what this woman did so long as she stayed put, and so long as the picture was finished on time. The director, Philip Rosen, did not however take too kindly to being ordered around by 'a bunch of spooks', and he came close to throwing in the towel the first time he walked into the star's dressing room without knocking – to find Rudy squatting on a table, stark-naked, chanting to Black Feather.

The Young Rajah owed much of its appeal, in fact, to Rambova's curious costumes. As a Hindu, Amos Judd wears a skimpy loincloth to which are attached pompoms, jewels, and dozens of strings of pearls which are wound about his thighs and legs. Two scenes from the film were considered too 'hot' for some parts of America and were vetoed. In the scene where Amos dons his Hindu costume and climbs into his swan-shaped barge with co-star Wanda Hawley, he reclines and raises one leg, revealing an unprecedented expanse of thigh which had Will Hays fuming down the telephone to Jesse Lasky. And in the earlier Harvard scene, where he and a fellow student are carrying the college boat over their heads, the outline of his penis is clearly defined through his ripped, skin-tight towelling shorts. Philip Rosen, assuming that he had allowed himself to develop an erection expressly to shock the large crowd of extras and spectators, ordered him off the set to take a cold shower ... so Rudy dropped his shorts and revealed to all and sundry that 'it' was in its normal state! Astonishingly, when Paramount were selecting shots from the film to be used on publicity posters, they chose this one, though few stayed pasted to the billboards for very long! The ones which were not ripped down by irate detractors were removed by fans, who of course were only interested in having *that* part of Rudy's anatomy mounted in their scrapbooks.

On 5 August 1922, a few days after *The Young Rajah* had finished shooting, *Blood And Sand* opened in Los Angeles. The press, many of whom had already seen the rushes, declared it Valentino's best film since *The Sheik*, if not better. Even Jesse Lasky was sufficiently impressed to present Rudy with a set of gold-plated golfclubs. Rudy, however, following a telephone call to Rambova, told Lasky that he would not be attending this or the film's New York première the following week – adding haughtily, 'This is my first *artistic* film, and I will not resort to having my clothes ripped off my body by females of little or no intelligence!' He then reminded Lasky of his earlier, cutting 'You're only the actor!' quip, declaring that henceforth until his Paramount contract expired at the beginning of 1924, *he* would be exercising his *actor's* rights to script, director and co-star approval – either that or he would sue Lasky personally for breach of contract. Then, whilst the mogul was ordering him to sit down and control himself, he turned on his heels and strode out of his office.

No one had ever walked out on Jesse Lasky before, and the next morning a studio aide was dispatched to Rambova's duplex to look for him. Rudy, however, was not there and when the aide arrived at Whitley Heights he was told by a workman that the actor had that morning spoken of catching the train to New York. Lasky was furious, and sent two of his henchmen to the station to bring Rudy back to the Paramount office, using force if necessary. The train, which was about to leave the platform, was held up for several minutes whilst the two men searched amongst the passengers for the missing star. Rudy *was* there, sitting next to Douglas Gerrard: both were wearing old clothes, dark glasses and thick false beards.

A few days later, the two friends arrived at the Hudnutts' 1200-acre estate, where Rambova's parents welcomed Rudy like a prodigal son. They were also incredibly naive. Under the terms of the bigamy hearing Rudy was not allowed to spend any time with Rambova unless someone 'responsible' was there to keep a watchful eye on him. Thus, when Gerrard suggested to the Hudnutts that maybe *he* should sleep in Rudy's room to prevent anything 'untoward' from happening, they readily agreed, wholly unaware of what was really happening.

For Rudy, the next few weeks were gloriously happy. Away from the film-world, Natacha Rambova was a completely different person to the 'hard-bitten bitch' of Jesse Lasky's very worst nightmares: warm, caring, and blessed with a surprising off-beat sense of humour. The trio's days were filled by exploring the huge Foxlair estate, boating on the lake, skinny-dipping by moonlight, shooting and golfing. In the evening they would read or recite poetry to each other, or play cards. This idyll was short-lived, however, when Jesse Lasky – still outraged by Rudy's walk-out – hired two private investigators to infiltrate Foxlair and hopefully catch the couple in a compromising position. According to Mrs Hudnutt's unpublished memoirs, the trio were playing cards one stormy night when they observed one of the intruders, and Gerrard went after the man with a gun. A fight ensued, during which the actor-director was flung twelve feet over the porch railings, though he was unhurt and managed to fire several shots, wounding the man in the foot.

Rudy was both angry and frightened. If these were the tactics employed by Paramount against their stars, he told himself, then he would personally sort out Jesse Lasky once and for all. Prior to this seemingly inevitable showdown, on 2 September he gave a statement to the New York press, accusing Lasky of having him trailed like a common thief, and declaring that *he* alone had made Paramount the great studio it now was. In return, he argued, its executives had repaid him only with tyranny, arrogance and broken promises, whilst persistently undervaluing his worth, star quality and pulling power at the box-office. And, worst of all, they had been unspeakably cruel to the woman he loved.

Because of the inordinately long train journey back to Hollywood, Rudy's statement was read by Jesse Lasky well in advance of the two men meeting, allowing him sufficient time to discuss with the other Paramount chiefs exactly what was to be done with their biggest star, who had also suddenly become their biggest headache. Lasky was all for firing him, but he was overruled: Valentino should be given one last chance. He was therefore told that his salary could be upped to $7,000 a week – a staggering increase – but that first of all he would have to sign a document allowing the *studio* to choose his films, with little or no artistic control or script approval falling on himself. Secondly, he would be honour-bound to 'gag' his so-called wife.

Needless to say, when Lasky repeated this final condition, Rudy flew into a rage, cursing the air blue until the mogul threatened to call security and have him thrown out. That same day, 14 September 1922, the studio suspended him and applied for a court injunction: this decreed that Rudy would have to honour the terms of his contract, to the letter, or retire from making films until 7 February 1924, when it expired.

Rudy was faced with the biggest financial dilemma of his career. He was in debt to Paramount to the tune of $50,000 by now, and W I Gilbert, the lawyer who had represented him during his bigamy trial, was also threatening court action because Rudy could not afford to settle his account. His new lawyer, Arthur Butler Graham, would cost him $2,500 a week – more than twice the fee he had been earning with Paramount. And now, for the third time in less than a year, Rudy had to account for his actions in a court of law.

In principal, some credit has to be given to Natacha Rambova for supporting Rudy in his fight against Paramount, inasmuch as he *had* been persistently undervalued and underpaid ever since *The Four Horsemen Of The Apocalypse*. Her assumption, however, that his public would have better appreciated him in so-called 'artistic' productions may not have withstood the test. Nazimova, no less successful in exotic film melodramas than she had been on the classical stage, had failed miserably to combine the two. Her production of Ibsen's *A Doll's House*, which no studio had been prepared to back, had recently bombed at the box-office, losing the actress a fortune. *The Young Rajah*, too, which had premiered on 12 November, was not doing as well as everyone had expected.

Rambova was also wrong to push Rudy into another costly legal battle – though cynics might add that had he not been powerless to stand up to her, he might more easily have resolved some of his differences with Paramount and prevented himself from ultimately looking rather silly. Whilst Arthur Butler Graham accused them of denying his client 'the rightful facilities of the artist, adequate dressing-rooms, scripts and plots', all the studio had to declare was that Valentino had fared better at the box-office in the films *they* had chosen for him, as opposed to the 'turkey' that he had proposed. Witnesses on behalf of Jesse Lasky, Sam Wood and other directors also testified about the actor's 'uncontrollable temper' and 'extraneous demands for a third party' – Rambova – who had been in no way connected with the studio. The judge therefore ruled in favour of Paramount, and on 8 December 1922, their decision was re-confirmed by New York's Appellate Division: Rudy's suspension would stay. Only days after losing his case, Rudy's new lawyer also served him with a writ for $48,000!

Paramount's victory was, however, pyrrhic. Public support for the 'fallen' actor could not have been stronger and over the next seven days more than 50,000 cards and letters from well-wishers poured into his fan-club. So great was the wave of goodwill that Paul Ivano, who had stayed on in Hollywood to supervise the Whitley Heights renovations, had to take on extra helpers. Ivano took advantage of the situation and had Rudy's signature mounted onto a rubber stamp, and charged the fans 25c for an 'autographed' photograph of their idol. 'We were getting eight sacks of mail every day,' he recalled. 'All those quarters fed us when Rudy was not making films!'

Rudy also entered into negotiations with Joseph M Schenck, the president of United Artists, a bucolic, bad-mannered individual he would subsequently refer to as 'Mister Skunk'. Schenck wanted him to play Romeo – a role which would, of course, have suited him ideally – opposite his wife, Norma Talmadge, in a proposed adaptation of *Romeo And Juliet*. Rudy was more than willing, but the project had to be abandoned when Famous Players-Lasky demanded $1 million to release Rudy from his contract with them.

Rudy's 'cause' was given an unexpected boost with the publication of the December issue of *Photoplay*. For months, the magazine's Ruth Waterbury had been courting Rambova, hoping for an exclusive, and her persistence had finally paid off. 'She is subtle, is Natacha Rambova,' Waterbury enthused. 'She is white satin embroidered in gold, she is absinthe in a crystal glass. She is a copy of Swinburne bound in scarlet. She is beauty drugged with sophistication. And she will hate me for saying all that.'

Rambova's primary intention when submitting to her first major press interview had been to bolster Rudy's flagging spirit by attacking Paramount as much as was possible without being sued. Indeed, Waterbury edited out some of her less flattering comments about Jesse Lasky, who had himself thrown a fit when she had told an earlier press-conference, 'Mr Valentino is better off now that he's removed himself from this artistic desert. He's a fine actor, and as such should be allowed to share artistic control of his pictures with a director he can trust.' And now, in this feature headlined, WEDDED AND PARTED, Rambova disclosed how Paramount had treated Rudy like dirt and removed her from his life by forcibly exiling her to New York:

> He knows nothing whatever about business. When the company offered him his contract, he was so happy with his success after his bitter struggle that he believed the whole world was without guile. He signed his contract without investigating its phrasing ... They were forever creating rules and telling him that he had to obey them, and poor Rudy, who is so instinctively honest himself, believed it and was always dazedly trying to find his way about through them [feeling] that he must in some strange way be to blame for all of it. Then we ran away and got involved in that foolish marriage. I admit it was unwise but we surely had meant no harm in it, but the company treated Rudy as though he were a criminal. They packed me off East and when I called at the New York offices, by way of being comforting they announced that there was no way of saving Rudy from a prison term and that he would undoubtedly get ten years ... I nearly went to Europe as they requested. I realise now that they were only trying to get me out of the way as they believed that would improve Rudy's box-office value. They declared that I would be the ruin of his career and then finally they told me that Rudy had already forgotten me. Then I got mad. I knew Rudy. So, I didn't sail for Europe. I knew my job was right here.

Rambova also tugged the heartstrings of her readers by divulging that though the man himself *looked* tough, within the strapping, athletic form there lurked an unexpected vulnerability:

> There is really nothing sophisticated or seductive about Rudy ... he has a personality that comes out on the screen which is entirely different from the Rudy I know. Yet I believe it is part of him as the exotic quality of my sketches is part of me. But basically he is just a little boy. Things hurt him as they would hurt a child and he is quite as emotional. Also he is just as spontaneous and trustful. Yet with all that there is a remarkable matter-of-factness about him and sincerity. He is the most sincere person I have ever known.

Across America, women from all walks of life, who of course did not know the *real* 'Mrs Valentino', wept upon reading these words. The fact that this beautiful, sad young man, the idol of millions, whose on-screen lovemaking set pulses reeling by becoming fodder to any conceivable fantasy, had had the great love of his life wrenched from him by these heartless bigots was insupportable. How these women would have reacted, had they known that Rudy was being 'consoled' by a male lover is not hard to imagine.

Rudy had met Frank Menillo, of whom almost nothing is known, when he had been working as a 'white-button boy' at Maxim's, and Menillo had avidly followed his career since learning that Rudy had begun working in the movies – he had even joined his fan-club and received several signed photographs.

What may seem astonishing today is the naivety of the press and the watchdogs from the Hays Office, who since the bigamy hearing had been doing their utmost to ensure that the actor did not step out of line. It has to be remembered, however, that in these days, *such* was Valentino's reputation for being a womaniser – founded more or less on his appearance in just one film, *The Sheik* – that hardly anyone outside the closeted gay community would have known that physically he was only attracted to men. Had this been divulged during his lifetime, no one would have *believed* it ... just as Rock Hudson's sexuality was a secret which this extremely 'butch' actor almost succeeded in taking to the grave. Therefore, when Frank Menillo told the press that he had invited his favourite movie star to share his room at New York's Hôtel des Artistes so that he could 'keep an eye on him', no one so much as suspected that he was also keeping Rudy's bed warm at night. 'Paramount doesn't care what happens to Rudolph Valentino, what with Christmas just around the corner,' one newspaper reported, remembering the time when he had been taken in by Viola Dana. 'But at least one of his fans does. God really does move in mysterious ways!'

During the train journey from Hollywood, and with the utmost sincerity, Rudy had penned an open letter to his fans – thanking them for their thousands of messages of loyalty and support – that he had planned to publish in the *New York Times*. He had, however, signed a deal with *Photoplay* to serialise his autobiography, and the editor demanded that he should be the one to publish the letter. Appearing in the very next issue of the magazine after the Rambova exclusive, and on no account of Rudy's choosing, much of it served only to boost his appeal:

> It was you, the fans, who made me ... Your kindness came to me at a time when it seemed that things could not be more desolate. You made theatre managers know me and you caused film magazines and newspapers to be conscious of me. I am more grateful than you will ever know ... Idols are created to be shattered. My pedestal is at present a little too high to be entirely comfortable. I feel too humble for such an altitude. In the very nature of things I know that I cannot occupy such a position very long. But before I fall I hope to bring you my little best, as my gesture of thanks for all that you have brought to me. You write and tell me that I bring romance to your lives. You say I give you colour and beauty and dreams. I wish that I had more English words at my command to express to you what such a faith to me means ... The Rodolpho [sic] Valentino you have brought forth is very different from the Rudolph Valentino who actually is. I assure you he is quite a commonplace fellow. But this other

> Valentino, this shadow personality, must dedicate himself to the work you expect of him. For him there is only work, constant creative work. He must strive to be that character whom you want to see. He must try to show you the beauty and joy of love, the radiance of life and the tragedy of death. He must try to live for you those dreams that you may not have been able to work out for yourself. He can no longer belong entirely to himself. Were I an artist working in any other medium I would give to you as far as my ability would permit whatever product I desired. Were I a painter, I could choose my own colours. Were I a musician, I could play my own melodies. Were I a Rodin, I could try to create for you a 'Hand of God'. But I am only an actor on the screen. As such I am dependent on my producers ...

At this point, unfortunately perhaps, Rudy's letter went off at a tangent, taking up almost an entire page of *Photoplay* with another attack against Paramount. He was, he said, being paid just $1,250 a week – a sum which may have seemed like a fortune to most people, yet which was very little compared to the salaries of some colleagues, *and* from which had to be deducted the expenses for all the costumes he wore in his films, along with the cost of all those rubber-stamp autographed photographs his fan club was sending out to the very fans he was now thanking. Obviously, he had forgotten that the fans themselves were paying for these. The money, however, he concluded was relatively unimportant:

> I was willing to go on at the same salary if they would permit me to make real photoplays instead of cut-and-dried programme pictures that can be hacked and torn and compressed into a given number of feet of film to fit so many cans, like so many boxes of sardines ... I do not consider myself a great actor yet. But I did have in me a deep feeling for the art of the motion picture, gratitude to the public, and an overwhelming, almost terrifying responsibility to continue to appear in good pictures and to continue to be worthy of the praise that you heaped upon me ... I am not selfish for

> money – money means very little to me and I have gone without it long enough to be used to it – but I am selfish in wanting to make good pictures. I don't want to be a cog in a machine that grinds them out in a cut-and-dried fashion. Art cannot be measured in inches!

At around the time Rudy moved in with Frank Menillo, Rambova – still on Nazimova's payroll – took an apartment on West 67th Street, where she was joined by her aunt, Teresa Werner. It was here, over the festive season, that the two women contrived, out of concern, it has to be said, to boost Rudy's self-esteem by arranging for him to receive 'messages' from the spirit world. Rudy had not once lost faith in his familiar, Black Feather, and he would often don his brave's garb if he needed to find inner solace – sometimes when reading scripts, so that he could get into his part, but most often after making love. Ramon Novarro once told a friend, 'With Rudy, sex always came first, *then* the slushy talk. But when he was in one of his "Indian" moods, it would be sex with Valentino followed by sex with Black Feather.'

The messages sent to the West 67th Street apartment were from Gabrielle Guglielmi, reassuring her son that she, like his 'buddy', was looking out for him, and that he should lend himself to the precognitive dream – the fact that all *will* turn out well in the end, so long as this is what one wishes. Gabrielle 'advised' him what to say to his fans when he appeared on the radio on 22 December. The programme was entitled *The Truth About Myself*, though once more it was little more than an excuse to air his grievances with Paramount, and the broadcast concluded with him declaring in an angry voice, 'Seventy-five per cent of the pictures released in America today are a brazen insult to the public's intelligence!'

Guided by his 'voices', Rudy added the finishing touches to his 'autobiography' for *Photoplay*. *My Life Story*, ghosted by Herbert Howe, unfolded over several issues of the magazine during the spring of 1923; though much of what Rudy dictated to Howe – once the editor had eliminated his racy comments about his co-stars and so-called peers – was little more than a re-invention of his 'exotic' past. 'Naturally sensitive and inclined to introspection, I have tried above all to know myself,' he begins, adding somewhat longwindedly, 'but when I take what we call a "long-shot" at that self, starting forth in the world from a poor little village at the heel of Italy, travelling curious ups and down in early life and vacillating between occupational calls, sailing blithely off to win riches in America ... to experience the grilling poverty, loneliness and utter misery which make or break, arising a few years later to occupy a place in the esteem and affection of the American public – when I view *that* self of myself, I feel I haven't even a speaking acquaintance!'

On and on he rambles: romanticising his family life – 'My father was a quiet, studious man' – zipping through his early years to get to the by now compulsory attacks on Paramount, which resulted in the studio receiving thousands of letters of complaint from irate fans, many of which actually threatened Jesse Lasky with physical violence ... and, of course, there was over-indulgent praise of Rambova: 'Every day, somebody else comes out to say how they discovered me, yet *she* says nothing at all.'

Rudy's mother also 'instructed' him to invite Cora McGeachy – one of Rambova's costume-designer friends who was also a medium and an exponent of 'automatic' writing – to the West 67th Street apartment, where he was presented with a sheet of paper upon which were scribbled the names of several people from Castellaneta who had recently died. They too, Gabrielle said, were watching over him. Rudy's mother then informed him, with astonishing accuracy, that within the space of one year he would have resolved his differences with Paramount, but that *before* then his career would have reached an unprecedented high-point, following a tour of the United States.

Although Rudy was not permitted to make films or appear on the stage as an actor, nothing in his Paramount contract stipulated that he could not appear in vaudeville or in dance halls. It was to this end, during the first week of January 1923, that he was approached by S George Ullman, a public-relations official from the Mineralava Beauty Clay Company, who declared that he, too, had been guided in Rudy's direction by one of Cora McGeachy's spirits – though most likely he had read about one of her seances with Rudy in the New York press.

A shrewd individual with a good business head on his shoulders, Ullman made the couple an offer they could hardly refuse, considering Rudy's debts and Rambova's refusal to ask her stepfather for financial assistance: a 17-week, all-expenses paid tour of America and Canada, with a salary of $7,000 a week. They would even have their own three-roomed private railroad car, furnished with Oriental carpets, original works of art and gold-plated fixtures and fittings, and be waited on hand and foot by a butler, maid and Cordon-Bleu chef. And, in return for all this, the couple would be obliged to promote Mineralava's products by delivering a short speech after each performance. Even Rambova was unable to find fault with this contract, and the deal was clinched on 19 January 1923 – Rambova's twenty-sixth birthday – in the West 67th Street apartment, in the 'presence' of Rudy's mother.

At around the time that Ullman entered his life, Rudy became involved with Robert Florey, a young Frenchman who had arrived in Hollywood in November 1922 hoping to make his name in the movies, only to end up as Douglas Fairbanks' press-agent for his recently-released *Robin Hood*. In the thirties, Florey would achieve fame *behind* the camera, directing films for the likes of Bette Davis and Errol Flynn, but when Rudy first got to know him he was struggling to make a living and smarting after the collapse of a whirlwind affair with Paul Ivano ... prior to which he had been the lover of the great Russian actor, Ivan Mosjoukine.

Exactly where and how Florey met Rudy is not known, save that Rudy – whose two weaknesses, as will be seen, appear to have been handsome French men and strong-willed women – immediately took a shine to Florey and invited him to work for him. 'Initially, all I did was inform everybody how wonderful he was as an actor, which of course they knew already,' Florey recalled. 'Then I started clipping articles about him from French film magazines. The effect he had on me cannot be explained. I had intended returning to France after *Robin Hood*, but once we became close, I knew I would never desert him.'

Robert Florey would have nothing to do with the seances at

West 67th Street, though he did accompany Rudy on a visit to Professor Winton, his clairvoyant, whose tiny studio was wedged between a gift-shop and a shooting gallery on Ocean Front – but only because Rudy had promised him a slap-up feed at the nearby Joe's Greek Cafe. According to Florey, Winton's predictions were grim:

> Valentino asked for the works – $5 for forty-five minutes. Winton, whom many of the big stars consulted, told him that he would soon be going on a long journey, that he would see even greater glories in his career, but that his life would be short. 'It isn't the first time you've told me that,' Valentino said, 'I know my life-line is short, but I'm sure that I'll still be coming here in twenty years time.' 'I only wish that were so,' Winton replied. 'But sadly, that isn't what I read in your palm.' Later, I asked Valentino *why* he kept returning to his clairvoyant only to listen to bad news. Then he told me, 'Because everything else that he's told me *has* come true.'

8

The History of Love and its Justification

'They say that only poets and fools dare dream ... that is why I attempt to write poetry.'

Rudy's French friend, Jacques Hébertot, once confessed that the actor's presence was such that he could walk into a room and make even the most virulently homophobic man want to have an affair with him. This seems to have been the case with George Ullman, and though their relationship never progressed beyond the platonic, Ullman unquestionably fell for Rudy in a big way, as he indicated in his moving biography of 1926, *Valentino, As I Knew Him*.

> I was familiar with his pictures and thought of him as a handsome boy [but] I had no idea of his magnetism nor of the fine quality of his manhood. To say that I was enveloped by his personality with the first clasp of his sinewy hand and my first glance into his inscrutable eyes is to state it mildly. I was literally engulfed, swept off my feet, which is unusual between two men. Had he been a beautiful woman and I a bachelor, it would not have been so surprising. I am not an emotional man – I have in fact been referred to as cool-headed – but in this instance, meeting a real he-man, I found myself moved by the most powerful personality I had ever encountered in man *or* woman.

The tango, naturally, dominated the Mineralava tour, which began early in February 1923. Rudy wore a near-copy of Julio Desnoyers' gaucho costume from *The Four Horsemen Of The Apocalypse* and Rambova a Spanish dress of black taffeta and velvet, both outfits designed by her. The first stop was Omaha, Nebraska, where for several days the city had been brought to a standstill by blizzards. Even so, thousands of people who had not stepped out of their homes for more than a week, braved the sub-zero temperatures to greet the couple at the railway station – including a two-year old boy named Edward Montgomery Clift, who twenty-five years on would himself become an acting legend.

The tour progressed: Wichita, Montreal, and finally New York, where the manager of the Hotel Astor told the press that such had been the demand for tickets, the auditorium could have been filled ten times over. Here and elsewhere along the 'holy trail', as the tour was dubbed by Elinor Glyn, many schools were closed for the day to enable Rudy's younger fans to catch a glimpse of him as he dashed from his railroad car to the waiting limousine. Often there was such pandemonium that city-centres had to be closed to traffic to accommodate the crowds. In Salt Lake City, Rambova's home town which in direct contrast to Omaha was gripped by a heatwave, dozens of police were drafted in and part of the waterfront cordoned off when the Valentino party decided to cool off in the lake.

To maintain their all-important image, Rudy and Rambova stayed only in the most exclusive hotels – in separate rooms, of course – and they were accompanied by James Abbe, the society photographer who ran the Tin Pan Alley Studio on New York's 47th Street. Abbe, who baptised the actor 'King Rudolph of the Movies', executed a series of studies of the couple which are never less than stunning. One in particular achieved world fame: dubbed 'The Royal Portrait', it features an overlapping head and bare shoulders profile of the couple, as if they are posing for a postage stamp or medallion. 'Their joint popularity was so great at the time, one might imagine the double image appearing on our silver dollars,' Abbe wrote some years later.

The Valentino-Rambova performances were identical, down to the last step. Each began deliberately late, a completely unnecessary ploy devised by George Ullman to whip up public enthusiasm, which on one occasion almost precipitated a riot. The programme comprised a series of waltzes, followed by a Spanish folk-dance choreographed especially for the tour by Rudy, who then delivered his meticulously rehearsed but mumbled advertisement speech – in Montreal this had been in French – attributing Rambova's peaches-and-cream complexion solely to the application of Mineralava's products. Occasionally there were scoffs from some of the males in the audience, particularly in Chicago, where the *Tribune* reported that Rudy too liked using Mineralava Clay. A display of Oriental and European dancing was then followed by a beauty contest, which Rudy was invited to judge until he was accused of always picking the same type of woman – in other words, a Rambova lookalike – after which the winners, who were offered the chance of a screen-test, were selected by audience applause. And, of course, the programme always ended with the Argentinian tango.

Throughout the Mineralava tour, Rudy and Rambova regularly consulted with Mesalope and Black Feather, and attended seances in every city on the circuit. At each press-conference they slated Paramount – not just for the previous misdemeanours, but because whilst Rudy had been removed from the payroll, the studio was raking in a fortune by ensuring that as many Valentino films as possible were playing wherever he was appearing. Even the minor studios had climbed on to the bandwagon – re-releasing films such as *A Rogue's Romance*, and *Virtuous Sinners*, where Rudy had only had bit-parts, but now with his name heading the credits.

In Chicago, on 4 March 1923 – the day his divorce from Jean Acker should have become final – Rudy had anticipated his 'remarriage' to Rambova. The ceremony had been booked at the Blackstone Hotel, to be followed by a reception at the Marigold Gardens. When the proceedings were suddenly cancelled, however, the Chicago press – who would always cause Rudy great pain – took it upon themselves to hint that the wedding had been put off because 'the bride-to-be has seen the light of day concerning her intended's effeminate, overbearing ways'. This referred to an advertisement which had appeared in the *Tribune* which declared that Rudy had *admitted* to using Mineralava Clay, as a result of which every barber's shop in the city was displaying piles of the stuff in their windows, next to his hand-coloured photographs, which *did* make him look a little 'pink', and which were captioned, MINERALAVA MAKES FACES YOUNGER.

In fact, the couple *had* received Jean Acker's papers, but had been unable to marry in Chicago because the State of Illinois required an *additional* waiting period of twelve months after a divorce had been finalised.

Rudy, however, decided that he could not wait any longer, and the wedding was arranged to take place over the state line, at Crown Point, Indiana, on 14 March. Rudy then called Paul Ivano in Hollywood, and asked him to be one of the witnesses: the other was to be Aunt Teresa. Ivano stunned Rudy by turning the request down. The charade with Rambova had dragged on for far too long, he declared, adding that she alone was responsible for Rudy's severe financial difficulties. Ivano concluded that he would still honour his promise to look after the Whitley Heights properly until after the tour – but that if Rudy had not come to his senses by then and ditched this 'dangerous' woman, then he must no longer consider himself his friend.

Rudy was so besotted with Rambova, so under her spell, that he was *unable* to see sense, and the wedding went ahead as planned, with George Ullman replacing Ivano as second witness. The pair appeared on the front page of just about every newspaper in the country, smiling radiantly, if only for the benefit of the press. And, as Ivano had predicted, the charade indeed continued with the publication of *Daydreams*, an anthology of poems which Rudy claimed he had written during his enforced separation from his fiancée. 'I am not a poet nor a scholar, therefore you shall find neither poems nor prose,' he confessed in the book's preface, adding, 'While lying idle, not through choice but because forcibly kept from my preferred and actual field of activity, I took to dreams to forget the tediousness of worldly strife and the boredom of jurisprudence's pedantic etiquette.'

In fact, once one has ploughed through this awesomely gushing sea of slush which was *not* penned by Rudy, but allegedly Ullman himself, the poems themselves are not that bad – though the cynics scoffed, not surprisingly, when Rambova, asked by the press what the initials following each poem stood for, replied that the book had been 'dictated from the other side' by luminaries such as Robert and Elizabeth Browning, and Georges Sand. One publication even offered an 'exclusive' that the RB, EB and GS *actually* stood for Richard Barthelmess, Ethel Barrymore and Gloria Swanson!

Daydreams, which included such mini-gems as 'A Baby's Skin', 'To A Dog', and 'Dust To Dust', sold over 500,000 copies during the last weeks of the Mineralava tour, shooting straight to the top of the best-sellers. Its most famous poem, however, which appeared on the printed page deliberately in the shape of the actor's penis, incensing the Hays Office, who could do absolutely nothing about the situation because, according to several 'experts', poetry did not have to be set out in any conventional form, was a remarkable piece entitled 'You'.

You are the History of Love and its Justification
The Symbol of Devotion
The Blessedness of Womanhood
The Incentive of Chivalry
The Reality of Ideals
The Verity of Joy
Idolatry's Defence
The Proof of Goodness
The Power of Gentleness
Beauty's Acknowledgement
Vanity's Excuse
The Promise of Truth
The Melody of Life
The Caress of Romance
The Dream of Desire
The Sympathy of Understanding
My Heart's Home
The Proof of Faith
Sanctuary of my Soul
My Belief of Heaven
Eternity of all Happiness
My Prayers
You

When the tour reached San Antonio, Texas, Rudy asked George Ullman to become his personal manager. It was a strange request, and a long-shot considering that Ullman would legally require at least ten per cent of his earnings ... and that Rudy was currently $60,000 in debt. His commercial value was of course all-evident, and Ullman needed little persuading to accept the position, though only on *his* terms. If he handled Rudy's affairs, he would expect *full* control of his career and business deals, with absolutely no outside interference, especially from Mrs Valentino, to whom he had taken a sudden aversion. 'Natacha was conspicuously self-centered,' he wrote in his book. 'In my opinion, she was congenitally unable to feel much enthusiasm for any individual but herself. At first she appeared fond of her husband, though soon she became a great deal more interested in the power-behind-the-throne of the unparalleled Valentino than being a wife to Rudy.'

Reluctantly, Rudy agreed to Ullman's terms, and a few days later the tour ended with the Valentinos' performance at New York's Madison Square Garden. This time there were *three* prizes for the beauty contest, and in the filmed footage of the event, Rudy looks considerably more nervous than the winners.

On 14 May, Rudy cut his only known gramophone record for Brunswick: the Woodforde-Finden classic, 'Kashmiri Love Song', coupled with José Padilla's 'El Relicario' – 'The Memento'. Much has been said about the Valentino 'baritone', particularly as for the majority of his devotees, this was the only time they would ever get to hear his voice. His phrasing is contrived and he persistently waits for every cue so that sometimes the music starts without him, but his singing is not that bad, considering that he had no rehearsals – primarily because the recording was only made as a gimmick to be distributed amongst his friends, even if it subsequently sold hundreds of thousands of copies. One must also not forget that even the luminaries of the Roaring Twenties – Libby Holman, Joséphine Baker, Damia and even Bing Crosby – were far from adequately served by the primitive recording techniques of the day.

Five days after cutting this recording, Rudy wrote to his friend Robert Florey in New York, in what would be the first in a series of missives, in badly-spelt French, peppered with expletives: 'I've decided to fuck off to Europe after this tour. Whether this will be to make a film or purely as a holiday, I'm not yet sure, and to be honest, I don't give a fuck one way or the other.' Then, explaining that he had booked Florey a first-class cabin on the *Olympic* scheduled to sail on 11 July, he concluded, 'All I want you to do is to fuck off ahead of me to London, then Paris, to make all the arrangements, then return to London and meet me there.'

Yet no sooner had Florey read Rudy's letter than another arrived: the reservation had been cancelled, and he had now been booked on the *Aquetania*, which would sail on 1 July. There then followed a *third* letter, this time from a very worried, confused, but above all *spurned* Valentino. One of Florey's friends had called Rudy in New York with the devastating news that his handsome Frenchman was about to dump him and get married:

> How can you do this to me? And if you are going to be stupid enough to get married, then naturally it will only damage our affair, which will have to end. I therefore beg you, also as your buddy, *not* to get married when you have such a good and happy future ahead of you! It would be such a *waste*! So, for my sake put all such thoughts out of your head, and think of all the fucking we'll be doing in Europe!

Florey cabled Rudy at once, informing him that the news of his 'impending marriage' had been nothing more than a prank played on him by a male rival who should have known better, and the matter was resolved.

At the end of May, George Ullman settled Rudy's outstanding debts, including his lawyer's bill – then he appointed a lawyer the actor would be able to afford. Next, he paid back the money which Rudy owed Paramount and set up a meeting with J D Williams, president of the newly-formed Ritz-Carlton Pictures, an independent company which had shown a fleeting interest in Rudy at the time of his break from Paramount. Williams had worked for First National when Rudy had appeared in his first film, *Alimony*, back in 1918, but he had never got around to meeting the extras. Now,

Ullman gave him just ten seconds to decide whether he wanted to sign Valentino or not whilst Rudy, sitting at the back of Williams' office, was motioned to keep his mouth shut. Rambova had not even been allowed into the building.

The deal was clinched by a handshake. Ullman then set about pitting Williams against Jesse Lasky who, having received over half a million letters in support of the actor, was having some regrets about the way he had treated Rudy. Williams made the first move in offering to buy out what remained of Rudy's contract with Paramount. Lasky, however, had a better proposition: he would release his star to Ritz-Carlton in February 1924 when his contract expired, providing Rudy agreed to make more films for Paramount within the next year. Ullman then summoned Lasky and Joseph Zukor, the head of the studio, to New York for a meeting – Rudy had refused to 'humble' himself by travelling to Hollywood and he had also made it clear that he was not interested in filming there, either – and on 18 July 1923 the contracts were signed. Rudy would receive $7,500 a week from Paramount, effective immediately, but most importantly he would be given total control over the choice of his scripts, scriptwriters, directors, co-stars and even technicians. The films would be made at Paramount's Astoria Studios on Long Island. And, needless to say, Mrs Valentino would be on the Paramount payroll as her husband's technical adviser.

Within one hour of this monumental meeting, the press had been informed of its outcome, *and* of the fact that within the next few days the Valentinos would be leaving for Europe, where they would be enjoying a belated honeymoon. This news made the early evening editions, which hit the news-stands just as Rudy and Rambova were returning to the West 67th Street apartment ... which Frank Menillo left via a back entrance, only minutes later. By midnight, five thousand fans had gathered outside the building to welcome Rudy's return to the screen, and when they began chanting his name he appeared at the window and waved to them – instigating a near-riot which had to be brought under control by mounted police.

There were almost as many fans gathered on the quayside on 23 July when, accompanied by Aunt Teresa, the Valentinos boarded the *Aquitania*. Trailing behind was their 'chronicler' for the trip, James Abbe, who had so exquisitely photographed them during the Mineralava tour. Robert Florey, who was already in London, would supply the accompanying features for the American press.

The most authentic and interesting account of Rudy's 'European Adventure', however, comes from the actor himself. Rudy had only recently negotiated a deal with *Pictures And Picturegoer*, one of his favourite British magazines, to serialise his autobiography (this was eventually published at monthly intervals between July 1924 and October 1925, but never released as a complete volume). 'You will learn more about Valentino, the man, than a dozen interviews could tell you,' the editor promised in his introduction, adding, this time deservedly, 'The most fascinating personality on the screen today stands revealed as a 20th century Pepys.'

Unlike Rudy's earlier 'life-story' for *Photoplay*, this one was not far-fetched: it was written by Rudy himself, in the form of a diary. Parts of it are, admittedly, delivered haphazardly – for instance, when he suddenly remembers an event from his past and goes off at a tangent. Much of the time he writes floridly, with the air of an intelligent schoolboy on his first overseas trip with a scolding mother – aka Rambova – and many of his entries are unedited and, like his letters to Robert Florey, printed with all the spelling mistakes. Some paragraphs were also removed owing to their sexual content. 'I pinch myself a little in the good, old-fashioned way, to be sure that it isn't *all* a dream,' he begins. 'Sometimes I am afraid that I will awake again, a lonely, friendless boy, shivering on the borderland of a strange and alien land.'

For nine days, the Valentino party kept to themselves, refusing to participate in the ship's social activities. When the captain announced that the *Aquitania*'s most distinguished guests would be judging a dance contest which had been organised to raise funds for a children's charity, Rudy donated a large sum of money in lieu, and a number of signed photographs which were auctioned.

The ship's first port of call was Cherbourg, where the party bade a temporary farewell to Aunt Teresa, since she had arranged to travel straight to the Hudnutts' château at Juan-les-Pins. The

Aquitania then continued to Southampton, running straight into a storm, and Rudy's first glimpse of England was through a blinding sheet of rain. He then fell into a state of despondency when only twenty or so fans and a handful of reporters clustered around the gangplank as he disembarked. His spirits were lifted considerably, however, when the boat-train reached London, for the platform was packed with 2,000 screaming fans who had learned of his imminent arrival in a radio news-flash.

Wearing a grey felt hat and an ankle-length fur coat over his suit, Rudy spent more than an hour signing autographs in the station forecourt – mindless of the rain, and the fact that it was after midnight – whilst Rambova sat in the back of the hired limousine looking more than a little bored. 'I shall not be working whilst I am here,' he told reporters, in a voice which was surprisingly deep and bearing only a slight accent. He then unbuttoned his overcoat to reveal what he was wearing underneath, and added, 'What I mean is, I am here for a rest, and to buy myself a few decent suits. And, may I say how thrilled I am by this wonderful greeting. I only hope that you will all excuse me, and come and see me at my hotel tomorrow. I am *very* tired.'

The 'I' – never 'we' – would continue throughout Rudy's fifteen-day stay in the British capital. And of course, the fans and the press took him at his word, swooping on the Carlton Hall at the crack of dawn and making so much noise that he was forced to get out of bed and make an appearance on the balcony, like a visiting royal. 'I have the sensation of being alone in London,' he wrote in his diary. 'Rain falling, a London peopled by the ghosts of all the famous personages of Dickens and history – and friends, friends of mine, waving little white flags of a beautiful truce to welcome me in.'

For thirty minutes, Rudy waved and blew kisses. One hour later, wearing a Japanese dressing-gown over his purple pyjamas, and vivid red slippers – 'Russian, you know, like my lovely wife!' – he gave his first British press-conference, whilst Rambova sat on the couch beside him, still very much the glum consort. 'There is no denying that the man is devilish good-looking,' enthused the anonymous male scribe for *Pictures And Picturegoer*. 'But if he carries the conceit that usually goes with good looks, he dissembles very cleverly. For he is quiet and shy and sensible, with not so much as a ha'porth of side about him!'

The questions were routine: these journalists had been warned against getting too personal by Robert Florey, and they also knew that this man was well and truly terrified of his wife – a snobbish, surly individual who very quickly laid *her* cards on the table by announcing flatly, before the interview began, 'We've had absolutely no privacy at all since our wedding. *Now* it's about time we got on with our honeymoon.' But if the questions were mundane, the replies were not always so:

Q: How many suits will you buy in London?
A: As many as I can afford!
Q: Do you play a musical instrument?
A: I once had an Irish wolfhound, but it grew too big for the apartment, so I gave it to a friend.
Q: What do you think about jazz?
A: The Americans must have *something* to excite them, I guess, seeing as they're no longer allowed liquor!
Q: How long will your honeymoon last?
A: This afternoon I shall be visiting Windsor Castle.
Q: Do you find Italian and English women more beautiful than American women?
A: Beauty does not apply to a particular country. Beauty will be found *everywhere*!

That evening in his diary – primarily because Rambova was checking his entries – Rudy amended his response to the latter question. On the whole, he wrote, the American girl led the way in the beauty stakes, simply because she was a composite of all the races which had filtered into America over the centuries. 'I should say that in other countries, one out of every fifty women will be beautiful,' he concluded. 'Whereas in America, one out of every fifty will be plain.'

The clothes, Rudy did *not* have to buy, for the next morning he was inundated with so many tailors that Robert Florey suggested that he should allow himself to be measured just the once, and details of his vital statistics should be posted in the foyer of the Carlton Hotel! Within forty-eight hours, over two hundred shirts, suits, overcoats and pairs of boots had been delivered to the hotel from dozens of small businesses whose prestige would be boosted considerably by being unofficially 'sponsored' by Rudolph Valentino!

To say that Rudy had come to England for a rest was very much an overstatement and in the next two weeks, he and Rambova did anything but relax. Each morning after breakfast – resisting pressure from his wife to ignore such 'meaningless piffle' – Rudy signed the mountain of autograph books which had been deposited at the hotel's reception desk ... Robert Florey had requested that these be restricted to five hundred a day!

For three days, trailed everywhere by photographers, Rudy and Rambova took in all the major tourist attractions: Hampton Court, Westminster Abbey, the Tower of London, St Paul's Cathedral. When Rudy remarked that he had acquired a taste for stout, he was invited to partake of his favourite beverage at Cumberland Place, the London home of Edward Cecil Guinness, the brewer of the most famous stout in the British Isles. Here he listened to an impromptu recital by the pianist Artur Rubinstein, and met Lord and Lady Birkenhead. The former, the Conservative politician and ex-Lord Chancellor who had played a major role in 1921 in opposing Irish Home Rule, surprised everyone at the gathering by tapping Rudy sharply on the shoulder and demanding, 'Young man, should I *know* you?' ... adding, after Rudy had politely introduced himself, '*Valentino*? Never ruddy heard of him!'

Rudy was 'defended' by the peer's daughter, Lady Pamela Smith, who at the age of twelve was already an ardent Valentino fan. 'A fair, lovely little thing, she interested me at once, as all little girls do,' he wrote, describing how he and she had ignored most of the other guests at Cumberland Place to chat about the movies, concluding, 'It was one of the most interesting talks I had in London.'

In London, there were two visits to the theatre. Firstly to see

Gladys Cooper in *Kiki*. Rudy is said to have enjoyed the play, or what bits of it he had been able to understand, though the actress upset him as he was leaving her dressing-room after the performance by telling him, 'Don't worry about the crowd outside the stage-door, dear. They're waiting for me and they won't know who *you* are!' Cooper was wrong, for the instant Rudy stepped out into the street he was mobbed by dozens of fans, most of them young men.

A few evenings later, the Valentinos went to Wyndham's Theatre to see the actor-manager Gerald du Maurier and the outrageously vulgar Tallulah Bankhead, then the toast of London, in *The Dancers*. This was du Maurier's own play and its plot was so contrived that most of the critics and even the cast had not even bothered trying to work it out, putting it down as 'far-fetched'. Even so, the play would run to over 300 performances, and Rudy only asked to see it in the first place because he had read that Tallulah appeared on stage wearing a buckskin dress and a Red Indian headdress – something which would appeal to Black Feather, he declared.

The evening certainly was an eye-opener, for Rudy was one of the few men in the almost exclusively lesbian audience, and afterwards Tallulah – bitterly disappointed that Rambova was present, for she had laid a bet with the rest of the cast that within five minutes she would have found out if the rumours about Rudy's being 'hung' were true – told him, 'You're not the *only* one capable of making the ladies swoon, Rudy darling!' She took an instant dislike to Mrs Valentino, however. After the pair had left the theatre she told her co-star, Audrey Carten, 'Imagine the poor darling, having to fuck *that*. Is there any wonder he'd rather lick the other side of the stamp?'

During their last days in England, the Valentinos drove out to Leatherhead, in Surrey. If Rudy was going to drag her all the way to some remote corner of Italy to show her where *he* was born, Rambova declared, then she too wanted to visit the scene of the happiest days of her childhood. In August, of course, the school was closed, though there was some compensation: at nearby Bletchingley there were the Ashton Cross kennels, famed for their

Pekingese, and as his wife could not make up her mind which of the three pups for sale she liked best, Rudy bought them all.

On 15 August, Rudy took his first flight in a commercial aircraft – from Croydon to Le Bourget – an experience which so excited the speed-freak in him that he left his wife to cope with her airsickness and yapping dogs and spent the entire flight in the cockpit with the pilot. He even asked if he could take a turn at the controls, explaining that he too had once wanted to be a pilot. This, of course, was not possible. From Le Bourget, where he and Rambova were cheered by two hundred fans, the party were driven to Paris, where they moved into the Plaza-Athenée Hotel on the avenue Montaigne.

Rudy's 'guide' during his stay in Paris was Jacques Hébertot, in those days one of the most powerful impresarios in the city. Not only was he the director of the Théâtre des Champs-Elysées, virtually next door to Rudy's hotel, but he also managed several of the country's top music-hall stars, owned two nightclubs, and edited a number of important theatrical magazines.

A handsome man in his late-thirties, Hébertot had a penchant for plucking fragile looking young men off street-corners, bedding them, and turning them into stars. His most famous conquest, twenty years on, would be Gérard Philipe, France's best-loved actor. Another was Roger Normand, an actor-singer-dancer who succumbed to Hébertot's charms in 1945, when the entrepreneur was sixty and 'still going strong'. It was in Roger that Hébertot confided about his brief relationship with Valentino:

> His wife was an absolute cow, and I'll never understand why Rudy seemed to care for her so much. She was snooty towards everyone she met, she was rude to him in public and treated her dogs better than she treated him. He told me that he had slept with her many times, as would be expected of a man and his wife, but that she had always refused to allow him to have sex with her. When I met him for the first time he had been sleeping with his French publicist, and Natacha seemed perfectly at ease with the situation. As for Rudy and myself, there was an instant chemistry between us, and until

Valentino in 1920 aged 25, on the eve of fame just before making *The Four Horsemen of the Apocalypse*. *(David Bret/Joop van Dijk)*

Four publicity shots from Valentino's last and favourite film, *The Son of the Sheik* , with Vilma Banky, 1926. *(JVD)*

Valentino's favourite sport, boxing with Gene Delmont at the Los Angeles Sports Club, just six weeks before he died. The referee is the legendary Jack Dempsey. *(DB)*

Rudy with his co-stars: above left, with Nita Kaldi in *Cobra (JVD)*; above right, with Helena d'Algy in *A Sainted Devil (JVD)*; below left, with Nazimova in *Camille (DB)*; below right, with Rose Rosanova in *Blood and Sand. (DB)*

Above, Valentino with his second wife Natacha Rambova and his lover André Daven in Paris in 1924. *(JVD)*
Below, with Daven, whom he described as the greatest love of his life, in *Monsieur Beaucaire. (DB)*

As Juan Gallardo in *Blood and Sand. (DB)*

Above, Rudy with his family in Paris at the end of 1926. With him are his sister Maria, his brother Alberto, his nephew Jean and Kabar, the dog presented to him by Jacques Hébertot. Below, Valentino taking a break on the set of *A Sainted Devil* with Douglas Fairbanks and Jackie Coogan. Mary Pickford, Fairbanks' wife, refused to be in on the shot on account of her loathing of the man who had taken her husband's Hollywood crown. *(DB)*

Valentino's favourite photograph, as Don Alonzo de Castro in *A Sainted Devil*. *(DB)*

> André Daven came along, we could not get enough of each other. I personally believe that had Valentino been based in France, where such things are not frowned upon or considered unnatural, he would have lived openly with another man and of course been that much happier.

André Daven was a twenty-four-year old, inordinately handsome reporter with *Bonsoir*, the Parisian evening newspaper, who had been dispatched to one of Rudy's press-conferences at the Plaza-Athenée in the hope of getting an exclusive – hardly likely, of course, considering that thirty others had turned up with the same thing in mind. But if Daven failed to acquire his scoop, he did end up with the man, as Jacques Hébertot explained:

> I saw their eyes meet across that crowded room, and instinctively knew what both men were thinking. Rudy later told me that Daven was probably the most beautiful man to have ever walked God's earth, and added how on their first rendezvous he had become so overcome with emotion that he had been unable to prevent himself from bursting into tears. But Daven was a spirited young thing. He told Rudy, 'If you want to have your way with me, then you've got to promise me a part in one of your films!' To which Rudy replied, 'If I can have my way with *you*, you can have a part in *all* of my films!'

Incredibly, it was *Rambova* who insisted that Rudy should write about Daven in his memoirs – about the man who, according to most of the close friends who were taken into the actor's confidence, was *the* love of his life, though several of the subsequent paragraphs were removed from his autobiography before it went to print:

> The minute he came into the room, I spotted him as a 'type'. I am constantly on the look out for types because I know them to be so very important to the screen. Young Daven is an extraordinarily good-looking chap with amazing eyes, fine physique, and general bearing out of the ordinary, and of a

> compelling attraction. Almost any man can spot a beautiful woman, but very few men can recognise the unusual or the attractive in another man. I *am* different in that respect. I have watched other such men rise in screen fame: Barthelmess, Novarro, Glenn Hunter and chaps like them have given some thought to the part 'type' plays in a man's screen success. Perhaps I would make a fine casting-director if I were not an actor … and if I did not have a wife with even acuter and finer capabilities than mine in this particular field.

With Hébertot and Daven, Rudy saw only the Paris he had wanted to see. He had particularly wanted to meet and dance with Mistinguett, France's most famous revue artiste, but she was touring South America. He did enjoy a reunion with Damia at Le-Boeuf-sur-le-Toit, the famous nightclub on the rue Boissy d'Anglas, then the haunt of the cream of Parisian society. The great chanteuse introduced him to Jean Cocteau and his boy-lover, Raymond Radiquet, who a few months later would succumb to typhoid, aged just twenty. He also met the painters Man Ray and Marie Laurencin and *refused* to sit for them … and he bumped into Harry Pilcer, whom he pretended not to have heard of. Pilcer was now a huge star in France, but Rudy would never forgive the dancer for rejecting him that afternoon in Maxim's. He also spent an evening at the Folies-Bergère, and naturally went to hear Damia's recital at the Olympia, where her repertoire included 'La Garde de Nuit à l'Yser', a stunning evocation of the horrors of trench warfare which had been inspired by the closing scenes of *The Four Horsemen Of The Apocalypse*.

Rudy was actually invited to tour some of the battlefields, but refused, telling a reporter that as a confirmed pacifist he could only condemn and abhor what had happened in Europe. He wrote in his diary that, to him, France was symbolised by a proud, beautiful woman through whose veins coursed the blood of undying courage. 'And France despoiled,' he concluded, 'is like a beautiful woman despoiled by vandal hands – a desecration.'

One man who fascinated Rudy was the playboy couturier, Paul Poiret, a self-made millionaire who had designed costumes for just about every major star in Paris. The son of a well-heeled Catholic family, Poiret had nevertheless left home at fourteen to establish an umbrella stall in a department store, after which he had served an apprenticeship with Worth and Doucet. He was enthralled by the East, and repeated to Rudy and Rambova the same story that he told everyone and which naturally 'appeased' Mesalope and Black Feather: in a previous incarnation he had been an Eastern prince. His costumes therefore were more colourful than those of his contemporaries, with an abundance of scarlet, gold, gilt and beads. 'Anything pale, washed out or insipid had been the rage for years,' he wrote in his memoirs, some years after his vast fortune had been squandered on reckless living, adding, 'All I did was set the wolves loose amongst the lambs – reds, purples and royal blues which taught the world how to sing!'

The Valentinos would never get over their first visit to Paul Poiret's mansion on the Faubourg St-Honoré. The couturier, despite his notoriety as a womaniser, was not an attractive man. Immensely fat, he greeted his guests dressed as a sultan, in cloth-of-gold robes and turban, and sitting upon a throne. He then offered the pair a list of his credentials: he had created exquisite *meneuse-de-revue* gowns for Mistinguett, Gaby Deslys and Mata Hari, he had written several plays and regularly held floating exhibitions of his Art Deco paintings on the Seine, and he had designed a black, windowless room for Isadora Duncan. Rambova waved all this aside and urged Poiret to share with her his experiences of the spirit world ... almost swooning when he told her, 'You remind me of a beautiful Tartar princess I once knew, centuries ago!'

Poiret was the first couturier to employ live models as a means of displaying his gowns, and when he suggested that Rambova would make the perfect mannequin, she readily agreed to advertise any of his creations so long as she could keep the originals. One of these, baptised 'Le Crimée', comprised of a white satin and velvet wraparound gown sewn together with hundreds of pearls and surmounted with a chinchilla redincote – in 1923 it was valued at a staggering $20,000.

Rambova, of course, was not the only one with expensive tastes. Whilst he was in Paris, Rudy ordered a custom-built, four-seater, four-cylinder Avion Voisin racing-car, upholstered in cherry-red leather. André Daven and Jacques Hébertot accompanied him to the salesroom and watched open-mouthed as he wrote out a cheque for the equivalent of $14,000. Then, because his car would not be ready for at least six months, the company loaned him a chauffeur-driven Voisin Tourer, free of charge, for the rest of his stay in France. Rudy accepted the car, but dismissed the driver.

The Valentinos had planned on leaving Paris the next day for the Hudnutts' château, but they agreed to alter their schedule when Jacques Hébertot invited them to spend the weekend at his villa in Deauville. André Daven's tiny saloon car led the convoy, with Robert Florey in the back, squashed amongst the luggage. Rudy and his wife, who, of course, insisted upon travelling in one of her beautiful Poiret gowns, followed in the tourer – trailing behind were Hébertot and Robert Florey, with the Pekingese pups.

Since the party's arrival in France, the weather had been nothing short of glorious, yet within an hour of their hitting the open road the heavens opened and, in their open car, Rudy and Rambova were very quickly soaked to the skin. Matters only became worse when, in a lay-by, Robert Florey offered to change places with her. Clambering over the suitcases in the back of Daven's car, having already lost a shoe in the mud, Rambova ripped her dress, causing Rudy to have a fit of the giggles. By the time the party reached the villa, the couple were not speaking to each other and there was more drama when they discovered that the people who had been looking after the place had left only enough provisions for two. Also, there was no electricity, the only water had to be drawn from a well at the bottom of the garden, and in spite of it being summer the building was damp and cold. Rudy was undeterred, and whilst the others headed off in the direction of the nearest hotel, he and Daven stayed put. 'We chopped wood, made a fire, and spent most of the weekend making love, pretending that we were the only people in the world,' Rudy later told Hébertot, adding, 'I cannot remember the last time I felt so happy!'

The pair did emerge from their love-nest, just the once on 9 August, to escort Rambova to the Casino, an occasion which allowed her to show off one of her Poiret 'paradoxes'. Rudy dismissed the evening as dull. The Casino was full of po-faced tourists, dinner was lousy and, he concluded, getting dressed up had been a waste of time as no one else had apparently bothered to make the effort. He did not purchase a single chip, and after watching one man lose three million francs in less than an hour, he left and returned to the villa with André Daven.

When the party returned to Paris, Rudy and Daven took a suite at the Plaza-Athenée – again, Rambova slept in the next room – and at six the next morning the two men were awakened by a curious scratching at the door. When Daven got out of the bed to investigate the noise, the door burst open and a grinning Jacques Hébertot unleashed a half-grown Doberman-Pinscher which sprang on to the bed and began licking Rudy's face. 'This was my own personal way of thanking Rudy for the tremendous joy he had brought for so many Frenchmen and women during those few weeks,' he later said. 'A man's dog – for a man's man!'

The Valentino's marriage was placed under some strain during the long drive between Paris and Nice. Declaring that the 'traditional' route through Lyons would only prove boring, Rudy decided that he would drive across the Alps and through Grenoble, where the snaking, narrow mountain roads, many with sheer drops to one side, would be more exciting. Driving at break-neck speeds and overtaking everything in sight – leaving André Daven's saloon, with Robert Florey and James Abbe in the back, way behind – he put the fear of God into his wife. Rambova was in the back, with the luggage and the dogs, trying her best not to let Kabar, the Doberman, jump out of the car! At one stage Rudy miscalculated a bend, screeching to a halt with the rear of the car dangling over a precipice. Neither did he help matters by telling her that they had only missed ending up at the bottom of the ravine because Black Feather had intervened!

The party stayed with the Hudnutts for ten days before setting off for Italy. Rudy and Rambova were still arguing much of the time, mostly about his driving, but the waters were calmed somewhat by the presence of Aunt Teresa. There were problems at the border when Customs officers asked everyone if they had any contraband to declare. Rudy lost his temper with them when they failed to recognise him, and this resulted in his luggage being searched – a lengthy process, for strapped to the car were eight valises, a large steamer trunk, innumerable hat and costume-boxes, and four cases containing Rudy's photographic equipment. Because of his dislike of Italian tobacco, Rudy had bought a large quantity of cigarettes in France, and when these were discovered in his luggage, he was made to pay a hefty surcharge before being allowed into Italy.

Having to persistently *tell* people who he was disappointed Rudy throughout his Italian trip. Most of his films had not been distributed there, or rather they had not been put on general release, so outside of the big cities he was virtually unknown. In Genoa, though *The Conquering Power* had been showing at a small cinema, Rudy had been astonished to learn that that season's big hit was *Joan The Woman*, starring Geraldine Farrar – a film which had been given its American release in 1917! 'Ten years from now, I *will* be popular in Italy,' he observed, 'but they don't know me now.'

Rudy's diary entry for 22 August 1923 read, 'I have often noted about women that they can stand up under the most tremendous strains, the most devastating calamities, and will break under some slight thing – such as motoring on one wheel, for instance!' Besides demonstrating his latest technique – to impress Aunt Teresa, who was almost as much of a speed-freak as Rudy, and who derived pleasure out of watching her niece turn green – on long empty stretches of the road to Genoa he had broken his own speed-record of 90 miles an hour. 'But what is a man to do when the dream of speed possesses him?' he had asked, and when the party reached its destination, at midnight, Rambova collapsed in her hotel room with what appears to have been a nervous breakdown.

Rudy, who until now had looked upon his wife as one degree short of invincible, did not know how to handle such a situation. The pair had planned a sightseeing tour of the city for the next day, as well as lunch with several local dignitaries. This was now cancelled, and after Rambova had eaten in her room, Rudy decided to take her on a drive into the country ... to the

Agricultural College he had attended some ten years before! The rest of the party, including André Daven, worn out not just by the journey but by the ceaseless bickering, opted to stay in Genoa to look after the dogs, but Aunt Teresa went along 'for the hell of it'.

Such was Rudy's excitement about seeing his old college that he never stopped to think that the place would be closed for the summer holidays. He did however bump into an old man named Luigi who was in charge of the *suisserie*, the stables where the thoroughbred bulls and horses were kept. Luigi recognised Rudy at once – not as Valentino, the film star, but as Guglielmi, the wayward youth whose troublemaking had been only marginally tolerated on account of his footballing prowess. For Rambova and Aunt Teresa, the afternoon must have been dreadfully boring. Italian was the only language spoken, and Rudy insisted on 'chatting' to every animal, greeting each one like some long-lost friend.

The next stop on the road was Milan, where Rudy had arranged to meet up with his sister. He had cabled her from Genoa, informing her that he had decided to stay on in the city for a few more days: unfortunately, Maria had not received the message, and at around the time Rudy set off for Milan, she left for Genoa, worrying that something had happened to him. Because of this, the reunion which took place two days later was more emotional than it might have been, and as had happened with Luigi, Rambova found herself once more shunted aside. Maria, a plain, soberly-dressed, no-nonsense young woman, took an instant dislike to her sister-in-law, criticising her for wearing a glove over her wedding ring, and even going so far as to tell her that only 'a certain type of woman' used powder and paint. For several days, therefore, Rambova explored Milan with Aunt Teresa – whilst Rudy and Maria caught up on all the gossip of the last ten years. He wrote in his diary, 'I saw not only my sister, but all of our childish scenes together, our pranks, larks, quarrels and makings-up.'

From Milan, the Valentino party – with André Daven and Robert Florey struggling to keep up with Rudy in the former's saloon – took the straight, 300-mile Roman road to Bologna. Here, on the outskirts of the town, driving steadily for once, Rudy crashed into a telegraph pole – and blamed his wife for distracting him! Fortunately, no damage was done to the car or its occupants. Then, only hours later, whilst another car was overtaking him on a bend, he swerved to the side of the road and hit a cart, causing it to shed its load, but again hurting no one. That evening he wrote, 'The old woman started cursing me in Italian. She may be there cursing me yet. And if her vocabulary of profanity and ferocity of her anger are any omens, she probably is!'

Crossing the Apennines towards Florence, where the roads were at their most treacherous, Rudy made a conscientious effort to drive carefully, though he set everyone's nerves on edge when he saw another cart, this time being drawn by two long-horned cattle. Screeching to a halt, causing André Daven to slam on his brakes and miss running into the back of him by a fraction of an inch, he leapt out of his car and shouted for someone to take his photograph whilst, fearlessly, he stopped the cart and posed between the huge beasts, the points of whose horns reached way above his head. Daven captured the moment for posterity, as Rambova quipped in a rare outburst of humour, 'Two big bullocks – and an even bigger prick between them!'

From Florence, where the Valentinos spent a small fortune on costume books – one, a first edition published around 1500, set them back $2,000 – the party drove to Rome, where Rudy had booked suites at the Excelsior Hotel. Here, their official guide was Baron Fassini, the former President of the Italian Cinematographic Union, and the emphasis for once was not on shopping. The pair were invited to spend a whole day on the set of *Quo Vadis?* where they met the great German actor, Emil Jannings, who despite his popularity in America had yet to visit that country.

In the evening, the Valentinos drove out to Fassini's castle at Nettuno, a former medieval stronghold overlooking the sea which impressed Rudy no end with its dungeons, secret passages, draughty halls and creaking staircases. Fassini told him that should he ever decide to make a film in Italy, he would be more than willing to put the place at his disposal, and Rudy promised that he would keep this in mind. Much more important from Rudy's point of view was the fact that the castle was favoured by Mussolini, who often came there, and whom Rudy wanted to meet more than anyone else in Italy. Whilst the Valentinos were in Nettuno, Fassini actually contacted Mussolini, and a rendez-vous was fixed for 12 September. However, as this was the day that Rudy was to be reunited with his brother at Campobasso, 120 miles south-east of Rome, the meeting had to be cancelled.

It was in Rome that the Valentinos had the most furious quarrel thus far in their marriage, one which resulted in Rambova throwing a sulk and taking the early evening train back to Nice. 'Natacha has gone,' Rudy lamented. 'I am alone today for the first time in many months. I could write a dissertation on loneliness ... it is like a mist from the sea, striking chill to the bone.'

He was of course only saying this for the benefit of his fans, who would take in his every written or spoken word as if it were some religious sermon. Aunt Teresa, who until now had never taken sides in these 'lovers' tiffs', had elected to stay with Rudy, and he still had André Daven, who had heard so much about Castellaneta from his lover over the last few weeks that he was just as eager to see the place as he was.

In Campobasso, Rudy met Alberto's wife and their nine-year old son, Jean, for the first time. Because the boy was spirited and mischievous, and more interested in 'driving' Rudy's car than he was in getting to know his new uncle, Rudy baptised him 'Mercurio' – the Italian word for quicksilver. Alberto was Secretary General of the town, and had recently been decorated with the Cross of the Chevalier. He was, however, less impressed by seeing his brother for the first time in ten years than he was in using his celebrity as a means of self-promotion. He had never seen one of Rudy's films, and only agreed to do so when Rudy suggested organising a gala-performance of *The Four Horsemen Of The Apocalypse* so that the proceeds could go towards erecting a memorial in honour of Campobasso's war dead. Alberto also refused to accompany him to Castellaneta, as did Maria, declaring that such a journey would prove but a waste of time – visiting a backwater which would be exactly the same as when he had left it, and driving over dirt-roads which would only damage a car which was not his.

On the morning of 20 September, Rudy sped into the town of

his birth, anticipating that the entire population would be out in the streets to welcome him. This was not to be. The locals knew that *someone* of importance had arrived when they saw the huge Voisin tourer pull up outside the town hall, followed by André Daven's saloon. No one, however, could put a name to the tall, elegantly-suited man who was the focus of his fellow travellers' attention: the cameraman who recorded his every movement, the photographer who began taking shots of a group of children, the middle-aged lady who flung them a handful of sweets, and the dark-haired young man scribbling in a notebook.

It was the latter, André Daven, his command of Italian no better than his English, who explained – by holding aloft a copy of *Photoplay* with Rudy's picture on the cover – that this was Rudolph Valentino, the world's most celebrated film star, returning to his roots ... only to be told by the mayor, who spoke French, that as the nearest cinema was in Taranto, hardly anyone in Castellaneta had ever seen a film, let alone heard of any of the actors who had appeared in one! Rudy did, of course, get a little further with the locals when he explained that he was the son of their former vet, Giovanni Guglielmi, now made good, though this only resulted in him being pestered for money, and when he refused on principle to dip his hand into his pocket, all he received was abuse.

The drama continued when the party moved on to Taranto, when Rudy and Daven – his 'valet' – checked into their hotel. Not only did their room not have a bath, they were told by the manager that the establishment had never had a call for such 'refinements' as there were reputable Turkish baths just around the corner! The last straw, however, came the next morning when – leaving the others resting in their rooms – Rudy took Daven to the tiny bistro he had frequented as a youth. The decor, the furnishings, the people behind the counter, the customers and even the crockery were exactly the same as they had been ten years before. 'These familiar faces,' he recalled. 'They had seemed so splendid to me then. Now, here they were, still talking the same language in the same way, still exchanging the same smallness of intellect. And as I watched them, I realised that the luckiest thing that had ever happened to me was getting away and going to America. I might so easily have become one of them.'

After spending a few days in Naples, and visiting Pompeii, the party drove to Nice, arriving at the Hudnutts' château on the last day of September. Rambova was fully recovered from her 'indisposition' and had arranged for a young woman reporter to witness her 'tearful reunion' with her husband. What is amazing is the fact that Rudy would have anything to do with a scenario which was so obviously contrived. Mrs Hudnutt served the trio tea on the lawn, whilst Rudy's 'pals' rushed off to write letters to their girls back home, Rambova's Pekingeses massacred the flowerbeds, and Kabar, Rudy's Doberman, persistently licked his master's face. The first question – 'Mr Valentino, have you *danced* much at all during your travels?' – meant only one thing, and received a suitably sarcastic reply, 'I haven't *danced*, my dear, I haven't *flirted*, and I've been neither a social nor a professional butterfly!' 'But,' the reporter pressed, getting to the crux of the matter, 'Are you *really* happily married? And how do you think a wife *should* be treated?' Rudy had to ponder over this one: he realised now that this young woman had been briefed by Rambova as to which questions to ask, that the whole world probably knew by now that his marriage had suffered a setback. His response, however, would only make matters worse:

> Marriage is pretty much like dancing. So long as the couple are in tune, the technique is of relatively little importance. I believe in giving a woman her way, but only in trivialities – *never* in the fundamental issues. A *man* should be the master and head of his house. In my country, men are *always* the masters, and women are happier for it!

9
The Melody of Life

'Natacha has said that I'm like a child, and I suppose I am. Isn't every artist? If we lose the questing spirit, the child's belief that something new, enthralling and delightful waits for us just around each corner, we lose more than half the joy of living.'

The Valentinos had planned on spending another week at the Hudnutt's château before returning to Paris, then going on to London where they were to be joined by J D Williams, who was on vacation. On 3 October 1923, however, Williams cabled Rudy, demanding that they meet in Cherbourg immediately regarding 'a matter of grave and pressing import'.

'At this stage in my career,' Rudy wrote, 'one cannot disregard the grave and the pressing. Things are hanging by the well-known hair.' The party set off, with Rambova agreeing to travel with Rudy only if someone else was behind the wheel. André Daven refused – he would not, he declared, allow anyone else to drive *his* car – and, as both James Abbe and Robert Florey were terrified of the huge Voisin, Rudy had no option but to hire a driver from the company, who turned out to be even madder on the road than he was. Because of his reckless driving, which resulted in several flat tyres, the party arrived in Cherbourg during the middle of the night to find that the ferry transporting passengers to the *Leviathan* had left without them. As a result of this, Rudy lost his temper: the pair ended up brawling on the quayside and had to be parted by André Daven and a young docker, who was finally persuaded not to call the police when Rudy promised him a signed photograph!

The young man – for a price, of course – then told Rudy that he would get them across the harbour to the *Leviathan* because he had access to a motor-boat. Under normal circumstances, Rudy would have been willing to wait another day and catch the next boat to Southampton. He was, however, concerned about the cable from J D Williams, so he pitched in and helped load his luggage into the boat – only to be told by customs officials after he had stacked the last of the party's sixty or so cases and trunks in the bottom of the vessel that everything would have to be unloaded again for inspection! As with the earlier incident at the Italian border, Rudy's 'I am Valentino!' ploy did not work. Two valuable 17th century Gobelins tapestries had been stolen from the palace at Versailles, and the authorities had demanded that everyone's luggage be checked, even that of famous film stars!

Eventually, the motor-boat set off across the harbour, just as a storm was brewing. The young man steering the boat was confident that they would make it to the ship in time, but half a mile from the shore it began raining heavily, and the sea turned exceedingly rough, affecting everyone but Rudy, who really did have a cast-iron constitution. When a huge wave suddenly engulfed the boat, however, the party had no option but to turn around and head back towards the quay. Several pieces of luggage had been washed overboard and, terrified that the boat was about to capsize and that everyone would have to swim for it, Rudy flung Rambova's jewellery case the ten yards or so onto the now departed *Leviathan*'s service-boat, also on its way back, where it was miraculously caught by a sailor. 'Jewels mean singularly little when your lives, like the frailest of reeds, are palpitating beneath an ominous sky and a hungry sea,' he wrote in his diary – incredibly, at five in the morning when he was shivering over a mug of coffee in a dockside bistro, by which time his wife had been reunited with her jewels.

Five days later, the Valentino party reached London, where they eventually caught up with J D Williams, who explained what all the 'urgency' had been about: Williams, who had heard about their argument in Rome, had wanted their tour to end on a happier note, so he had arranged for a surprise party aboard the *Leviathan*, complete with a dance-band! Rudy told him, still shuddering after his brush with death, 'Just consider yourself lucky that your *band* didn't end up playing Chopin's "Funeral March!" '

On 21 October, the Valentinos arrived in New York, and the very next morning Rudy met with Paramount's executives to decide upon his comeback film. Several projects had been proposed before his trip to Europe, but the two which had interested him the most had been *Captain Blood*, based on the pirate novel by Rafael Sabatini, and Booth Tarkington's romp through 18th century France, *Monsieur Beaucaire*. Rudy was now fervently in favour of the former. He had read and enjoyed Sabatini's *Scaramouche* and *The Sea Hawk*, and the script called for several fighting scenes for which he would strip to the waist. Rambova, however, argued that there had been enough high-seas drama in *Moran Of The Lady Letty* to last Rudy a lifetime, so *she* decided that he would do *Monsieur Beaucaire*. Tarkington, she declared, was not just any ordinary writer. He was an artist who had *twice* won the Pulitzer Prize (with *The Magnificent Ambersons* and *Alice Adams*), so who better to play the eponymous hero than the finest actor of his generation, with costumes designed by his wife? Then, offering Jesse Lasky a taster of what was to come now that she was *officially* listed as Valentino's artistic director, she dismissed the script as 'claptrap' and gave instructions for it to be rewritten. Then, as this was going to take several weeks she, Rudy and Daven returned to France to spend the festive season with the Hudnutts. Paramount, naturally, paid for the trip.

The visit to Juan-les-Pins was not a success. Rudy had insisted on an all-American Christmas, and had brought over a huge trunk filled with glass baubles, tinsel, streamers and scented candles. On Christmas Eve, a huge pine was cut from the Hudnutt estate and the entire gathering spent several hours decorating it. Rudy himself lit the candles – and set fire to the tree, though no great damage was done until he decided to extinguish it with the garden hose and flooded the room. New Year's Eve was spent at the plush

Negresco Hotel, in Nice, where Rudy and André Daven got very drunk and took to the dance floor with two pretty blondes in Charleston dresses ... actually two chorus-boys from the nearby Perroquet Club, to which the party relocated, raging until well into the next afternoon when Rudy, still inebriated, had to be half-carried on to the *Leviathan* for the journey home.

In New York, the Valentinos and Daven were given a suite at the Ritz-Carlton, where Rambova immediately began reading and amending the revised script for *Monsieur Beaucaire*. Encouraged by Daven, whose knowledge of the French music-hall was second to none, she had engaged Georges Barbier as her personal adviser. Barbier, an almost legendary designer and musician who had worked with Mistiniguett at the Folies-Bergère, was an expensive commodity that Jesse Lasky could have done without, particularly as Rambova had also commissioned *sixty* costumes from Paul Poiret! The film's budget soared even higher, however, when she began selecting her 'team' which would eventually comprise *two* assistant directors, a fencing coach, four wardrobe assistants, a make-up supervisor ...and a professional violinist to soothe Rudy's nerves by playing his favourite classical pieces whilst he was relaxing between takes. And when Lasky asked, sarcastically, if this was all, Rambova acidly added that whilst he was obviously in a benevolent mood, he could also hire an English poetry-reader so that everyone else connected with the film – most of whom, she declared, would not know *how* to read – might be entertained with readings from *Daydreams*!

Rudy had been looking forward to showing André Daven around New York, particularly as there had been no time to do so during his lover's first visit to the city. Initially, the fans prevented this, since more than a thousand of them surrounded the Ritz-Carlton, day and night, with a constant stream of them breaking through the already stringent security, posing as reporters, photographers and studio personnel. Eventually, J D Williams called the Chief of Police, who assigned Rudy a small team of bodyguards to protect him around the clock. Both Rudy and Daven became amorously interested in one of these – a burly, thirty-year old policeman named Luther Mahoney.

One evening, Rudy and Daven spent several hours chatting up Mahoney – taking a risk, though Daven later said that he had been 'sympathetic' – in the hope of wooing him back to their suite after his shift. The young cop, however, soon put paid to their designs. Explaining that although he did not disapprove of homosexuals – adding that half the men he had met from the movie fraternity were thus inclined – he concluded that he personally had no intention of 'turning the other way', and that in any case he was married with two small children. Rudy apologised for his oversight, and the atmosphere remained amicable. Mahoney explained that he was beginning to tire of police work, especially hazardous in the days of Prohibition, and that he was thinking of setting up a trucking business in Los Angeles with his brother, who was also a policeman. Rudy told him, 'If you do, and if you're ever in Hollywood, please look me up.'

The fact that Rudy's new film was to be shot on Long Island had done wonders for the rented property market. Greedy estate agents doubled and sometimes trebled their fees, yet within two days of Rudy's return there was not so much as a vacant single room within a twenty-five mile radius of the studio. Fans who could not afford to be fleeced in such a way simply braved the elements and camped overnight outside the studio gates, refusing to budge even when the police were drafted in. More often than not, their idol would be suffering the after-effects of the previous evening's visit to a speakeasy with André Daven and Luther Mahoney, followed by a discreet, costly visit to one of New York's infamous 'glory-hole' clubs, once Mahoney had gone home to his family. Yet, all Rudy had to do was fake a smile or pop his eyes for everyone, male and female, to set off shrieking. Rambova loathed this overzealous idolatry, and each morning tried her utmost to dispel the screaming horde who surrounded his car whilst he patiently signed autographs.

The fans were not Rudy's only concern, for when Rambova read in a tabloid gossip-column that her husband's last trip to Europe had been to enable him to have treatment for venereal disease, she *banned* all reporters, photographers and visitors from entering the lot or approaching studio personnel. This embargo was lifted two weeks into shooting, however, when Konstantin Stanislavsky, the famous Russian actor-teacher and the founder of the Method School of Acting, paid an impromptu visit to the set and demanded to be photographed with the actors. For Rambova, such an endorsement from so mighty a figure in the theatrical world – and a Russian to boot – was yet another of Mesalope's miracles, assuring her that this project could not fail.

Not unexpectedly, Rambova soon got on the wrong side of Sydney Olcott, the director of *Monsieur Beaucaire*, when she began contesting not just every decision he made, but also the acting abilities of Rudy's co-stars. She could not stand Bebe Daniels, whom Rudy had asked for to play the part of Princess Henriette, and persistently reminded her that she would be hard put to act her way out of a paper bag. No one, however, received the brunt of her criticism more than Rudy, for her remarks to him were so vile that he often ended up in tears. 'That was Rambova, through and through,' André Daven later reflected. 'The fact that she could make a big man like Rudy cry gave her some God Almighty power, and this is why so many men made fun of him. Rudy was paranoid about being considered effeminate, and would have fought any man to the death for saying such a thing, yet he was terrified of his wife.' The reason for this fear was explained by Daven's and Rudy's friend, Jacques Hébertot, who told Roger Normand, 'She knew he liked sleeping with other guys, much as she liked women, and of course had she decided to blow the whistle on him, his career would have been over in next to no time. So she got away with treating him like shit, on the pretext that if he ever complained, she would tell the world his best-kept secret.'

Of the cast of *Monsieur Beaucaire*, only Doris Kenyon, a long-forgotten actress who played the Lady Mary, met with Rambova's approval, and whilst Rudy was 'dilly-dallying' with his latest lover and even managing to elude his fans by taking André Daven to Bustanoby's, the two women spent some time together. Kenyon composed a 13-line poem in Rambova's honour, which she had published in *Motion Picture Classic*, and which began: 'She is an iris, swaying in its stem/ Poised, cool, elusive in the evening dusk.'

There was also a much-publicised incident when Sydney Olcott attempted to mediate in an argument between Rambova and the cameraman, Harry Fischbeck, whom she accused of deliberately photographing Rudy from all the wrong angles. When she yelled at Olcott, 'This idiot is trying to make Valentino look bad!' the director retorted dryly, 'That, Madam Valentino, appears to be your job!'

Eventually, like others before him, Olcott fronted Jesse Lasky with a 'her-or-me' ultimatum, and an uneasy truce was obtained ... after which Olcott, who had been contracted to direct Rudy's next film, told Lasky, 'I'd sooner drop down dead than work with Valentino again whilst that minx is around!' Lasky is also reported to have said, borrowing from June Mathis, 'Valentino alone *is* a dear, dear boy – but when teamed up with that damned wife of his, he's just one half of a double-hernia!'

Monsieur Beaucaire was, unintentionally, a high-camp extravaganza from start to finish. 18th century French noblemen *were* notoriously foppish and effeminate, endlessly bowing and scraping to one another whilst being introduced. And Rudy *was* a great actor, of this there is no doubt. Nevertheless, for his American detractors *no* role could have better set him up for their lampooning than the one where the World's Greatest Lover appeared on screen in silken breeches, powdered wigs, and sporting twin heart-shaped beautyspots, whilst his limp-wristed courtiers minced around him, one of whom pouts at the camera before fixing his lipstick and plucking his eyebrows! Of course, Rudy had worn a similar get-up in the flashback sequence in Nazimova's *Camille*, though few critics remembered this. The publicity poster, too, caused problems with the censor. Rudy is seen perched on a balustrade, plucking a ridiculously long phallic-shaped lute, which in an early scene of the film he does, admittedly, hold provocatively.

The macho Rudy, however, does come to the fore when his character, the Duc de Chartres, travels to England disguised as the French Ambassador's barber, and in the course of events very quickly ends up fighting a duel. Declaring that Rudy was only *attempting* to act at the expense of his personality, which had made him a sensation, *Photoplay*'s J R Quirk concluded, 'Except for one or two rattling good swordfights, the old spark disappears. He doesn't look a *bit* dangerous to women.'

This was of course but one opinion, and *Monsieur Beaucaire* was a great success upon its release that autumn. Rambova's work on the film was universally acclaimed, and deservedly so, in spite of the havoc she had caused. 'Never have such wondrous settings or beautiful costumes been seen in a photoplay!' enthused the *New York Times*, whilst *Bioscope* called it, 'A masterpiece of the united arts of the scene-builder, the decorator, the costumier and the cameraman.' The film also contained the obligatory, deliberately drawn-out dressing scene with André Daven, who was playing Rudy's on-screen brother, the Duc de Nemours. For several minutes, Rudy flexed his muscles and paraded his naked torso, fixing Daven with a look which was accurately interpreted by gay fans worldwide – another potently homo-erotic wrestling scene with Daven, at one stage of which the two men seem as though they are about to actually kiss, was cut from most of the finished prints.

The enthusiasm for *Monsieur Beaucaire*, of course, entitled Natacha Rambova to deliver a stridently public 'I told you so!' to Paramount, ultimately proving that Rudy's public demanded *art*, not fantasy. The production, however, had far exceeded its budget, and for Valentino's final picture with Paramount, Jesse Lasky was urged to keep the costs down. After some deliberation – and having read some of the poison-pen letters to Rudy which had been delivered to the studio by mistake, attacking him for playing a 'pink powder-puff' – Lasky plumped for *Rope's End*, a short story by Rex Beach which had first appeared in *Cosmopolitan* magazine during the summer of 1913. Scripted by Forrest Halsey, the man who had done a sterling job adapting *Monsieur Beaucaire*, it became *A Sainted Devil*.

Rambova hated the concept of Valentino, the world's archetypal hero and lover, playing a drunkard who rushes off to the South American jungle to rescue his wife from bandits, even though his leading lady was to be her friend, Nita Naldi. Lasky ignored her protests, however. Rudy had approved of the script and had a few ideas of his own how he should play Don Alonzo de Castro, and so far as he was concerned, nothing else mattered.

The sparks began flying on the set of *A Sainted Devil* when Lasky hired the exotic French actress, Jetta Goudal, to play Dona Florencia, one of Don Alonzo's love-interests. When Goudal watched in amazement as Nita Naldi walked onto the set, baring her magnificent breasts and demanding that everyone attest their firmness, from Rudy down to the junior technicians, she too began behaving lasciviously. However, whilst Rudy had always laughed off Naldi's advances because the woman *was* genuinely funny *and* only pulling his leg, he seemed to respond to Goudal – allegedly because of some of the taunts concerning his virility, following *Monsieur Beaucaire*. In other words, he wanted the world to *think* that he was sexually interested in women, when he was not.

The crunch came when Rambova called a set meeting to reveal her costume designs for the film, for Goudal laughed at them and told her, 'These clothes are obviously intended to be worn by effeminate men and deformed women – and *I* do not fit into any category, Madam Valentino!' Shoving her designs back into their folder, Rambova walked off the set. Later that evening she called the director, Joseph Henabery, at his home and informed him that unless Goudal was removed from the production, there would *be* no production. By the next morning the fearless but foolhardy Frenchwoman had been replaced by Dagmar Godowsky, the actress who, some years earlier, had orchestrated Rudy's first fateful meeting with Nazimova.

The rumours began circulating at once: Jetta Goudal had been dismissed from *A Sainted Devil* because she had failed to make a man out of Valentino. The truth, however, was far more sinister. The actress had informed Jesse Lasky of Rudy's relationship with André Daven. The repercussions of such a revelation being made public would, of course, have proved horrendous. Rudy's career would almost certainly have ended at once, and the Hays Office would have had no option *but* to prohibit the screening of his films, following an international scandal which would have relegated even those involving Fatty Arbuckle and Wallace Reid to the ranks. Lasky therefore offered what he hoped would be the ideal solution: one of his assistants would fix Rudy up with one of the whores employed by the studios exclusively to 'normalise' homosexual men, and subsequently broadcast the clinical details of their 'encounter' in such a way that there could be no further doubt that they were 'regular guys'. It was a ploy which hardly ever worked and one which must only be condemned for its sheer hypocrisy, considering it had been set up by the Hays Office, but especially because it resulted in a number of suicides – and it almost made Rudy the laughing-stock of the film world.

Appalled that a married man should be expected to prove his virility in such a way, Rudy begged André Daven to go with him to the young woman's apartment: a 'threesome' would curb the rumours which Jetta Goudal had spread about them *both*, he explained. This Daven would not do. He had only begun concealing his sexuality since arriving in America, and for Rudy's sake he would continue to do so, but he had never slept with a woman in his life and had no intention of doing so now. According to Jacques Hébertot he told Rudy, 'Just close your eyes and imagine you're making love to me, and everything will be all right.' Everything was *not* all right, however, and the next morning everyone on the lot had been informed that the World's Greatest Lover had been unable to 'rise to the occasion' with one of the most seductive women in New York.

Chaw Mank later affirmed that Rambova – who made no effort whatsoever to defend her 'investment' – was entirely responsible for her husband's misery at this time. He observed in his memoirs, 'If she had shown more affection toward Valentino in public and on the set, gossip that the Great Lover could only love on the screen might not have been so prevalent.' Rudy himself coped with his dilemma the only way he knew how: when a technician asked him outright if he really *was* a 'fairy', Rudy smacked him in the mouth.

In July 1924, whilst *Monsieur Beaucaire* and *A Sainted Devil* were awaiting release, the Valentinos were summoned to a meeting with Ritz-Carlton's J D Williams to discuss Rudy's debut film with the studio. Rambova very quickly monopolised the proceedings when Williams – described by Jesse Lasky as, 'One poor son-of-a-bitch who's just inherited America's Number One Headache'

– read out a list of possible projects. He was only halfway through this when Rambova banged her fist on his desk. Valentino's contracts now stipulated that *he* alone had complete control over the choice of his material, co-stars and studio personnel, and as his standards as a first-rate artist were exceedingly high, he would no longer be prepared to accept 'fourth-rate drivel' concocted by illiterate studio chiefs! Before Williams could interject, she then announced that Rudy – described at this stage in his life by Chaw Mank as 'acting like Rambova's well-trained performing monkey,' – had already commissioned June Mathis to write the screenplay for *The Scarlet Power*, Rambova's own tale of daring-do and swashbuckling between the Moors and Christians of medieval Spain, which she had written under the pseudonym of Justice Layne. She then added that Rudy had *insisted* that she be the film's set and costume designer, technical adviser *and* director, that the production should have a budget of not less than $1 million, and that Williams should release $40,000 of this immediately so that the couple could travel to Spain – where, incidentally, the film would be shot in an authentic Moorish location – to purchase the props, costumes and some of the sets, and to execute the research necessary to make *this* film the most successful and spectacular of Valentino's career. Rudy's co-star, in conclusion, would be Nita Naldi. In a decision which he would bitterly regret, Williams agreed to every one of these demands.

In August, the Valentinos, André Daven and James Abbe, along with Rudy's Doberman and his wife's trio of Pekingese, arrived in Paris. Here there was a brief reunion with Jacques Hébertot, and Rudy collected his new Voison. Rambova, however, at once put her foot down when her husband announced that they would be touring in this, and an uneasy compromise was reached: he, Daven and James Abbe would take turns driving the vehicle to Juan-les-Pins, taking the conventional route this time and *never* exceeding the speed-limit. The car would then be garaged at the Hudnutts' château, and their travels would be continued by train.

In Juan-les-Pins, Rudy was reunited with his brother and sister; neither of whom went out of their way to be sociable with Rambova. This disappointed him, for he had rather hoped that they might go with him to Spain. Mrs Hudnutt, too, had not forgotten Rudy's last visit to her home when he had set fire to the Christmas tree, and this one was also not incident free. Rudy insisted on playing the gathering a preview of *Monsieur Beaucaire*, so a projector was sent over from Marseilles. Unfortunately, this was not in working order and Rudy – usually a wizard with mechanics and electrical appliances – blew all the fuses in the house on *two* consecutive evenings. Then, to make up for any trouble he had caused, he announced that he was taking everyone for a cruise along the Riviera, and hired a motor-boat ... which André Daven decided that *he* would navigate.

During his brief sojourn in the South of France, upon Rambova's insistence, Rudy grew a short goatee beard for his role in the new film, whose title had now been changed to *The Hooded Falcon*. She had seen what he looked like in a false beard, she declared, when he had visited her in New York during their separation, and he had made her cringe with embarrassment. He also spent as much time as he could sunbathing, hoping to acquire a 'Moorish' tan so that he would not have to have his skin darkened with make-up.

At the end of August, this time accompanied by Mrs Hudnutt, the Valentino party set off on what J D Williams later referred to as 'The Sacking of Spain' – arriving in Madrid with a mountain of luggage, including Rudy's two bulky movie cameras, which on account of a porters' strike they had had to heave on and off the train. Rudy had booked two suites at the Ritz: one for his wife and mother-in-law, the other for himself, Daven and Abbe, a sleeping pattern which would be repeated throughout their tour. The party stayed in Madrid for almost a week, sightseeing, filming the lovely Moorish architecture, and visiting antique shops – spending several thousand dollars on weapons, armour, Gothic chests and chairs, and jade artefacts for the film ... and several thousand more on antiques for their Whitley Heights home. Rudy was able to move around freely without being mobbed, since hardly anyone recognised him with a beard.

In Madrid, Rudy also met the celebrated painter, Federico Beltran-Masses, who was so taken up with him and Rambova –

and André Daven – that he wanted to do their portraits there and then. Rudy had a better idea. As he was pushed for time, would it not be better for Beltran-Masses to pay a visit to Hollywood, where he would find a wealth of celebrities to paint? The artist agreed.

The next stop on the road was Seville, where the matador upon whom Ibanez had based his character, Juan Gallardo, had allegedly lived. Naturally, Rudy tracked down the supposed address – a filthy house in a run-down suburb of the city – though there was some compensation when he stumbled upon a shop in the vicinity which sold the costumes of matadors who had died in the ring. Such items of apparel were considered unlucky by the Spanish, and Rudy was able to acquire a dozen of the most beautiful embroidered suits for next to nothing. King Alfonso XIII and most of the Spanish royal family were also in Seville, and they invited the Valentinos to a bullfight. Throughout the entire colourful but gruesome spectacle, Rambova kept her eyes tightly shut and covered her ears, and when it was over she told Alfonso that protocol had forced her to endure the most abhorrent afternoon of her life.

During the next week, Rudy and Rambova – their shopping spree way over budget already – filmed the Alcazar and the Alhambra, the huge 14th century fortified palace built by the Moorish kings in Granada. Here, Rambova loaned $10,000 of Ritz-Carlton's money to purchase a consignment of exquisite Spanish shawls, which she hoped she might be able to re-sell to some of the chic New York department stores. The following day, whilst she and Mrs Hudnutt stayed in their suite to wrap and crate these, ready to be shipped back to New York, James Abbe told Rudy that he would like to do several pre-publicity shots for *The Hooded Falcon*. Abbe photographed Rudy looking Christ-like in Moorish robes, and whilst he was developing these, Rudy and his lover 'blitzed' the antiques and costume shops, spending $30,000 on jewellery, ivory ornaments and Moorish costumes. 'The Valentinos' expedition was more like the Huns sacking the art treasures of ancient Rome than an actor and writer selecting necessary properties for their next film,' observed Chaw Mank.

At the end of September, having spent Ritz-Carlton's $40,000 and an additional $60,000 of the studio's money, the Valentinos journeyed back to Juan-les-Pins, where they bade farewell to Mrs Hudnutt. Maria and Alberto Guglielmi, anticipating Rambova's return, had already left for Italy. Then the party drove up to Paris, where they met up with Nita Naldi, who was having her costumes for *The Hooded Falcon* made up by Paul Poiret's seamstresses. In Paris Rudy received a cable from J D Williams: he and his wife were well on their way towards bankrupting his studio, and they were requested to return home at once. Rambova cabled back with the message that they would leave Europe when they were good and ready, and next morning – taking Nita Naldi with them – the party set off for the Loire Valley and a tour of the châteaux.

It was in Chaumont that Naldi, who thus far had managed to keep her exhibitionism under control, finally let rip during a guided tour of the castle. When the courier pointed to the bed which had been slept in by Catherine de Medici and one of her many lovers, Naldi exposed her breasts to the room full of tourists and quipped, 'I'll bet *she* didn't have tits like these!'

Mercifully, in a country famed for its *demi-mondaine* actresses, this incident went largely unnoticed by the French press, whereas the 'new-look' Valentino, photographed descending the gangplank of the *Leviathan* after it had docked in New York, two weeks later, caused a national outcry – not just from Rudy's fans, but from the Master Barbers Association. The former refused to even *consider* accepting their idol with a beard, and bombarded his fan club, Paramount *and* Ritz-Carlton with thousands of letters of complaint. The latter, fearing that half the men in America would follow Rudy's example, took more stringent action, issuing a public statement: until the offending whiskers were removed, the association's barbers, together with their families and friends, were expressly forbidden from seeing any Valentino films. The statement concluded, 'Such a fashion as a beard will not only cause injury to barbers, it will utterly deface our country and make American citizens difficult to distinguish from Russians.' Rudy shaved the beard off at once.

Two days after arriving in New York, the Valentinos incurred

J D Williams' wrath by taking out a one-year lease – using Ritz-Carlton's money – on a plush apartment at 270 Park Avenue, on the pretext that they expected to be working in New York for at least this long. One week later they took over the Ambassador Hotel for what was to be the party of the year, inviting seemingly every film personality who happened to be in town at the time, and many more who considered the occasion well worth the five-day train journey from Hollywood. Mae Murray, Lillian and Dorothy Gish, Alma Rubens, Barbara La Marr, the Talmadge sisters, Bebe Daniels, Mary Pickford and Marion Davies all competed against 'Madam Valentino' – as she insisted upon being called, never Natacha – in the fashion stakes, losing miserably when Rambova made an entrance down the grand staircase, bedecked as an Oriental princess ... with a lounge-suited Rudy trailing several paces behind, like a lackey.

Friends such as the scriptwriter, Adela Rogers St Johns, later declared that Rambova had staged the party 'so that the world could observe that in the Valentino household, the woman wore the pants'. According to Jacques Hébertot, however, the guest list had been drawn up by Rudy himself, who told André Daven whilst they were on their way to the bash, 'Tonight you're going to meet all of my fucks – past, present and future!' In the course of the evening, Daven was introduced to several of Rudy's men, most of them now married: Charles Farrell, Richard Arlen, Thomas Meighan, Richard Barthelmess, Milton Sills and, of course, George O'Brien, who immediately took a shine to the dashing young Frenchman. The most important man of all, however, was not there: Paul Ivano still would have nothing to do with Rudy whilst Rambova was around.

When J D Williams complained again that the Valentinos' spending was nudging his studio towards bankruptcy, Rambova told him not to worry – *The Hooded Falcon* would prove *so* profitable that inside six months, Ritz-Carlton would be giving all the major studios a run for their money. By the end of October, however, Williams had summoned the pair to his office and delivered the not so pleasing news: his backers were no longer sure of the projected film, particularly as Rudy had told the press that he had every intention of growing another beard for his role, and they had forced him to reduce its budget to $500,000. This meant that shooting it on location in Spain would now be out of the question – like *Blood And Sand*, it would have to be made in Hollywood. Rambova's immediate reaction was to have a fit, but Williams read the signs and nipped this in the bud. Pushing June Mathis's script across the desk, he explained that, whilst *The Hooded Falcon* most definitely *would* be made, the studio would have to be given time to relocate to the West, and in the interim period he saw no reason why Rudy should not consider doing another film for Ritz-Carlton to occupy his time.

The suggested project was Anthony Coldeways' reworking of Martin Brown's stage play, *Cobra*, which had enjoyed a hugely successful run on Broadway with Louis Calhern and Judith Anderson. Rambova, of course, would have nothing to do with the film, and stunned Williams by telling him that if Rudy really wanted to appear in such 'trash', then she would not dissuade him. Rudy skipped through the précis. *Cobra* was a contemporary drama, and in the original play the role of Count Torriani – an Italian nobleman whose dwindling fortune compels him to seek employment in a Bronx antiques-shop – was not inordinately large. Coldeways had, however, expanded it considerably, adding several boxing sequences. Rudy, having been given a rare opportunity to make up his own mind, announced that he would love to do the film, provided its release could be held back until after the première of *The Hooded Falcon*. Williams gave his word on this, but added that as new backers would have to be found for the film, shooting would probably not start until late in the spring of 1925. This Rudy did not mind, for he would now have the opportunity to add the finishing touches to his Whitley Heights home, and move in.

10
Sanctuary of my Soul

'The public expects me to be one of the romantic heroes I play on the screen, and the real Valentino isn't one bit like that.'

During the train journey back to Hollywood, the Valentinos dissected June Mathis's script for *The Hooded Falcon*, but whereas Rudy agreed that a few *minor* adjustments might have to be made, Rambova dismissed the entire script as inadequate and cabled George Ullman with the instructions to order a rewrite, at no extra cost to the studio, or else. Mathis's reaction to such a threat drove the first serious wedge between the couple; she told Ullman that she never wanted to see, hear or speak to either of them again.

Utterly devastated, Rudy slumped into another period of neurasthenia and near reclusion, much as had happened after his bigamy trial. This time, however, he had absolutely no one to turn to and confide in. Paul Ivano was gone from his life, or so Rudy was convinced, and André Daven had stayed on at the Park Avenue apartment since many of the antiques which the Valentinos had bought in Europe were stored there, and the lease still had another eleven months to run before it expired.

Once again, Rudy began searching for company at the Torch Club: two weeks of one-night stands until he engaged in another brief fling with Richard Arlen – any excuse, it would appear, to prevent him from spending too much time with his wife, who still insisted upon extravagant living even though the pair were deeply in debt.

Another occasional lover was Mario Caracciolo, a handsome Neapolitan in his mid-thirties who had formerly been an officer with the Italian cavalry, though at the time of his meeting with Rudy, Caracciolo was working as a physiotherapist-masseur at the Los Angeles Athletic Club. In the autumn of 1924, he became Rudy's personal fitness adviser, subjecting him to a rigorous training programme which even he found tough, initially. His problem, Caracciolo told Rudy, was that he was eating all the wrong foods and smoking far too many of the strong, monogrammed cigarettes which he had especially made in London and sent over by the crate. Other friends had, of course, been telling him this for years, to no effect, but when Caracciolo informed him that he was 'too flabby around the middle' – his weight had gone up to 190 pounds – Rudy agreed to a compromise. He would not cut down on his eating and smoking, but he *would* submit to whatever training programme Caracciolo devised for him. This involved getting up each morning at five, eating a light breakfast of fruit, then spending an hour riding one of his horses before undertaking a thirty-minute workout with weights, followed by a two-mile run. After this came the enjoyable part of the regime – a massage and rub-down by the beefy Caracciolo, followed by a brunch which might quite easily have fed three men. Then, in the evening, the entire routine was repeated and – so Rudy said – bed at nine.

Mario Caracciolo's intervention did wonders for the already remarkable Valentino physique, though it did little to ease his troubled mind. It was whilst he was at such a low ebb that Luther Mahoney, the young policeman Rudy had befriended in New York at the time of *Monsieur Beaucaire*, re-entered his life. A few months after their meeting, Mahoney had indeed left the New York City Police and moved West, but the business venture with his brother had never got off the ground and he had taken a job – as a carpenter and car mechanic with United Artists!

Upon his arrival in Hollywood, Mahoney had remembered his promise to Rudy, and he had tried to contact him, only to be told by J D Williams' secretary that the Valentinos had been in Europe, collecting the props for their next film, *The Hooded Falcon* ... and, yes, the secretary confirmed, the character Rudy was going to portray *was* supposed to be an expert falconer!

Now, in November 1924, Mahoney did not bother trying to contact Rudy through the studio. He drove straight to Whitley Heights, where he found the actor looking very un-Valentino-like – dirty, dishevelled and miserable – much as he had when June Mathis rescued him not so long before. And over a quart of illicit whisky which saw both men very much the worse for wear, Rudy poured out his heart: he was up to his eyes in debt, his lover – André Daven – was hundreds of miles away and similarly lonely, and he was experiencing tremendous difficulties within his marriage on account of Rambova's constant interference in his career.

Mahoney explained that he, too, was at a financial low, for the job with United Artists did not pay that well, and his wife was about to have another baby. As for becoming Rudy's lover, Mahoney had already made that *very* clear back in New York, and repeated it once more, just in case. He added that he *could*, however, prove useful as the Valentinos' factotum. United Artists could already vouch for his talents as a carpenter, painter and decorator, he was an expert landscape gardener and he knew how to handle horses, dogs, falcons *and* difficult women. Rudy hired him on the spot to manage the Whitley Heights estate, without even discussing the matter with Rambova ... yet if he had anticipated fireworks by making so important a decision without consulting her, he was pleasantly surprised when Rambova expressed an immediate fondness for the young man. More than this, several days later *she* engaged Mahoney to help out on the sets for *Cobra*, and asked him to design and construct a fishpond and aviary as a gift for Rudy!

Two weeks before the Christmas of 1924 – almost two years since Rudy had bought the house – the Valentinos moved in. The grounds had been beautifully laid out with Italian cypress trees and rare shrubs, and a high wall built along the pavement side of the two-storey property, surmounted by a wire fence, to keep the fans out. The exterior had been finished off in Spanish-style stucco, and a garage incorporated into the upper level. Rudy had also constructed what is generally believed to have been Hollywood's first barbecue pit, an idea which he had picked up in a Far Eastern travel-guide whilst researching *The Sheik*. The house's interior was designed by Rambova. Its huge living room had a black marble sunken floor, over which she had scattered dozens of black Oriental rugs. The furniture too was mostly black-lacquered, offset by walls of buttercup yellow. The two bathrooms were fitted with costly multi-headed showers, and the Valentinos' toilet was a near replica of Paul Poiret's elevated 'throne', with a gold-edged seat. The two master bedrooms were fitted with electrified incense dispensers.

One of the first visitors to Whitley Heights was George O'Brien, himself now a major Hollywood star. Since his last 'encounter' with Rudy, George had taken the bull by the horns and rented a small apartment with Torch Club regular Gary Cooper – not yet a big name, but working as a stuntman in Westerns. To curb the gossips, Mervyn LeRoy, a director friend of Nazimova's, had moved in with them. It was LeRoy who had encouraged George to test for one of the bit-parts in John Ford's railroad epic, *The Iron Horse*, scarcely believing his ears when the young man returned home and announced that Ford had engaged him to play the lead! Rudy was naturally pleased to see his former lover, and not in the least envious of the fact that *The Iron Horse* and not one of his own films had proved the box-office smash of the year.

George O'Brien was asked to spend Christmas with the Valentinos, and was witness to the exemplary act they put on for the benefit of the press, posing for photographers and holding day-long parties around the six-sided pool. Rudy gave his wife a diamond-encrusted moonstone wristwatch which remained her most treasured possession, even *after* the events of the next few years. She, however, only enabled him to court publicity of the worst kind when she presented him with a platinum slave bracelet of interlocking chains – a piece which she herself had designed and had made up at Tiffany's. Rudy's fans were so taken by this that thousands of them rushed out to buy cheaper versions of the piece when it was mass-produced, as they had with Julio's bolero and Amos Judd's turban. The press, however, accused Rudy of 'inciting unnatural behaviour' amongst his male admirers, and urged him to get rid of it. This he refused to do. 'It was quite a surprise to me, a *man* wearing a bracelet, but I didn't make any comment at the time,' recalled Luther Mahoney, who had bought the piece on Rambova's behalf, in a taped interview shortly before his death in 1967. 'Rudy agreed that it was a wonderful gift, and he wore it all the time. Many remarks were made about it ... but a man of his character never paid any attention to such comments from such people. Rudy was not used to making bad remarks about people, so they just rolled off him, like water off a duck's back.'

This falsified atmosphere of wedded bliss ended abruptly once the festive season was over. Rambova went back to rewriting the script for *The Hooded Falcon* – spending more of Ritz-Carlton's money by hiring William Cameron Menzies and Adrian for the sets and some of the costumes – whilst Rudy spent most of his days with Luther Mahoney, who was teaching him the art of falconry. Rudy had had six chicks shipped in from Seville, which he and Mahoney were permitted to train in Griffith Park – but adhering to the City of Los Angeles' regulations, as the birds were considered a dangerous species, a marksman always had to be in attendance in case they got out of control and attacked anyone. They never did, and Rudy became so expert at handling them that he soon began taking one with him to the studio. Then, early in February 1925, Joseph Henabery, the man who had directed *A Sainted Devil*, called Rudy to say that shooting was about to begin on *Cobra*.

Rambova's initial absence from the set of the new film enabled George Ullman to take advantage of Rudy's fallibility so far as important decisions were concerned. He had never liked 'the fake Russian', nor had he ever concealed his resentment. He alone had rescued Valentino in his hour of need by arranging the Mineralava tour ... so why not at least *attempt* to assume complete supremacy over him now?

To a certain extent, Ullman was responsible for the Valentinos' crippling debts, and the fact that the couple had never once been in the black. He had agreed to represent Rudy solely on the basis that he handle *all* Rudy's affairs: any money earned by the actor and his wife was paid directly to Ullman, who signed all the cheques for their expenditure or simply dolled out wads of notes whenever they were about to embark on one of their shopping sprees. *Only* Ullman knew exactly what was coming in, and had he so wished he could quite easily have curbed what was going out. The fact that he did not ultimately points to the fact that, like Jesse Lasky before him, Ullman knew that being in control of the finances of a living legend also meant being in control of his life. Ullman also knew that just as he would never achieve his goal whilst Mrs Valentino was still around, so Rudy would never get anywhere with a small, independent company like Ritz-Carlton. To this end, Ullman began setting the wheels in motion to relieve him of both.

Rambova had vowed to have nothing whatsoever to do with *Cobra*. 'Modern day stories bore me to tears,' she told the press. With her obsessive nature, however, it was impossible for her not to interfere, although her visits to the set were kept to a minimum on account of her involvement with *The Hooded Falcon*. She 'loaned' Rudy the services of William Cameron Menzies and Adrian in her place. Menzies had most recently designed the sets for Douglas Fairbanks' *The Thief Of Baghdad* and Adrian (né Adolph Greenberg) was, at twenty-three, already one of Hollywood's top costumiers. In later years he would dress Greta Garbo and Joan Crawford, amongst others, and enter into a 'twilight tandem' marriage with Janet Gaynor. After only a few days' shooting, however, Rudy was forced to admit that *Cobra* was not the most thrilling film he had ever worked on. It was also his least successful – the only film in which he played an Italian, and the only one where he failed to get the girl at the end. 'He limped through his part as if it were a death march,' observed Chaw Mank, who had recently formed the Rudolph Valentino Friendship, whose honorary presidents were Milton Sills and Warner Baxter.

Rudy did however enjoy working on the boxing sequences because they were 'choreographed' by the World Heavyweight Champion, Jack Dempsey. The press were allowed into the Los Angeles gymnasium where Rudy was observed lifting with one hand dumb-bells which most of them would not have been capable of lifting with two, swimming thirty lengths of the Olympic-sized pool without getting out of breath, and going eight rounds with 'Society' Kid Hogan and Gene Delmont, the young boxer he was to fight in the film. The pictures of Rudy in tight shorts and an athletic vest reveal what a superb specimen of masculinity he really was, and compelled one sympathetic publication to observe, 'Notice Valentino's muscles – and who could not help it? Now you'll understand why Rudy is willing to fight ten rounds with *any* critic who pans him unfairly!'

One of these practice bouts was filmed. Rudy is extremely agile, ducking and bouncing all over the canvas and taking no punches himself, save one in the midriff which winds him slightly, forcing him to stagger backwards clutching his stomach, albeit laughingly. In the not too distant future when this was shown on cinema newsreels around the world, in view of the tragedy still to come, few of his admirers would feel like laughing with him.

When it came to the actual filming of these sequences, however, Rudy ignored the moves Dempsey had taught him, attacking his opponent, Gene Delmont, as though this was a fight to the death. 'He really did give me a battering,' Delmont later said, adding, 'And *still* some of the critics called him a pansy because he was afraid of his wife. Maybe if he'd punched her every now and then the way he punched me, she'd have stopped bitching at him!'

In May 1925, the painter Federico Beltran-Masses arrived in Hollywood, and immediately took up residence at the Ambassador Hotel where, in a military uniform and displaying his dozens of gallantry medals, he was photographed with Rudy, Douglas Fairbanks, and Marion Davies – who had already engaged him to begin working on her portrait the next day. This perturbed Rudy, whose idea it had been for the artist to come to America in the first place, and who had wanted his wife to be first. However, after a hurried discussion in Spanish – enabling Rudy to make a few unflattering comments about Davies under her very nose – it was decided that Beltran-Masses would work concurrently on portraits of Valentino, Rambova *and* Davies, before moving on to whoever could afford his inordinate fees.

Over the course of the next two months, Beltran-Masses would complete four portraits of the Valentinos, which one critic hailed as 'modern-day Goyaesque masterpieces': Rudy looking the picture of sartorial elegance, though to the delight of some detractors hand-on-hip and flaunting his slave bracelet, in his gaucho costume; a bearded Rudy in his Moorish robes and armour for his role in *The Hooded Falcon*, a servant crouching at his feet; Rambova in Spanish dress; and a portrait of Rambova which Beltran-Masses called 'La Gitana', where she is reclining, semi-nude, in a mantilla. She hated it when she saw the finished result; she had not posed naked, and she threatened to sue the artist if he said otherwise. Rudy merely declared that *he* could do better, and copied the painting (which *does* look better than the original) which he purchased from Beltran-Masses and eventually hung in his bedroom at Falcon Lair.

As soon as *Cobra* had been completed, Rudy and Rambova drove to Palm Springs, where they had planned a four-week vacation at the home of their friend, Floretta White. Whilst they were there, a call came through from George Ullman. Ritz-Carlton had called in the receiver, solely on account of the Valentinos' over-indulgences for *The Hooded Falcon*, and although J D Williams was still confident that Rudy's popularity would get him his money back, his backers had refused to stand by him upon learning that Valentino *would* still be sporting a beard in the film. 'The public will never accept Rudy with whiskers,' Williams had told Rambova a few days before the couple had left for Palm Springs, to which she had testily replied, 'Valentino wears a beard for his role, or he *doesn't* do the picture!' Now, their contract had been terminated.

Ordering Rudy to stay put, Rambova returned to Hollywood, intending to give Ullman a piece of her mind. She certainly told June Mathis what she thought of her, over the telephone, declaring that *she* alone was responsible for Rudy's dilemma, inasmuch as had Mathis written an efficient script in the first place, none of this would have happened. For once, however, Ullman's Machiavellian charm won her over. When he informed her that he had already entered into negotiations for a contract with Joseph Schenck, the president of United Artists who had earlier wanted Rudy to play Romeo, Rambova returned to Palm Springs, satisfied that their financial future would now be assured. United Artists had originally been formed to accommodate Hollywood's quartet of 'goldmine' stars: Chaplin, Pickford, Fairbanks and Norma Talmadge, along with D W Griffith.

In his bid to 'woo' Rudy into joining United Artists – not that he needed any incentive – Joseph Schenck told him that he would loan him the money for the 16-room, Mediterranean-style property he had recently viewed. Rudy would much rather have preferred to live in the country. Recently, he had written in his diary, 'With what the Americans call great open spaces stretching like Edens around us, why do we huddle and struggle in cities, wearing our brains and our bodies out?' The country, however, was impractical, so he settled for this two-level house at 2 Bella Drive, in Beverly Hills, on a commanding hillside position not far from Benedict Canyon Road. Only completed in 1923, it was set in eight and a half acres of landscaped grounds. There was a garage large enough to house four cars, surmounted by a six-room servants' quarters, along with an extensive kennels and stable area. Apart from an undeveloped acreage adjoining the property, everything was in pristine condition and Schenck agreed that the asking price was a 'snip' at $175,000. Rudy bought the place, hired a small redecorating team, and baptised it Falcon Lair.

Once he had swallowed the bait, so to speak, Rudy was summoned to a meeting with Schenck, to which he was accompanied by George Ullman, who informed him that as the press were going to be there, to let him do all the talking. Unfortunately, Rambova's instructions had been more explicit. Rudy was to sit at the back of the office, and keep his mouth shut whilst *she* discussed the terms of his contract. The afternoon was certainly memorable. United Artists were willing to offer Rudy $10,000 a week for a three-picture deal, together with 42 per cent of the studio's profits from these – effectively, a deal worth well over a million dollars a year. On top of this, in common with the other United Artists stars, for the duration of his contract he would be supplied with a furnished bungalow, along with the services of a maid, dresser and personal chef. There was, however, one condition which would have to be strictly observed, added Schenck. Natacha Rambova was to have absolutely *no* say in any aspect of these films ... more than this, she was to be prohibited from entering the set. Schenck told her that if she should so much as set one foot inside his studio gates, he would have her arrested.

Rambova hit the roof, hurling every form of abuse at Ullman and Schenck, accusing them of conspiring behind her back to remove her from Rudy's life – which of course was true – and screaming that he would never be party to any deal which did not involve her as his personal and technical adviser. Initially, Rudy remembered his 'orders' and said little other than a polite, 'Mr Schenck, I think you're being very unfair to the woman I love. Please, I beg you, reconsider!'

Earlier, Ullman had reminded him that his debts were such that he could hardly afford *not* to sign the contract, which quite probably would make him the highest-paid actor in Hollywood after Chaplin. Rambova went *too* far, however, this time by saying in front of reporters, 'Valentino is *unable* to perform unless I'm there to advise him. And who would choose the appropriate material for the furthering of his career if I weren't around? Not him, that's for sure. *He's* incapable of doing things for himself!' Upon hearing this, Rudy strode across the room, grabbed Rambova by the shoulders and shook her like a rag, then flung her back into her chair. Then, for the benefit of the press *he* bellowed, 'You have humiliated me in public and cost me the respect of my friends. You have mocked my work and abused my talent, but now I will do things *my* way. My job is to make films. Yours is making *babies*!' Then, whilst Rambova was still trembling, Rudy grabbed Ullman's pen and signed the contract.

Rambova's first act of revenge on Rudy was to call Elizabeth Redfield, a feminist reporter from *Liberty*. The fact that the subsequent interview, headed 'May A Wife Deny Her Husband Children?' did not appear until the January 1926 issue of the magazine, when the Valentino's marriage was virtually over, enabled it to lose a great deal of its clout. 'I *love* children,' Rudy had confessed in the instalment of his autobiography that had been published in September 1924. 'Children *are* romance. They are the beginning and they are the end. They are romance before the bright wings are clipped, before they have trailed in the dry dust of disillusion.'

Rambova complained how Rudy, like most foreign men, regarded women as subordinates – she would never forgive him for the comments he had made to the young woman reporter in Nice, at the end of the European tour – and she added that in her opinion, to introduce children into such an 'unbalanced' set-up was wrong, particularly as Valentino was not interested in siring a daughter, but a son whom he hoped to raise as 'a mirror-image of his own magnificent masculinity'. As an American woman, she concluded, she resented her husband's attitude, and though she too adored children, she would not sacrifice her career to bear them for a man who clearly did not regard her as his equal.

From Redfield's point of view, of course, and that of most of the American public who read the article, Rambova appeared to have a valid point, though these people were unaware that the Valentinos' marriage had not actually been consummated – not through any fault of Rudy's who, according to his confession to Jacques Hébertot, had *tried* to make love to her on numerous occasions, only to have her turn her back on him. 'He only wanted to have sex with her for reasons of procreation,' Hébertot confirmed. 'Natacha didn't want to be tied down with children whilst artistically she was at her peak, but neither did she want him getting anybody else pregnant. Rudy wouldn't have wanted a bastard child. He would have divorced Natacha and married the mother. That's why she always turned a blind eye to him having sex with other men, but always went almost insane if he so much as looked at another woman.'

Elizabeth Redfield, however, had her own opinion regarding Rambova's apparent lack of maternal instincts, particularly as Nita Naldi, by the beginning of 1926 no longer Rambova's friend, had given an 'authentic' story to the press concerning 'Mrs Valentino's three abortions', of which more later. The fact was here was a woman who cared for dogs, and a particular breed of dog, more than children. Redfield concluded, 'By some uncanny psychology, cold-blooded and self-interested women choose to love tiny, yipping dogs who have the smallest cranial capacity of all the canine family. The Pekingese has become a symbol for a certain type of childless wife. Is Mrs Valentino such a type?'

After giving this interview, without Rudy's knowledge, Rambova told him that, seeing as she could no longer be legally involved in the making of his films, it was now his duty as a husband – and in recompense for all *she* had done for him – to set her up with her own production company! Rudy was so overcome with guilt that after discussing the matter with George Ullman, who privately considered the deal cheap at half the price just to get her off Rudy's back for a while, he agreed to finance any project of her choosing with $30,000. Within days, she had begun working on *What Price Beauty?* and recruited Nita Naldi as its star and Alan Hale Sr to direct.

Basically, it was a silly film, and much too artistic to be understood by anyone who was not on Rambova's particular wavelength. A satire on the cosmetics industry, it told the story of a raunchy vamp (Naldi) who competes with a poor country girl for the love of the handsome manager of a beauty parlour, though the true stars of the film were the extraordinary gowns which Rambova had commissioned from Adrian. These all too quickly sent the budget soaring to over $100,000, which of course came out of Rudy's pocket.

One of the bit-parts in *What Price Beauty?* was played by a nineteen-year old dancer from Montana named Myrna Adele Williams, who at around this time changed her name to Myrna Loy. Rambova had discovered Loy – described by one acid-tongued hack as 'a twin-edged Gillette that cuts both ways' – some months before, when Loy had been working in the chorus at Grauman's Chinese Theatre, and on behalf of J D Williams she had offered her a screen-test for a small part in *Cobra*, which she had failed. During the filming of *What Price Beauty?* Loy fell for Rambova in a big way. 'She was absolutely beautiful, the most beautiful woman I had ever seen,' she recalled in her memoirs, some sixty years later. For her brief appearance in the film, Adrian had designed her a skintight red pyjama-suit, to which was attached a sweeping, fur-edged train, and this was complemented by a curious blonde wig, bobbed at the back and brought to three points across her forehead. 'Natacha dubbed me "the intellectual type of vampire, without race, creed or country," ' Loy concluded. But whereas Myrna Loy loved the film and later sang its praises, some years later when asked for *her* opinion, Nita Naldi could only scoff, 'She thought she could become another Nazimova, with all this arty-farty rubbish. That film was the worst piece of damned shit I ever appeared in!'

Rudy was a frequent visitor to the set of *What Price Beauty?* – much to George Ullman's annoyance, for Rudy's manager was terrified that Rambova might wish to return the compliment when Rudy began working on his first film for United Artists. This was to be *The Eagle*, Hans Kraly's adaptation of Alexander Pushkin's unfinished novel, *Dubrovsky*. Ullman's and Joseph Schenck's fear of Rambova's re-interference in her husband's career would lead to them having nothing to do with the subsequent distribution of her film. As Luther Mahoney explained, 'Their whole thought was that if the picture *was* a success, then Mrs Valentino would be a success. She would then start producing under the Rudolph Valentino Production Company. This nobody wanted, except herself and Mr Valentino.'

What Price Beauty? was premièred a few weeks after its completion at a small cinema in Pasadena, though it would take another three years for Rambova to get it properly distributed. Not unexpectedly, it bombed at the box-office.

During the early summer of 1925, with no further projects lined up for the foreseeable future now that she and her husband were 'artistically separated', Rambova lapsed into a state of severe depression. She would often absent herself from Whitley Heights for days at a time, and there were reports in the press that she had resorted to taking drugs. She was still involved with Myrna Loy, though her real tower of strength was a young cameraman who had worked on her film. Rudy was well aware of both relationships, though this did not prevent George Ullman from hiring a private detective from the Burns Agency and having her followed in the hope of discrediting her name ... a foolish move, considering Rudy's own nocturnal activities. Luther Mahoney, the ex-cop, was the first to find out about this, and he informed Rudy. This resulted in the first major bust-up between Rudy and his manager, and a rare act of weakness from the usually iron-willed Rambova, who confided in Luther Mahoney that this time she really *was* at the end of her tether. 'Natacha told me she wanted to build a boat, that she would like to go to some island where she could do what she wanted, and start afresh,' Mahoney recalled.

Rudy knew only too well that once his wife had made up her mind to do a thing, she was unstoppable, and whilst Mahoney advised her on a brief separation to allow herself and Rudy space to sort out their differences, Rudy – not even thinking where the money was to come from – drove out to a boatyard in San Pedro, where he commissioned a 32-foot, six-berth Fellows-Craft cabin cruiser.

At the end of July, Rudy began shooting *The Eagle*. The film was directed by Clarence Brown, then enjoying great acclaim with *The Goose Woman*, starring Louise Dresser, who was also to star in this film as the man-hungry Czarina, Catherine II. Nine years later she would portray her predecessor, Empress Elizabeth, opposite Marlene Dietrich's Catherine in *The Scarlet Empress*. In years to come, Clarence Brown would become Greta Garbo's most-preferred director, it is said because of his ability to placate temperamental stars and keep them happy. Rudy certainly smiles a lot in this one, and to some extent the 'powder-puff' rumours abated with his macho interpretation of Vladimir Dubrovsky, the self-parodying, swashbuckling Cossack – even more so when United Artists 'leaked' a story to the press that he was having a passionate affair with his Hungarian-born co-star, Vilma Banky, whom Sam Goldwyn had discovered during a recent trip to Budapest. This most of them found hard to swallow, although Rudy *was* seen in public with Banky on numerous occasions, they were always accompanied by Aunt Teresa and usually by André Daven and Mario Caracciolo, both of whom had been given bit-parts in the new film. The latter, urged by Rudy, had also made his name pronouncable by changing it to Carillo.

Neither did the press know much about Vilma Banky who, according to Sam Goldwyn, had been working as a typist when he first saw her. Born in 1898, she had left Budapest in 1920 to begin her film career in Austria, returning a few years later to live openly with another woman. In Hollywood, of course, such things were actively discouraged, and in 1927, in the studios' attempts to rescue both their flagging careers, she would be pushed into a 'twilight-tandem' marriage with another gay star, Rod La Rocque. Astonishingly, this union would prove a happy one, ending only with La Rocque's death in 1969.

The Eagle begins with the butch-looking Czarina inspecting her regiment, which is described as the handsomest in all Russia – not surprisingly, because her officers were hand-picked, and many of them ended up as her lovers. When a sudden gun salute causes the horse she is about to mount to bolt, Dubrovsky, a young lieutenant, leaps into its saddle to tear after a runaway carriage, which he restrains, impressing its pretty occupant, Mascha (Banky). The Czarina, even more taken with him, rewards Dubrovsky by giving him the horse, and by inviting him to supper. Here, she attempts to seduce him, only to be thwarted: he falls to his knees and kisses her hand, tries to get up and is pushed down again, and whilst the expression on her face gives the impression that she is having an orgasm, he dodges to one side and leaves her hand patting thin air. For a moment, she pauses to sign someone's death-warrant, then kisses him and walks off to change out of her man's uniform. Dubrovsky wipes his mouth in disgust and leaves, telling a friend, 'I enlisted for war services only!' Unaccustomed to being rejected, the Czarina orders his apprehension, dead or alive.

Meanwhile, Dubrovsky has more pressing problems. His father's enemy, Kyrilla Troekouroff (James Marcus) has seized his house and his estates, and the old man is dying. Dubrovsky swears vengeance, and assumes the guise of the Black Eagle, a masked Robin Hood-type avenger who, with his brigands, whilst attempting to rid the townspeople of oppression, robs the rich and gives to the needy. When his men capture Mascha, the usual Valentino sado-masochism is played down: instead of whipping the lady, he whips his lieutenant and declares, 'The Black Eagle does not wage war against women!' Later he discovers that she is Kyrilla's daughter, though this does not deter him from plotting to kill the tyrant. His plan nears fruition when he meets Mascha's new French tutor,

Monsieur Leblanc, who has arrived in town to take up his position – the pair share a carriage, and during the ensuing journey, Dubrovsky assumes the other man's identity.

In the next few scenes, Dubrovsky turns Kyrilla into a shivering wreck by leaving messages from the Black Eagle. Kyrilla then decides that the only man capable of protecting him from his persecutor is Leblanc, whose bravery has been tested by being sent to fetch a bottle of wine from the cellar, which is guarded by a wild bear. Dubrovsky killed the bear, which recognised him, because it had attacked Mascha, and she has now guessed both his identity and realised that her father is living in *his* home. When Dubrovsky asks her what she thinks of him, she screams, 'I hate you!' whilst he turns to the camera and makes a face as if to say, 'We'll soon see about that!' However, when she threatens to tell her father who he is, Dubrovsky believes her, and owns up to being the Black Eagle. At this stage, Mascha admits to him that she loves him, and they escape together, only to be captured by the Czarina's guards. Sentenced to face the firing-squad, Dubrovsky's last wish is that he and Mascha be married, and in a scene where Valentino's facial expression may only be described as heartbreaking, he is led out to meet his death. We then hear gunfire, and the camera transfers to the bullet-holes in cardboard cut-outs – for the uncharacteristically sympathetic Czarina has sentenced *Dubrovsky* to be shot and not Monsieur Leblanc. The latter is spirited out of the country with his bride!

11
The Power of Gentleness

'I should like to know my house, to make a shrine of it where all the beautiful things I am able to garner from the four corners of the globe would find abiding places. Where friends might come to remember me, where I might die, at last, after the storm and stress.'

The Hollywood scandalmongers had a field-day when, in the first week of August 1925, Rudy took up residence at Falcon Lair and his wife refused to move in with him, probably still convinced that *he* and not George Ullman had had her trailed by the Burns Agency. In truth, now that she was no longer involved with his career and therefore no longer part of his personal life – to Rambova's way of thinking, the two could *only* go hand in glove – she herself could quite easily have gone to the newspapers and given them the story of the decade: Valentino, the World's Greatest Lover and the idol of millions of women was a closeted, promiscuous homosexual. It was not as if she would have had much difficulty proving such an allegation! A stubborn mixture of common sense and pride prevented this, however, for in 'outing' her husband she would make herself a laughing-stock, and plenty of witnesses would be willing to testify to the fact that she, too, had engaged in love affairs which had not conformed to the norm. She would also be responsible for an extremely unpleasant Hays Office witchhunt, compared to which the Arbuckle and Reid scandals would appear tame, and which would result in the destruction of many careers besides hers and Rudy's.

Rudy spared no expense in making his home his haven on earth. Unlike the other big stars in Hollywood, he rarely socialised: this he declared would have meant putting on an act, as most of them did, when acting *should* have been reserved for the set. 'Why should I force myself to smile when I don't feel like it?' he once asked. 'And why should I be expected to be seen in public with a lot of people I can't stand, or who cannot stand me? I'd much rather stay at home and entertain my friends.'

Much of Falcon Lair's interior was done out in Rudy's favourite dark red leather – an obsession which had begun when he had ordered the upholstery for his Voisin – and the main bathroom had the same colour marble fittings. The Venetian china and Bohemian cut glass were worth thousands of dollars, as was his collection of medieval armour, most of which was kept in the library, with his equally precious first editions, paintings, jade and ivory ornaments, and his matador costumes. The antiques he and Rambova had purchased in Europe had been transfered from the Park Avenue apartment, and his stables and garages filled to their capacity: four Arabian steeds which he, Daven and Paul Ivano rode most mornings, and his and their cars. And yet, surrounded by the Valhalla of opulence, Rudy still felt that something was missing from his life, so a few days after moving into Falcon Lair – 'He must have been off his head!' André Daven said – he made one final, desperate attempt to get back into Rambova's good books. This woman, his most torturous nightmare who had spent most of their marriage making his life an absolute misery, was *still* in control, despite everyone's attempts to exorcise her demon . . . yet in his self-created impossible-to-live-with, impossible-to-live-without situation, he could not bear to lose her or imagine any future without her.

The occasion was a reception at the Ambassador Hotel for Federico Beltran-Masses, arranged by Rudy and Marion Davies to thank the painter for 'humbling' himself amongst the Hollywood community – a trip for which he had received free accomodation and food, not to mention $100,000 in fees.

The bash was attended by a galaxy of stars, including Tom Mix, Gloria Swanson, Mae Murray, Irving Thalberg and Norma

Shearer, the Fairbanks, and Bebe Daniels. Rudy also invited his friend, Adela Rogers St Johns, to cover the event in her newspaper column. What he did not reckon on was Rambova's obstinacy, the fact that for once she was not interested in showing off her latest creation or in flaunting her power over her husband in public . . . indeed, there *was* no power left for her to flaunt. For two hours, Rudy pleaded with her to go, and Rambova only backed down when he reminded her that, as hostess for the evening, she would be branded unspeakably rude by every columnist in Hollywood if she did not turn up. This of course caused problems for the *real* hostess, Marion Davies: the Valentinos arrived at the Ambassador Hotel two hours late, whilst some guests were leaving, and as Rambova's 'fashion parade' took over an hour – with Rudy reduced to his usual lackey status several paces behind – most of the exquisite food paid for by Davies had to be thrown away.

The next morning Rudy, accompanied by Luther Mahoney, Beltran-Masses and George Ullman, set off for the boatyard in San Pedro to see how they were getting along with Rambova's cabin-cruiser. Rudy was driving the Voisin through Pasadena, exceedinq the speed-limit as usual, when another car cut in front of him, causing him to swerve into a telegraph pole. Within seconds, a traffic-cop was on the scene. In all probability he had been trailing Rudy all the way from Falcon Lair, aware of his lunatic driving and hopeful of making a 'celebrity bust' and scoring a few more points towards promotion. Rudy and his passengers were badly shaken, but unhurt, and whilst the actor was arguing with the cop that it had not been entirely his fault, Mahoney found a telephone-box and called the studio for a replacement car to get the party to San Pedro, then arranged for the Voisin to be towed to the nearest garage. When Rudy noticed what had happened to his 'baby' – the car had two buckled front wheels, a smashed fender and a busted radiator, and would eventually set him back $7,500 for repairs, more than half of its original cost – he completely lost his temper with the policeman and threatened to sock him in the jaw for calling him a 'dago road-hog'. For his pains he was given a speeding ticket, and served with a court summons.

The crash and what might have happened, along with Adela

Rogers St Johns' scathing attack on Rudy's wife for her snooty attitude towards her peers at the Beltran-Masses reception, pushed Rambova towards the brink. The following evening she told Rudy that she had arranged to leave him – not for good, but until they had both had time to sort out their marital problems. She would, she said, travel to New York, where hopefully she would find a reputable distributor for *What Price Beauty?*, and then she would sail for France, for a holiday with her parents. She promised to return as soon as Rudy had finished working on *The Eagle*.

Rudy made one last desperate attempt to keep his wife by his side. He did not mind her not wishing to live at Falcon Lair – indeed, if she loathed the place so much, he would sell it and find them somewhere else! Also, he added, he intended setting up his own production company once his contract with United Artists had expired and he had settled his debts. His first independent project would be James Branch Cabell's *The Silver Stallion* a medieval adventure set in the imaginary 13th century kingdom of Poictesme, which she would of course design and adapt for the screen. Rambova again assured him that she would be coming back, and told him not to worry. She even suggested that at the end of the year, they would be able to travel to Europe together and spend Christmas at the Hudnutts' château, as they had done before.

On 13 August 1925, Luther Mahoney drove the Valentinos, George Ullman and Aunt Teresa to the railway station, where there was alteady a massive crowd of fans and press. The couple hugged and kissed for the benefit of the movie cameras: Rambova giggled, and playfully wiped her lipstick off Rudy's face, before Aunt Teresa and George Ullman joined her on the train. The trio then stood on the observation platform at the rear of the vehicle, and as it began moving away from the platform, Rudy clung to the rail and ran behind it until he was out of breath. Then he stood in the middle of the track, waving his hat until it was out of sight. Returning to the platform, he turned to a reporter and muttered, 'There she goes, the love of my life!'

He would never see Natacha Rambova again.

That the scene at the railway station had been little more than publicity-seeking play-acting became obvious a few days later, when the Valentinos began bitching at each other in newspapers at opposite ends of the country. Rambova started the ball rolling during the actual journey to New York by confessing to a reporter that she had never intended going to Nice in the first place – at least not until she had found somewhere to live in New York and put her career back on the rails. And when asked if she would *ever* be returning to her husband, she shook her head and replied, 'I will not be a parasite. I won't sit and twiddle my fingers, waiting for a husband who goes to work at five in the morning and gets home at midnight to read mail from girls in Oshkoch and Kalamazoo!'

There was of course the apartment at 270 Park Avenue, still being looked after by André Daven, still housing many of the antiques the Valentinos had bought in Europe. When asked why she would not be moving there, she explained that the place would hold too many sad memories. What she did not know was that Rudy had called Daven, and that the young Frenchman was already en route for Hollywood, as were former lovers Paul Ivano and Douglas Gerrard, who had been waiting for this call-to-arms for some time. After spending a few weeks in a hotel, Rambova and Aunt Teresa moved into an apartment on West 81st Street.

Rudy was not in a particularly forgiving frame of mind when *his* turn came to speak to the press. 'We can't always order our lives the way we would like to have them,' he told a clutch of reporters who were allowed on to the set of *The Eagle*, adding, 'Mrs Valentino can't have a career and be my wife at the same time. She understood this before she left here.' And, when asked if divorce might be on the cards, he shrugged his shoulders and levelled as honestly as only he could, 'Who knows? I'm beginning to feel that I was as well off single as I am married. I don't know definitely if we'll be reconciled or divorced, but I *do* know one thing, Natacha cannot come back here as my wife whilstever she's seeking a career in pictures.' Rambova's response to this was a surly, 'And he knows what *I* was like before he married me. If Mr Valentino wants a housewife and babies, he'll have to find somebody else!'

During these early days of freedom, Rudy found the unlikeliest of bedmates in Federico Beltran-Masses – a chubby, balding man in his early forties who was not his type at all, and who later boasted to the the press that he had saved Rudy from suicide. According to the painter, he had found Rudy sitting in the library at Falcon Lair with a loaded revolver pointed at his head – which he had subsequently knocked out of his hand. This story was dismissed by several of the actor's friends, including Jacques Hébertot, who declared that as Rudy was narcissistic towards the point of absurdity, *had* he wished to take his own life, he would not have mutilated *any* part of his all-perfect body, let alone blow his head off!

Rudy *did* attempt to call his wife in New York, not because he was missing her, but because he wanted to know one way or another how they stood. His calls were not returned. Rambova had been signed to play the lead in a film opposite Clive Brook, the actor who seven years later appeared in *Shanghai Express* with Marlene Dietrich. Based on a story by Laura Jean Libby, its title, *When Love Grows Cold*, could hardly have been more appropriate, and neither could its theme: a wife who has been shunted aside by a husband who has suddenly found fame. George Ullman had pulled the strings to get her the part, his way, of course, of getting back at her for the problems she had caused him, though his revenge did not stop here. When the film was released early in 1926, following Elizabeth Redfield's article in *Liberty*, Ullman gave instructions for the name Natacha Rambova to be inserted in brackets on the playbills, whilst 'MRS RUDOLPH VALENTINO' appeared in much larger letters underneath. Then, just to make sure she received the message he personally penned the film's first intertitle: 'This is a powerful heart-rending story of a woman's supreme devotion and sacrifice for a man who paid the penalty of forgetting when success came to him.' Rambova threatened to sue Ullman, gave him a sound ticking-off over the telephone instead, and swore that she would have no more to do with the movie business . . . a promise she would keep.

Meanwhile, on 12 September 1925, shooting was completed on *The Eagle*. Still in his Cossack costume, Rudy drove to a courthouse where he was fined $50 for dangerous driving, following the crash in Pasadena. Then, with time on his hands before his next project, he embarked on a series of 'boys-only' vacations with a dozen male friends – former and current lovers – aboard the *Phoenix*, the cabin-cruiser he had had built for Rambova. 'I think there must have been sailors in my family,' he wrote in in his diary. 'For the sea pounds in my veins with a tune I still remember, and know that I could not have remembered in *this* life.'

Four weekends in succession, Rudy took the boat out to Catalina Island, where some of the photographs taken by Paul Ivano are real eye-openers: Rudy, Ivano, Carillo, Beltran-Masses, George O'Brien and Robert Florey, all camping it up in blazers, flannels and top hats – then, when they were out of sight of the coast, in leotards or nothing at all. His other 'guests' included the actors Jack Warren Kerrigan and Eugene O'Brien, and occasional lovers Manuel Reachie, then married to Agnes Ayres, and Jean de Limur, a French bit-part player who later directed Edith Piaf's first film, *La Garçonne*, in which André Daven had a small role.

At Falcon Lair, between voyages, the parties raged on for days. 'Rudy was trying to recreate the ambiance of the Torch Club right there in his own back yard,' Daven recalled. 'There were naked men everywhere. Rudy especially liked to make love on top of his car – it was the nearest we ever got to being in the driving seat, one might say – whilst the wind-up gramophone thrashed out 'My Man' or 'Cry-Baby Blues'.'

Robert Florey, too, remembered these 'quiet nights' at home: 'Rudy would dismiss the servants and we would look after ourselves. No women were ever allowed at our parties – well, apart from Alla Nazimova, and that lady was so off this planet, I'm sure she had no idea what day of the week it was. Fridays, however, were different. Some of we Catholics don't eat meat on Fridays, but during that fall of 1925, Rudy designated Friday as a 'no-fuck day' and we would pile into our cars and go see the boxing matches at the American Legion Club. But as soon as it struck midnight back at Falcon Lair, off we were again!' Daven and Florey also described how, on outings to clubs and speakeasies such as the Plantation, in Culver City, the friends always 'covered' themselves by ensuring that they were seen and photographed with 'dates' such as Vilma Banky, Mae Murray – and Nita Naldi, who had coined the not-so-polite term, 'Rudy's fag-hags', for his female pals.

On 8 November 1925, Rudy travelled to New York for the première of *The Eagle*. At every stop of the journey the train had been besieged by fans, causing it to reach its destination twelve hours late. Reporters everywhere had pestered him with questions concerning his marriage, but he had remained tight-lipped, even when a representative from one newspaper told him that he had it 'on good authority' that Rambova, who had sailed for Europe after completing *What Price Beauty?*, was on her way back right now . . . to beg him to forgive her!

Outside the Mark Strand Theatre, 10,000 fans screamed his name as a team of bodyquards manhandled Rudy, Ivano, Daven, Vilma Banky and United Artists' press-attaché, Beulah Livingstone, from their limousines into the foyer. Before the lights dimmed for the film to begin, Rudy walked on to the stage to thank everyone for their support, and during the ten-minute standing ovation he was clearly on the verge of tears.

Two days later, Rudy applied for American citizenship, on the very day that Rambova arrived back from Europe. The two did not meet, and both faced a barrage of press who were only interested in knowing one thing. Was their marriage over? Both declined to comment. Then, on 12 November, Rudy received a visit from his wife's lawyer. Whilst in France, Rambova had applied for a divorce on the grounds that for the last two years her husband had failed in his duty to support her! Two days after this, having decided not to stay on in New York for the *Cobra* première at the end of the month – this film was slated by the same critics who declared that *The Eagle* was the best he had ever made – he boarded the *Leviathan* for England, and the London première of *The Eagle*.

The continuing pressures of his personal life on his all-important public image are now known to have contributed to a sudden decline in Rudy's health. He had always been a nervous, unpredictable young man, feeling on top of the world one minute, only to fall into the blackest depression the next. Friends have said that his acute neurasthenia could have been treated and even cured, had he taken the trouble to seek help. In fact, until the end of 1925 Rudy had never *had* a doctor. 'Self-cure is the only cure for all ills,' he had once said. Crossing the Atlantic, however, he became dreadfully ill with seasickness – something that had never happened before – and after a great deal of yelling at André Daven, he allowed his lover to summon the *Leviathan*'s physician, who diagnosed a suspected gastric ulcer.

Rudy felt *so* ill that it was a supreme effort for him to attend the new film's première at the Marble Arch Pavilion, yet as soon as he saw the 5,000 cheering fans, his spirits at least were lifted. A press-conference had been arranged to follow the screening, but André Daven – his publicist for the evening – advised him to cancel this and return straight to their hotel. Rudy would not agree, though Daven did restrict the number of people attending to just ten reporters and twenty cinema staff.

Rudy surveyed this meagre gathering, and told one young woman who began scribbling, 'Just remember, dear, that I'm an *American* now!' Yet even his humour and radiant smile did not fool another reporter, who asked him if it was true that he was not feeling well. 'I'm fine,' he replied. 'It's just that I don't like making public appearances. It's so difficult to know what is exactly the right thing to do. If I smile and bow in return for a welcome from a crowd, someone is sure to think me conceited. If I'm just cool and casual, someone else will probably think me up-stage. It's an ordeal, either way!'

The next morning, Rudy went to see a Harley Street specialist who confirmed that he did have a gastric ulcer. He was advised to give up his 60 cigarettes a day habit, and to drink only milk – which, of course, would only have brought more ridicule from the press. He was also told to cut down on his massive intake of food – the double portions of pasta and fatty meats which were always washed down with entire bottles of rich red wine, and the two *pounds* of bacon he often devoured in a morning after his work-out. Rudy paid the specialist his hefty fee, promised that he would start taking care of himself . . . then went to the nearest street corner and bought four bowls of jellied eels.

In the evening, Rudy and Daven dined at the Mayfair Hotel, at which several journalists were present, though purely by chance. Delighted to have been given such an unexpected scoop, one of these made his move – only to be told by Daven that this was strictly a private function, *not* to be shared by the press. 'Lunching next to the World's Greatest Lover was an *extremely* dubious pleasure,' one of them reported, all the same. 'And I can assure you, this was one "romantic" episode that I'd rather not experience again!' Having discarded the cutlery to eat everything with his fingers – even the pudding and custard – Rudy had wiped his hands and mouth on the tablecloth and blown his nose into his napkin, then stood up, broken wind loudly and pronounced, 'Better out than in!'

Rudy had planned on spending a week in London before leaving for Paris. Terrified of some of the stories Rambova might give to the press if put under pressure, he had decided not to contest their divorce, and to facilitate the proceedings he had agreed to submit to temporary residence in France. However, when he learned that Mae Murray was in Paris and allegedly down on her luck following *her* divorce from Robert Z Leonard, he chartered a small plane to take himself and Daven across the Channel.

Rudy found Mae Murray in a state of nervous exhaustion not unlike his own, though this soon changed when the trio hit the town. Over the next few days, Rudy was able to push his problems to the back of his mind, spending like there was no tomorrow and ignoring the telegrams from George Ullman which streamed into the Plaza-Athenée Hotel, informing him that his debts were once again getting out of control.

Between bouts of crippling abdominal pain which Rudy attempted to 'cure' by swallowing an emetic after particularly heavy meals, he and Daven escorted Mae Murray to parties hosted by the Dolly Sisters and Cécile Sorel, the doyenne of the *Comédie Française*.

And naturally, Rudy insisted on seeing Damia's recital at the Théâtre des Champs Elysées, though he did not care for the second half – Paris' latest import from the United States, Joséphine Baker, in *La Revue Nègre*. 'There was too much tap-dancing, and I came away from the theatre with a thumping headache,' he complained. He did, however, enjoy meeting Mistinguett at last, as well as José

Padilla, the composer of 'El Relicario' and Mistinguett's latest success, 'Valencia'.

Early in December, amused by the report in a French tabloid newspaper that she was about to become 'the next-Madame Valentino', Mae Murray returned to New York, whilst Rudy and Daven continued to paint the town red with Jacques Hébertot. It was the latter who arranged for the pair to have a private box at Les Ambassadeurs, where the South American tango-singer, Carlos Gardel, as big in France as Rudy was in America, was topping the bill. 'He just sat there open-mouthed, clutching the back of the seat in front of him until his knuckles turned white,' Hébertot recalled. 'Then, as the lights went up after Gardel's curtain-call, Rudy turned to me and said, "More than anything in the world, I want to fuck that man. Would you please arrange for us to meet?" '

Carlos Gardel had actually been born in Toulouse in 1890, but his childhood and youth, of which almost nothing is known, had been spent in Abasto, Argentina. His rise to fame had been swift: from bar-crooner to headlining star virtually overnight, and with looks and a physique almost comparable to Valentino's, his songs and macho appeal had always been targeted at female audiences, in spite of the fact that Gardel was rampantly homosexual and out of the closet. He was, however, an extremely reclusive, neurotic and unpleasant individual who rarely smiled unless taking a bow, who hardly ever met his fans or gave interviews. Although his recordings sold in vast quantities – 70,000 copies in Paris alone, during his month-long season at Les Ambassadeurs – he is alleged never to have listened to any of them.

Before leaving the theatre, Rudy scribbled a note in Spanish, and Jacques Hébertot delivered it to the singer's dressing room. Gardel's response was that he could not meet his favourite actor right now, and by way of an apology he sent him tickets for the next evening's recital. 'The same thing happened, three nights in succession, but this legendary meeting of loins never took place,' Hébertot added. 'Rudy even asked *me* to sleep with Gardel, then describe to him over the telephone what had happened, whilst he got himself off. But that never happened either.'

Carlos Gardel, like Hébertot, only ever had sex with young men who were brought to his dressing room or hotel suite, and he once confessed that he would never consider engaging in a relationship or even a one-night stand with anyone as remotely famous as himself, let alone Rudolph Valentino. It has also been stated that Gardel's only *true* pleasure in life was his torturous solitude, and when he died ten years later in a plane crash, at forty-four, the one million distraught fans who followed his funeral cortège still knew very little about his life away from the stage.

Snubbed by one of the world's most beautiful men, and as if aware that time was running out – *and* taking advantage of a break from the virulent American press – Rudy flung himself with frenetic abandon into what Jacques Hébertot later referred to as 'Valentino's fifteen-day fuckathon'. Retaining their suite at the Plaza-Athenée for press and publicity purposes, Rudy and Daven transferred to their new 'headquarters', a *maison-close* on the rue Lauriston. 'Hot and cold running women!' was how one publication described the new set-up. The building's 'employees', however, were all male.

The pair's evenings were spent visiting the haunts of Rudy's apache days, though Claude Rambeau and Martin et Coco were long gone. At the notorious Jockey Club, Rudy was asked by the manager to select the prettiest person in the room to partner him in the Argentinian tango. He chose André Daven. At the Cabaret Fyscher, more than a little inebriated, he was persuaded to stand on a table and croon 'O Sole Mio'. His favourite establishment in Paris, however, was a gay club not far from the Place de l'Opèra, frequented by the Paris Ballet Company. After sharing several members of the chorus with his lover, Rudy fell for the hunky, Gardel-lookalike choreographer – announcing that, as he had been unable to have the genuine article, second-best would have to do. He was then informed of this particular choreographer's long-standing tradition, the fact that in order to 'hit the jackpot', so to speak, Rudy would have to compete with the rest of the corps by submitting to *la loi de la règle* . . . in other words, the choreographer often decided who would be keeping his bed warm that night by getting his boys to stand in line, and to attention, whilst he went to work with his ruler. As Chaw Mank recalled, 'Rudy won . . . by producing an organ of Herculean proportions.'

Outside the Alcazar music-hall, a few evenings before Christmas, Rudy and Daven were accosted by Baron Imre Lukács, the Hungarian tycoon to whom Vilma Banky had been allegedly engaged before stardom had beckoned her to Hollywood. Lukács, who had already told the French press that his greatest ambition was 'to kill the man in the bangle', began insulting Rudy. Accusing him of stealing his woman, he demanded immediate satisfaction. Never one to disappoint, Rudy delivered a pretty mean uppercut and laid him out on the pavement . . . then hauled him to his feet and challenged him to a duel – swords at dawn, in the Bois de Boulogne! André Daven begged him to reconsider, only to have Rudy appoint him his second, and at seven the next morning, Christmas Eve, the actor turned up at the venue to defend his honour. The duel, fortunately, never took place. Lukács had telephoned a director friend in Hollywood who had been willing to swear, on his own life, that any relationship between Valentino and Banky had been strictly reserved for the screen. Upon hearing this, Rudy embraced his opponent . . . and asked him to lunch at the Plaza-Athenée!

In Paris, Rudy was also reunited with his brother and sister, a meeting which was so tearful that he begged them to seriously consider taking up residence in Hollywood so that they need never be separated again. Alberto did not want this. On the strength of Rudy's name he had recently been appointed United Artists' Italian representative – but he did accept an invitation to spend a lengthy vacation at Falcon Lair now that Rambova was out of the way. Maria had decided to settle in Paris, where Paul Poiret had offered her employment as a seamstress, and she told Rudy that she did not even wish to *see* America.

After the Christmas holidays, Rudy and Daven spent a few days with Jacques Hébertot at his villa in Deauville, before catching the train to Nice. In spite of his impending divorce, the Hudnutts were no less fond of him. They might not have accepted Daven into their home, however, had they read his comment in the press regarding Rudy's soon-to-be bachelor status, 'Valentino doesn't need to be married to a cow to get all the milk he wants!'. They insisted that Rudy spend some time with them before returning to the United States, where he was scheduled to begin work on his second United Artists film in the middle of February.

In her unpublished memoirs, Mrs Hudnutt referred to Rudy as 'the same sweet loving boy of old', and recalled how he had spent many hours alone in their daughter's room – before burying his head into her lap and sobbing like a child. And yet, when his divorce was announced – on 19 January, Rambova's twenty-ninth birthday, when he was in Cherbourg and about to board the *Leviathan* – he told a reporter, 'This is the happiest day of my life. I vow that I will never marry again!'

Rudy had sworn exactly the same thing at a press-conference in Paris, on New Year's Eve, and to hammer home the point he had even taken out a $10,000 bet, registered at 5–1 with the Sporting-Club de Monte Carlo, that he would still be a bachelor at the end of the decade. Robert Florey later explained why a man who was so obviously attracted to his own sex, and unashamed of the fact, was still searching for a *woman* to share his life with, and why he would never succeed in finding one:

> He was always dreaming of the ideal companion, some ethereal wife who would be there not to *inflime* his desires, but to elevate him in the eyes of the public. He wanted a woman who would be graceful, delicate, beautiful, and above all unposessive and subservient. In short, the kind of woman he was looking for did not exist, certainly not in *this* world.

At around this time, reports began circulating in the American press concerning Natacha Rambova's alleged abortions, along with reports that she had suffered a miscarriage in the South of France on account of Rudy's reckless driving. Nita Naldi, for so long one of Rambova's closest friends, had turned against her, accusing her of publicly humiliating her husband once too often. The rumours were of course untrue, and were hotly disputed by Aunt Teresa, who declared that as she had been almost constantly by Rambova's side during her marriage to Valentino, *she* more than anyone would have been aware of one pregnancy, let alone three.

Neither did these fabrications displease Rudy, for those detractors who had doubted his virility now had 'proof' that he had had a sexual relationship with his wife, albeit that his close friends and a large section of the movie industry knew otherwise. Naldi's outpourings had been two-fold: getting even with Rambova because she believed that Rudy was 'too much of a gentleman to put the bitch over his knee and give her a damned good spanking!' – and because she was hoping to discredit Rambova, the *actress*, on the eve of her first venture on the legitimate stage. For this Rambova had chosen a one-act play, *The Purple Vial*, which opened in Bridgeport, Connecticut, at the end of January 1926, transferring two weeks later to the Palace Theatre in New York. Here, Nita Naldi's attacks fell on deaf ears. Largely because the playbills still hailed her as 'Mrs Valentino', the play was moderately successful, and the reviews generally favourable. 'She have a performance that was a revelation for one coming out of a silent drama for her first speaking role,' enthused *Variety.*

The Purple Vial, however, had come close to being cancelled when the manager of the Palace Theatre had wanted to stage it in the second half of a programme which was to have begun with *The Eagle*. 'You can have Valentino in your theatre if it'll make you happy,' Rambova declared, 'but you won't have me!'

12
The Proof of Faith

'If we do not suffer, if we have never known the pain of body, the pain of heart, mind and soul, if we have never wept over a bier or crushed out bitter breaths against a vanquished hope, then we have never really lived at all.'

It was in a relaxed state of mind, even though George Ullman had informed him that he was on the verge of bankruptcy, that Rudy returned home to make what would be his last film. *The Son Of The Sheik* was based on Edith Maude Hull's *Sons Of The Sheik* sequel to her original story, with both characters rolled into one for Hollywood's benefit, and with the added attraction of Rudy donning a beard – this time a false one – and playing his own father. Agnes Ayres was brought in to play his mother, Diana, the role she had created in the original film. It was a Valentino production in all but name. With Rambova gone – though he is still seen wearing her slave bracelet throughout the film – Rudy no longer found it necessary to *demand*, merely politely request, for his every wish to be granted. Joseph Schenck hired Frances Marion to write the screenplay – she would later adapt *Dinner At Eight* and more famously, *Anna Karenina*. Vilma Banky was engaged as his co-star, William Cameron Menzies as his art director, and playing the part of his sidekick, Ramadan, was the gawky, Copenhagen-born actor Karl Dane, who had triumphed the previous year in King Vidor's epic, *The Big Parade*. And, after years of fruitless wrangling, Rudy was finally going to be directed by George Fitzmaurice.

In *The Son Of The Sheik*, this particular young Arab is meaner-looking, moodier, and considerably more sexually menacing than his predecessor. The film opens with the dancing-girl, Yasmin (Banky) reflecting on her meeting with Ahmed, several days before in the small Algerian town of Touggourt – the camera zooms in on her face, which is slowly transformed into his. Then, she had told him how she had been compelled to dance, even when tired, because she and her father were so poor – refusing Ahmed's offer of gold, with the excuse that her father and his gang of cut-throats would only gamble it away. Ahmed therefore gave her a friendship ring, and the pair have since met at Yasmin's favourite moonlight haunt, a cluster of ruined buildings surrounded by palm trees. Here, they have fallen in love.

And now, after this brief flashback, the lovers meet again, and Yasmin tells Ahmed that she does not even know his name, to which he responds, 'I am he who loves you. Is that not name enough?' He then proceeds to seduce her, complying with her request to first remove his pistol belt – delivering a series of impish pecks to her neck, cheeks and lips, before the lengthy kiss which slowly and sensually extends from her shoulder, all the way along her arm to her fingertips. The mere expression on Rudy's face during this one scene caused havoc with the censor, and almost ended up on the cutting-room floor. 'He exceeds the bounds of mere concupiscence and seems to be having an orgasm,' remarked the critic Paul Roen, sixty years later in his hugely entertaining study of the genre, *High-Camp Film Guide*.

What the lovers do not know is that Yasmin has been followed to their rendezvous by a band of thugs led by Ghabar the Moor (Montague Love), the man whom her father has chosen to be her husband, and who now intends capturing Ahmed so that he may demand a ransom from his wealthy father. Ahmed puts up the most tremendous fight – flinging adversaries up into the air as if they are weightless, and almost strangling one of them with his feet – though eventually he is overpowered and knocked unconscious. When he comes to, he is strapped to a grating: his shirt has been ripped to reveal as much glistening torso as George Fitzmaurice thought he could get away with, and Rudy's muscles are only enhanced by the fact that his hands are tied above his head and dangling, an indisposition that also enables him to wear the expression of a would-be Christian martyr so beloved by his fans. He is then told by Ghabar the lie that Yasmin was merely the bait to lure him into this trap, something she has often done before . . . then lashed with a bullwhip, in a scene which Rudy emphasised should be played for real.

Freed by his men, Ahmed is taken back to Touggourt, where he recovers from his wounds and plots his revenge on Yasmin. When he learns that she is dancing at a local cafe he goes there, starts a brawl, and during the ensuing mayhem abducts her – riding off with her to his desert lair, where he unceremoniously flings her onto his divan. She cowers with fear – and lusty anticipation – as he narrows his almost lizardous eyes. Casually, he lights a cigarette, then strips off his cloak and bejewelled belt. Momentarily he appears to be on the verge of tears, then his expression changes into a sardonic grin as he pronounces, 'So, my young charmer. Your mission in life is to lure men into lonely ruins – to be robbed and tortured!' Then, flexing his mighty biceps he spits out, in what was to become *the* catchphrase of the year, 'I may not be the first victim – but, by Allah, I shall be the one you'll remember!'

At this, Yasmin cowers again, though by this time she is perhaps more excited by the prospect of what may be about to happen than actually afraid of the dark-skinned stud, who opens his shirt to display his wounds and levels, 'An eye for an eye – a hate for a hate. That is the law of my father!' At this, Yasmin begs him to stay, clinging to his thigh as he walks away as if her very life depends on his ravishing her, dragging on to him until she is flung aside like a rag. Borrowing her own line from *The Eagle*, Banky/Yasmin tells him that *she* hates him, but this only amuses him. Arms folded across his chest, Ahmed ponders, stares coldly, and advances. 'Your gang will not collect from me this time,' he says. 'For once, your kisses are free!' Yasmin makes one last bid to get away, but the entrance to the tent is guarded, and as the picture fades Ahmed manoeuvres her back towards the divan where, we assume, he finally gets around to bedding her.

The action now transfers to the sumptuous villa of Ahmed's

father, Sheik Ahmed Ben Hassan, where he and Diana, his wife (Agnes Ayres) are worried about the young man's whereabouts. Diana has received a letter from her son's intended – for a marriage that has been arranged by the Sheik. Her name is Clara, and the photograph we see is that of Clara Bow! 'Allah help him when I've done with him!' the Sheik exclaims, as he sets out to look for his son. Meanwhile, we are witness to the latest exchange between the young couple, who have obviously spent the night together. 'I'll hate you with my dying breath,' Yasmin cries, following a half-hearted attempt at stabbing him, whilst he counteracts this with, 'And you'll have *more* reason to hate me before I've finished with you!' – suggesting that more of the same is about to come, though his machinations are momentarily halted by the arrival of his father, and another altercation wherein Ahmed declares that he will never submit to an arranged marriage. Vowing that he will *bend* him to his will, the Sheik demonstrates his power by bending an iron bar double – only to have Ahmed pick it up and bend it back into shape. The Sheik realises that his wayward son is a force to be reckoned with: nevertheless he does manage to convince Ahmed to reluctantly set Yasmin free.

En route to Touggourt, however, Yasmin is captured by Ghabar and taken to the Café Maure, a dive frequented by cut-throats and whores. Ahmed and his father – by now reconciled to the fact that his son should do as he did, and marry for *love* – set off to save her. Ahmed enters the establishment wearing a disguise – one of the costumes purchased for *The Hooded Falcon* – and, mistaking him for a wealthy traveller, Ghabar forces Yasmin to dance for him. When he reveals himself, she confesses that although she has *tried* to hate him, her heart has prevented her from doing so.

An all-out scrap ensues, resulting in a swashbuckling episode not even matched by the Errol Flynn epics of the next decade. Using table-tops, chairs, and even a massive barrel for a shield, and dodging daggers – one of which misses him and plunges into a man's buttocks – the eponymous hero and his father fight off their enemies a dozen at a time, with Rudy executing *all* of his own stunts: charging up and down staircases whilst swishing away with an uncapped sword, delivering nifty uppercuts which caused genuine injury to the unfortunate extras, and finally making the most spectacular headfirst leap from a balcony, on to a chandelier from which he swings precariously for several seconds before dropping effortlessly the fifteen feet to the ground, bouncing up like a sprite to dash up another staircase and dispatch another handful of villains . . . and all of this whilst clutching a non-prop, razor-sharp dagger between his teeth!

The climax to this unprecedented, unbridled masterpiece of homo-eroticism comes with Ahmed chasing Ghabar – who has escaped with Yasmin during the chaos – across the rolling sands of the desert, engaging in yet more swordfighting whilst their horses are galloping at full-speed, until Ahmed unhorses Ghabar, drags him to the ground and strangles him . . . whilst two of the Moor's captured men, half-naked and tied together on the back of a mule, bite and nip each other. Ahmed then rides off with his love after one final flexing of his redeeming biceps, into the sunset.

During the shooting of *The Son Of The Sheik*, Rudy toned down his sexual activities considerably. There were no all-gay parties at Falcon Lair or aboard the *Phoenix*, no trips to his favourite hang-outs in Santa Monica – primarily because Alberto, his wife and their eleven-years old son were living under the same roof, though he was still sleeping with Paul Ivano and André Daven, more often than not as a threesome. The image of the World's Greatest Lover, however, had to be maintained. In one of their last rows, Rambova had threatened to 'spill the beans' about his sexuality, and Ivano more than anyone was terrified that she would be as good as her word. For this reason, he arranged for Rudy to meet one of the film community's most alluring sirens . . . Pola Negri.

Apolonia Chalupec had studied dance at the Rozmaitosci School in Warsaw, appearing in a handful of self-financed films before moving to Berlin in 1917, where she had met Ernst Lubitsch, then a student of Max Reinhardt. The following year, Lubitsch had put her into *The Eyes Of The Mummy* and *Gypsy Blood*. In 1922 she had signed a lucrative contract with Famous Players-Lasky and sailed to America, where the Hollywood publicity machine had been put into overdrive. Jesse Lasky had 'arranged' for her to be mobbed at the New York docks, and for her car to be preceded by a police escort with wailing sirens and flashing lights as it edged through the rush hour traffic along Fifth Avenue. 'Her arrival could hardly have been topped by the Second Coming,' Jesse Lasky Jr observed in his memoirs.

In her first American press interview, Negri had, like Valentino, revealed a predilection for bending the truth . . . boasting that she had been the last great European to have been born in the nineteenth century – 'Just before midnight, dear, on New Year's Eve, 1899!' Recent research, however, suggests that she had probably been born in 1894, though some sources have suggested 1886, making her over forty when she met Valentino.

Pola Negri had caused a sensation with her first Hollywood film, *Bella Donna*, and the subsequent *Forbidden Paradise* had made her a household name. Commanding fabulous fees, she had moved into a mansion on Beverly Drive, whose central feature was a sunken Roman bath in the living-room. One of the loveliest women in films at the time, and one of the most volatile, no one courted publicity quite like Negri, who was very quickly 'rumbled' by Nita Naldi and awarded the somewhat inglorious title, 'Tinsel Town's Number One Fag-Hag'. In 1933 she would become 'involved' with the former silent star, William Haines, having been instructed – and paid – to do so by Louis B Mayer. Haines, who unlike Rudy and most of his friends had never been *in* the closet, had been seen loitering in Pershing Square in downtown Los Angeles, a well-known gay pick-up spot, and Mayer wanted to make sure that one of his biggest stars, who had survived the transition to sound, stayed big at the box-office. Negri and Haines would subsequently be photographed everywhere: at the glitziest parties and receptions, at premières, and even buying the king-sized bed which, they told the press, would not be used until after the wedding . . . a union which would be called off, with some feasible excuse, once Haines had completed his next film. Such had been Negri's ability to play the role that for a time she had actually believed that she and Haines would marry . . . until one month after their 'engagement' he was arrested by the vice-squad and his Hollywood career ground to a halt.

During the late spring of 1926, abetted by Paul Ivano, and more than a gentle shove from Joseph Schenck, Rudy began his 'affair' with Pola Negri, a series of publicity stunts which would increase their box-office standing, yet enable both partners to remain as promiscuous as they had always been. They met at one of Marion Davies' parties, an event – like the one with Rambova at the New York railway station – which inspired sterling performances from the pair and almost convinced Ivano that they were *not* the pawns in a Schenck-directed game of chess. Rudy kissed Negri's palm and loudly enthused that she was one of the most beautiful creatures he had ever seen, and minutes later she was overheard telling a reporter, 'Once Valentino has experienced *my* love, he'll forget about all other women. I vow that we will be married by the end of the year!' Not so long before she had said the same thing about Chaplin, with whom she had engaged in a genuine affair. Then, just before midnight – pretending that she had to be on set by six the next morning – Negri left the party, followed a few minutes later by Rudy and Ivano, who later 'confessed' that his friend had driven to Falcon Lair (to change!), then headed off to Negri's house for 'a night of unbridled passion'. André Daven, who was at Falcon Lair looking after Rudy's sick Doberman, Kabar, later stated that Rudy *had* driven to Negri's place, but that this had only been for the benefit of the reporters who had trailed him from Marion Davies' party, and that he had returned to Falcon Lair by another route after giving them the slip.

Rudy may not have been interested in becoming Pola Negri's lover, but he certainly treasured her friendship. Once again he believed he had found a surrogate mother figure he felt he could lean on, though unlike June Mathis who had never breathed one word of his confidences to the outside world, Negri would make him out to be some superstud whose animal passions were limitless. Jean Acker and Natacha Rambova had spoken of Valentino's inadequacies in the bedroom: Negri complained to friends such as Hollywood's resident hack, Louella Parsons, that if Rudy could only make love *four* times on the trot, it was because he was having a bad night. When the pair attended a reception for the playwright, Michael Arlen, at the Biltmore Hotel – Rudy wearing his Juan

Gallardo costume, and Rambova's slave bracelet which, he told the press, had never left his wrist since she had gone, and Negri dressed as a Spanish gypsy – one of the picture captions read, 'Valentino says one thing. Pola says another. And Hollywood makes up its own mind!'

In truth, Negri was not sexually attracted to Rudy at all, and it was perhaps because there were no amorous complications that their friendship worked so well, though sadly it had begun too late in his all too short life. Her respect for him was such, however, that she persisted with her pretence for more than half a century after his death – though to be thought of as Valentino's lover *did* of course offer one certain prestige. In *Memoirs Of A Star*, her ghostwritten autobiography of 1970, she denied his homosexuality by declaring, 'Valentino's true sexuality reached out and captured me. I was fascinated by the way in which he used his body in a perfect act of love . . . Call it fatalism, but from our first meeting I was aware that this man had the power to destroy my life, or to change its course so irrevocably that it would never be the same again.' She also described in great detail how Rudy had been fond of strewing rose petals across her bed as a prelude to love-making, confirming what other lovers have also said – Valentino liked to have sex first, *then* get down to the business of small talk. Unfortunately, Pola Negri's 'revelations' were more the working of an over-active imagination than fact.

In June 1926, Rudy made up with June Mathis: driving to her apartment, he entered without knocking, took her in his arms and kissed her more passionately than he had any of his leading ladies, then fell to his knees and begged her forgiveness! Mathis later admitted that no apology had been necessary. She had felt compelled to turn her back on Rudy because even her tremendous fondness for him had been overshadowed by her loathing of the woman who had wrecked his life, and she had been confident that he would run back to her once Rambova had deserted him. Mathis also said that Rudy had wanted to show her a good time – dancing, wining and dining – before leaving for the New York première of *The Son Of The Sheik*, because he had had a premonition that they would never see each other again. 'He didn't have to say anything. I just knew. The dear, dear boy was a bundle of nerves, not at all like the Rudy of old.'

Robert Florey was also convinced that Rudy had foreseen his own demise. 'He told me that he had at first worried about Professor Winton's prediction that he would die young,' Florey wrote, some years later. 'Then he said that, after giving the matter careful consideration, he'd come to the conclusion that death was but the beginning of another, better life. "My soul will live on long after I'm gone," he said, adding, "I don't know if I'll be able to stay in touch with my friends, but I'm happy with the knowledge that I *will* be leaving them many lovely memories." '

It was after Rudy had invited June Mathis for a spin in his new 'baby' – a huge, gleaming five-seater Isotta Fraschini limousine – and subsequently frightened the life out of her, that she begged him to give up driving until he was feeling a little better. Rudy gave her his word that he would, and even went to the trouble of hiring a chauffeur. This worked well, until an outing to San Francisco at the end of June, when Rudy yelled so much at the young man for 'driving like a snail' that he stopped the car, got out, and climbed into the back of the vehicle with André Daven and Douglas Gerrard. The journey was completed with Rudy at the wheel, and for once he kept within the speed-limit. On the way back to Hollywood, however, according to Daven he 'just freaked out', slamming his foot against the accelerator. It had started to rain, and tearing through San Luis Obispo, he did not see the level crossing ahead of him, or the oncoming Southern Express: hurtling over the tracks and missing the train by several feet, he skidded across the wet tarmac on the other side, wrapping the front of the car around a telegraph pole. 'My third and lucky one,' he joked with a paramedic before passing out from shock. Incredibly, neither Rudy nor Douglas Gerrard, who had been sitting next to him, suffered so much as a scratch, though the chauffeur received facial abrasions, and André Daven was detained in hospital overnight with two cracked ribs.

The Hollywood première of *The Son Of The Sheik* took place at Grauman's Million Dollar Theatre on 9 July, where the special guests were Mae Murray and Prince David Mdivani, whose wedding Rudy and Pola Negri had recently attended. This marriage which would turn out to be as farcical as both of Rudy's had been, for Mdivani had no money, and his 'château' on the Russian–Persian border was little more than a crumbling heap of stones which had not been lived in for years. Rudy arrived on Negri's arm, smiling radiantly for the fans but occasionally grimacing. The previous evening he had suffered a violent bout of vomiting at Negri's house, but had refused to allow her to call a doctor, claiming that his 'malady' had been caused by the side-effects of a potion he had been prescribed by a backstreet quack to combat premature baldness. To cheer him up, his escort had arranged for a huge floral display to be erected in the theatre's foyer: a bank of scarlet gladioli, against which his name was spelled out in white carnations. Rudy pretended to be thrilled by the gesture – he did not wish to hurt Negri's feelings by informing her that, like most of the theatrical community, he considered the mixing of red and white flowers an unlucky omen.

There was a further première of the film in San Francisco, where the Mayor presented Rudy with a spaniel puppy – bringing the total number of dogs in the Falcon Lair kennels to fourteen – before he boarded the train for Chicago, on the first stage of his journey to New York for the film's East Coast première. Curiously, causing many people who knew him to retrospectively support June Mathis's premonition theory, Rudy did not allow any of those who had been closest to him over the last few years to accompany him on the tour. André Daven, Douglas Gerrard, Paul Ivano and Federico Beltran-Masses would never see him again.

It would be a gruelling schedule. There were few days when Rudy did not suffer bouts of extreme nausea, and the intense heatwave gripping most of America did not help, though what really aggravated his condition was the now infamous 'Pink Powder Puffs' article in the *Chicago Tribune*, which Rudy read whilst he was breakfasting in his suite at the city's Blackstone Hotel.

The journalist responsible for the piece had recently visited a new public ballroom on Chicago's north side, with which he had been suitably impressed – until stepping into the men's lavatories, where he had seen a slot-machine on the wall which dispensed solid blocks of pink face powder. Below had been printed the instruction, 'INSERT COIN. HOLD PERSONAL PUFF BENEATH TUBE. PULL LEVER.' And now, he concluded:

> It is a strange social phenomenon, one that is running its course not only here in America, but in Europe as well. Chicago may have its powder puffs – London has its dancing men, and Paris its gigolos. But *Hollywood* is the national school of masculinity. Rudy, the beautiful gardener's boy, is the prototype of the American 'male'. Hell's bells! Oh, Sugar!

On 18 July 1926, when this offensive, wholly unwarranted article first appeared, the journalist responsible for it begged the editor of the *Chicago Tribune* not to divulge his name – not just through fear of reprisal from Rudy's fans and friends, but from the actor himself who had already made it clear that he would 'thrash the daylights' out of anyone who dared question his virility. Had he known that the culprit was D Dorgan, the author of the earlier 'Song Of Hate' attack in *Photoplay*, and the man who had called his mother a 'wop', he would have demanded satisfaction there and then and the matter might have been resolved effectively, as had happened in Paris with Baron Lukács. Unfortunately, despite several frantic calls to the *Tribune*, George Ullman never found out who had written the piece until many years later and Rudy, cut to the core – mindless of his manager's protests that he would only make matters worse – had a piece inserted in the *Tribune*'s rival publication, the *Herald-Examiner*:

> To the 'man' who wrote the editorial 'Pink Powder Puffs' in the *Chicago Tribune*:
>
> The above-mentioned editorial is at least the second scurrilous personal attack you have made upon me, my race, and my father's name. You slur my Italian ancestry, you cast ridicule on my Italian name, you cast doubt upon my manhood. I call you in return a contemptible coward, and to prove which of us is the better man I challenge you to a

personal contest . . . to meet me in the boxing or wrestling arena to prove, in typically American fashion (for I am an *American* citizen) which of us is more a man. I prefer this test of honour to be private, so that I may give you the beating you deserve, and because I want to make it absolutely plain that this challenge is not for purposes of publicity. I am handing copies of this to the newspapers simply because I doubt that anyone so cowardly as to write about me as you have done would respond to a challenge unless forced by the press to do so. I do not know who you are or how big you are, but this challenge stands even if you are as big as Jack Dempsey. I will meet you immediately, or give you reasonable time in which to prepare, for I assume that your muscles must be flabby and weak, judging by your cowardly mentality, and that you will have to replace the vitriol in your veins with red blood, if there be a place in such a body as yours for red blood and manly muscle. I welcome criticism of my work as an actor, but I will resent with every muscle in my body attacks upon my manhood and ancestry.

George Ullman had been right: had Rudy ignored the article – or even hired someone to write an equally sarcastic reply and play the detractor at his own game – its contents might not have been so widely broadcast. And now his challenge ended up being printed, alongside the original attack, in newspapers all over the world, along with a hard-hitting, no-nonsense postscript:

Hoping that I will have an opportunity to demonstrate to you that the wrist under a slave bracelet may snap a real fist into your sagging jaw, and that I may teach you respect of a man even though he prefers to keep his face clean. You may therefore send your answer to me in New York care of United Artists. I remain, with utter contempt, RUDOLPH VALENTINO.

The debacle with the *Chicago Tribune* had absolutely no effect on

Rudy's popularity: 5,000 screaming fans greeted him when his train pulled into New York's Central Station, and twenty police motorcycles escorted his limousine to the Ambassador Hotel. Even so, he would not let the 'Powder Puff' incident drop, and when the perpetrator failed to turn up, he took on a challenge – to fight two rounds on the gravel-covered roof of the Ambassador Hotel from Frank 'Buck' O'Neil, a loud-mouthed, tobacco-chewing boxing expert who wrote for the *New York Evening Journal*. O'Neil, a pal of Dick Dorgan, boasted to the press that Valentino would never dare face him in the ring: he was two inches taller than Rudy and a good thirty pounds heavier. Rudy so badly needed to get all the aggression out of his system that he would have taken on anyone. Dismissing his opponent as 'a flabby lump of lard', he peeled off his shirt and flexed his muscles for the cameramen – who, obeying the dictates of the Hays Office because Rudy had not shaved his chest since completing *The Son Of The Sheik*, were obliged to film him from behind honing in on 'his mighty biceps and potentially fatal right hook' . . . and of course, his slave bracelet.

The event was covered by dozens of pressmen. During the first round, Rudy took several sharp punches on the chin and another that bloodied his nose, but he bounced back in the second and floored O'Neil with a series of perfectly-aimed jabs . . . and as with Baron Lukács, the two men shook hands and went off to dine, with O'Neil telling reporters, truthfully, that the best and fittest man had won, adding, 'That boy has a punch like the kick of a mule!' Rudy, however, was far from satisfied and declared that he never would be until he had come face-to-face with the 'tyrant' who had insulted him in the first place.

Early the next morning, Rudy escorted his brother Alberto and his family to the docks, where they boarded the SS *France*. Ten minutes later he was photographed in another part of the harbour, shaking hands with Umberto Nobile, the aviator who had recently flown across the North Pole in the airship, *Norge*, and who was also returning to Europe. Again, to his naive way of thinking, Rudy believed that to be snapped alongside 'a regular he-man' would make his detractors think twice about calling him a pansy.

The following afternoon, with Aileen Pringle as his date, Rudy arrived at the Mark Strand Theatre amidst scenes of sheer lunacy. The temperature was 98° in the shade, and fans had queued most of the night for tickets, so tempers amongst the crowd were strained. George Ullman and a dozen bodyguards managed to get him inside the building unscathed, but when the time came for him to leave, Rudy's chauffeur was unable to back the car up against the stage-door. With four thousand hysterical fans who had broken through the barrier of mounted police to contend with, Rudy made a mad dash the few yards to the vehicle, whilst hands coming at him from every direction stripped him of his tie, hat, wrist-watch, cuff-links and buttons, and his jacket and shirt were ripped to shreds. Once, he would have found such an experience exhilirating. Now, however, all he wanted was the seclusion of his hotel suite.

Missing his friends terribly, and feeling far from well because of the heat and his bleeding ulcers – and heartily sick of being told by the studio who he should and should not date – Rudy called Jean Acker and invited her to dine with him at the former actress Mary 'Tex' Guinan's speakeasy. This was a favourite haunt of politicians and theatre people who were willing to fork out up to $100 for a bottle of the cheapest whisky or champagne, and was famous for its strip-shows and some of the wildest parties in town.

The evening was, of course, a feast for the press, who immediately began speculating that Rudy and his first wife were thinking about getting together again. No one appeared to notice that his old flame, Frank Menillo, was sitting at the same table . . . or indeed, who he was. Acker, however, smiled meekly and kept tight-lipped on the subject, whilst Rudy retorted sharply, 'We're good friends, and we always will be!' The press then focused their attention on the cabaret, a bravora performance from the Indian fakir, Ramin Bey, who invited Rudy to join him on the stage . . . to have him pass a steel needle through one side of his face to the other, without drawing blood or him feeling any pain! Rudy, of course, only jumped at this latest excuse to prove his manhood, though George Ullman was not sure that he should have been risking the most famous – not to mention the most valuable – profile in the movies, even for an apparent optical illusion. An enthusiastic

Rudy rolled up his sleeve and proffered his forearm instead . . . the one sporting the slave bracelet, of course. Ullman then gave the waiter a $50 tip to bring a glass of neat alcohol to cleanse the area, just in case.

A few days later, bidding a temporary farewell to Jean Acker and Frank Menillo, Rudy left for the Chicago première of *The Son Of The Sheik* at the city's Roosevelt Theatre. He was aggrieved that the author of the 'Powder Puffs' article still had not come forward, and issued a statement to the Associated Press which was published in just about every newspaper in America *but* the *Tribune*. Paying tribute to all the journalists who had treated him fairly in the past, but adding that there always had to be at least one exception to the rule, he concluded:

> It is evident that you cannot make a coward fight any more than you can draw blood out of a turnip. The heroic silence of the writer who chose to attack me without any provocation in the *Chicago Tribune* leaves no doubt as to the total absence of manliness in his whole makeup. I feel as I have been vindicated, because I consider his silence as a tacit retraction and an admission which I am forced to accept, even though it is not entirely to my liking.

On 1 August, Rudy attended the new film's première in Atlantic City, after which he was the star guest in Gus Edwards' revue at the Ritz-Carlton Hotel, where for twice the regular admission fee the audience were able to watch Valentino dance the Argentinian tango for the last time. Edwards then presented him with a pair of boxing gloves, should he ever discover the identity of the Chicago 'tyrant' and wish to take him on.

The next morning, Rudy returned to New York, where he again met up with Jean Acker and Frank Menillo. He had no further engagements until his film's Philadelphia première on the sixteenth, so George Ullman advised him to rest. Rudy promised to take things easy, continued swallowing vast quantities of sodium bicarbonate to combat his stomach pains, and pleased only himself. The next twelve days saw him hitting the town with near-suicidal vigour: speakeasies, clubs, parties, receptions – he and Menillo always returning to the Ambassador Hotel in the early hours, accompanied by a different pair of dancing-girls, for appearance's sake, who would always be 'paid off' once they were inside the building, having been seen by the ever-present reporters.

During this first week of August, Rudy gave his last press interview – though in the case of this particular journalist, Henry Louis Mencken, it retrospectively appears to have been a last confession. Known as 'The Sage of Baltimore', the highly eclectic Mencken had founded the satirical publications, *The Smart Set* and *American Mercury*, instruments with which he had attracted tremendous controversy due to his vicious attacks on what he called the 'booboisie': collectively the Bible-Belt and all forms of religion, politicians and public figures, traditionally-minded writers, Prohibitionists, anything British . . . and newspaper editors.

Curiously, Mencken had neither written about Valentino nor seen any of his films . . . even more strangely, he also later admitted how the actor had sent for *him*. The two men had a heart-to-heart over dinner at the Ambassador Hotel for over three hours, with Mencken uncovering so many 'emotions and personal details' of Rudy's life and loves that his could quite easily have been *the* scoop of Valentino's magnificent career. In the end little of what was actually said made it to the finished article, such was Mencken's wish not to blow his own trumpet, at someone else's expense . . . and such, of course, was the world's loss.

> He began by talking of his home, his people, his early youth. His words were simple, yet somehow eloquent. I could still see the mime before me, but now and then there was a flash of something else. That something else, I concluded, was what is commonly called, for want of a better name, a gentleman. Valentino's agony was the agony of a man of relatively civilised feelings thrown into a situation of intolerable vulgarity, destructive alike to his peace and to his dignity . . . It was not that trifling Chicago episode that was riding him, it was the whole grotesque futility of his life. Had he not achieved, out of nothing, a vast and dizzy success? Then that success

> was hollow as well as vast, a colossal and preposterous nothing, [for] every time the multitudes yelled, he felt himself blushing inside...Here was a young man who was living daily the dreams of millions of other young men. Here was one who was catnip to women. Here was one who had wealth and fame – and here was one who was *very unhappy*.

On the evening of Saturday 14 August, ignoring George Ullman's protestations, Rudy and Frank Menillo attended a party thrown in his honour at the apartment of a young broker pal, Barclay Warburton Jr, which raged on until the middle of the next morning. Two hours later, George Ullman found him on the floor of his hotel suite, clutching at his stomach and writhing in agony. Yet Rudy still refused to see a doctor, leaving his manager with no alternative but to call an ambulance. He was rushed to the city's Polyclinic Hospital, where a desperate search began to find someone willing to 'disfigure' the world's most celebrated, not to say valuable, torso. 'No one wanted to take the responsibility of operating on Valentino,' his brother Alberto recalled. 'They were waiting for some big, well-known surgeon to come along, and it took until six o'clock.'

An emergency operation was carried out for a burst gastric ulcer and a ruptured appendix – by *three* of the most distinguished surgeons in New York State: Doctors Harold Meeker, Paul Durham and Randolph Manning. Rudy was then taken to recuperate in a soundproofed suite on the ninth floor of the building, where George Ullman had organised a round-the-clock armed guard. His first words upon coming out of the anaesthetic were, 'Did I behave like a pink powder puff, or a man?'

The operation appears to have been initially successful – a faked photograph of the stricken star, said to have been taken inside the operating theatre, appeared on the front pages of newspapers, assuring fans that all was well. George Ullman thought so, too, telling the press how Rudy had been sitting up in bed only hours after surgery, discussing future projects. Earlier he had confessed, to the chagrin of thousands of admirers, that he envisaged perhaps another five years of 'lover' roles before he began tackling other more mature parts. He particularly wanted to play Cesare Borgia, Christopher Columbus and Cyrano de Bergerac, Ben Hur and Fu Manchu – for which he had already posed for pre-publicity photographs. High on his list too was a film about Max Dearly, the creator of of the apache.

Ullman also recounted how Rudy had asked for a mirror, saying, 'I want to see how I look when I'm sick. Then if I ever have to play the part in pictures, I'll know how to put on the right make-up!' He also issued a message to his fans, thanking them for their love and support.

Even Rudy's doctors were confident of him making a complete recovery; the removal of his appendix had been more or less a routine procedure. Then, two days before he was expected to be discharged, pleurisy set in, swiftly followed by peritonitis and septoendocarditis, a poisoning of the heart-wall. And when he developed a temperature of 104 and became delirious all hope of saving him faded.

Hospital bulletins, issued every hour on the hour and broadcast over the International News Service radio network, pronounced Rudy close to death, whilst much of America tottered on the brink of mourning. The press, by and large, were sympathetic, though some of the reports in the *New York Daily News* could not resist poking fun at him, even as his life was ebbing away . . . printing the words PINK EDITION in large letters next to the headlines. Rudy's last lover, Frank Menillo, went to see him every day, as did Joseph Schenck, though 'Mr Skunk' was privately less concerned for his 'dear buddy' than he was for United Artists' biggest investment. Natacha Rambova and Aunt Teresa sent a cable from the South of France. Jean Acker asked to see him, and Rudy nodded his approval. This hard-bitten woman had also engineered more than her share of misery, but their past was buried as she held his hand for the last time . . . clasping her own gold slave bracelet about his wrist.

Outside the hospital, an estimated 10,000 fans maintained an all-night vigil, and as prayers were said throughout the land, the hospital switchboard received 70,000 calls in just four days and had to take on extra staff. Flowers arrived by the truckload, and there was a constant stream of telegrams and get-well cards from every corner of the globe.

The end came, peacefully in his sleep, ten minutes after noon on Monday, 23 August 1926. Rudy was just thirty-one years old, and of the hundreds of obituaries, perhaps the most touching – and truthful – appeared in the *Newark News:*

> So he dies, while curious crowds throng the streets before the hospital, and his last breath is drawn within a circle of hired men and women attendants, without one relative at his bedside, perhaps without a single man or woman who loved him for himself.

Epilogue
You

'There is no such thing as death!'

The world had rarely known such an intensity of grief, as across the United States, flags were lowered to half-mast, and every film set in the country closed down for the day.

At once, rumours began circulating as to the cause of Rudy's demise. The general opinion was that strapping young men in their prime, who posed for health and strength pictures and who excelled at most sports, simply did not die from anything as ridiculously treatable as gastric ulcers. There were reports that he had been fed arsenic at the Warburton party by a wealthy woman spurned by him whilst shooting *The Son Of The Sheik* – alternatively, that the perforations discovered in his stomach lining during his operation were in fact bullet-holes, courtesy of a jealous husband. Another 'official' source stated that Rudy had succumbed to syphylis of the brain.

George Ullman and Joseph Schenck waged a war as to who could come up with the most marketable death-bed speech – copies of his final films for United Artists had already been dispatched to over 5,000 cinemas and theatres, and business at the box-office was brisker than ever. Ullman declared that Rudy's last words to him had been, 'Don't pull down the blinds, George. I feel fine. I want the sunlight to greet me!' To Schenck he is claimed to have said, 'Don't worry, chief. I'll be all right!' Pola Negri went one step further, claiming that she had received a letter from one of

Rudy's doctors, sent via Mary Pickford, wherein he had said, 'Tell Pola that I'm thinking of her.' It is quite probable that nothing was said at all: in an official statement, Dr Meeker told the press that the actor's last conscious words, in incomprehensible Italian, had been muttered at 3.30am, and that from 8am until the time of his death, he had been in a semi-coma. He also emphasised the fact that Rudy *had* died alone.

On and on it went, filling the front pages of newspapers for days. 'Statesmen and men of science, great teachers and men who have swayed the masses through the spoken and written word have been stricken and died with far less public notice,' observed the *New York Times*. More fake photographs appeared: 'Valentino Being Welcomed Into Heaven By Caruso', 'Valentino's Funeral Procession' – several days before the event took place. There was a new song, crooned by another Rudy, Rudy Vallee, over the nation's airwaves:

There's a new star at home
In that far starry dome!
Valentino, goodbye!
But way up in the sky,
There's a new star in heaven tonight!

The effects of his death rapidly reached epidemic proportions. Even before the body had been removed from the premises, over two thousand fans rioted outside the Polyclinic Hospital, sobbing hysterically – some tearing their hair out by the roots, one dying of a heart attack, and another attempting suicide by flinging herself under the hooves of a police horse. Two fans slit their throats in London, and a twenty-seven-year old British starlet named Peggy Scott – claiming that she had had a one-night stand with Rudy in the South of France, a claim which was disproved at her inquest – achieved the moment's fame which might otherwise have eluded her by swallowing a fatal dose of mercuric chloride. At the Ritz, in Paris, a bellboy with a similar claim on Rudy's affections was found dead in his basement room, naked and spreadeagled across a lovingly arranged display of *Sheik* memorabilia. One of the surgeons who had attended Rudy at the hospital suffered a coronary. Barclay Warburton Jr, who had half-carried him back to his suite prior to him becoming ill, was so overcome with grief that he ended up in an asylum.

Rudolph Valentino's funeral remains possibly the largest there has ever been for a popular personality (official figures state those of Edith Piaf, in 1963, and Princess Diana in 1997, to have been slightly smaller), with more than 20,000 half-crazed fans jostling outside Frank Campbell's Broadway Funeral Home, in the drizzle, ten hours *before* the doors were thrown open to the public, by which time they had increased five-fold. Within the building, Rudy's silver and bronze casket was protected day and night by mock-Fascist guards, a publicity stunt dreamed up by United Artists, who wanted to keep Rudy big at the box-office for as long as possible in the days when the popularity of movie stars usually waned with their demise. Complementing the guards was a wreath, allegedly from Mussolini – in the guise of Joseph Schenck, whose studio rival, Jesse Lasky, had paid for dozens of 'shriekers' to be strategically placed amongst the mourners.

Mass panic occurred when, during a sudden forward surge by the crowd, the front window of the funeral parlour shattered, showering dozens of people with lethal shards of plate-glass. Added to the confusion of fainting, heart-attacks, and random tramplings and beatings from mounted police wielding batons was the rain, now forming a solid sheet. Eventually, Rudy's casket had to be moved to another viewing-room, whilst the downstairs Chapel of Rest was turned into an emergency-room to cater for the constant stream of casualties . . . upwards of 250 an hour, though fortunately most of these were not serious.

As many as 9,000 people an hour, ten hours a day for three days, filed past Rudy during his lying-in-state within Campbell's plush Gold Room. The studios had wanted to add to the farce by dressing him in his *Sheik* costume, but George Ullman had put his foot down, and he had been dressed formally and the casket placed behind a screen of reinforced glass. The catafalque was surrounded by the accoutrements of the Catholic Church, from which he had long since lapsed: a statue of the Virgin Mary, two huge altar candles, and a copy of the Vulgate Bible. The Vatican had been expected to send a message of sympathy, but issued a condemning statement instead: 'This is collective madness, incarnating the tragi-comedy of a new fetishism.'

On the morning of Tuesday 31 August, a requiem Mass was held at St Malachy's Church in New York, outside which were gathered 6,000 fans – fifty times as many had lined the funerary route from Campbell's. The mourners were led by Jean Acker, who without any fuss had carried out her former husband's apparent wishes by clasping *her* slave bracelet about his wrist. Both she and Pola Negri, who walked beside her into the church, collapsed during the ceremony and had to be revived by paramedics. Behind them came George Ullman, June Mathis and Alberto Guglielmi, who had set off from Europe as soon as he had heard about Rudy's illness, only to arrive too late. George Ullman had sent Natacha Rambova a cable informing her of Rudy's death, but she had made no attempt to be present at his funeral: neither had his sister, Maria. Further behind were those Rudy had *truly* loved: George O'Brien, Richard Barthelmess, Ramon Novarro, Frank Menillo and a dozen or so extras, stagehands and dancers who had known him intimately at some stage of his all too brief career, and whose grief was no less intense than that of Rudy's dubious female conquests.

On the eve of the funeral, there had been a series of heated quarrels amongst the chief mourners. Pola Negri had arrived at New York's Grand Central Station decked out in the most fashionable mourning weeds which, she told the press, had set her back $3,000. Then, after plugging her next film, *Hotel Imperial* – she had been working on this upon hearing of Rudy's death – she had broken down completely, declaring between sobs that Valentino had been the greatest love of her life – adding, now that there was no one around to refute the claim, that they had been engaged to be married. 'I loved the irresistible appeal of his charm, the wonderful enthusiasm of his mind and soul,' she had continued. 'I didn't realise how ill he was. He never told me.' This much was certainly true, but what angered George Ullman and Ben Lyon, the husband of Bebe Daniels who for some reason had been roped in to help with the arrangements, was that Negri had commissioned an 11-by-6-foot blanket of scarlet roses, upon which was spelled the name POLA in white carnations, and that she had given instruction for this to be draped over his casket. At the première of Rudy's last film, such a gesture had been appreciated, but not now. Lyon accused the actress of trying to turn Rudy's funeral into a farce, and attempted to have the blanket removed from the funeral parlour. Alberto Guglielmi also hit out at her for using his brother's fame as a 'publicity-crutch' . . . then promptly told the press that he had applied to change his name to Valentino. At this Negri flew into a rage, declaring that she and Rudy's genuine loved ones had always been there to help him through his every hour of need, whilst he had hardly ever spoken about his family. The flowers stayed put.

Earlier in the week, Alberto had upset everyone by *demanding* that his brother's body be returned to Italy for burial, but in this particular argument he had been overruled by George Ullman and every single one of Rudy's friends. *America* had made Valentino, declared Ullman. It and its people had captured his heart: the last time Rudy had visited the country of his birth, hardly anyone had recognised him. Ullman had then added that, in any case, the Guglielmis had no say in Rudy's affairs – when he had signed his will, Valentino had nominated Ullman as his executor and the administrator of his estate. In fact, he *was* remembered in Castellaneta: the priest officiating at the Mass in the little town at around the same time as the one in New York hailed him as, 'That sublime interpreter of earthly passion.' Some years later he would be honoured with a statue, a cinema and bar, and a Via Valentino. After the ceremony in New York, Rudy's casket – accompanied by Jean Acker, Alberto, Pola Negri and the Ullmans – was conveyed by train to Hollywood, for entombment in the Memorial Park Cemetery. There were lengthy stops along the way at Chicago, Kansas City, El Paso, Yuma and Colton, each one greeted with mass hysteria. In one little town the train was forced to stop because a contingent of Italian mandolinists wanted to pay tribute to Rudy by playing him a medley of Neapolitan love-songs. 'The emotion was virtually unbearable,' Alberto remembered, in 1977.

'Even now, fifty years on, I get a lump in my throat thinking about that day.'

In Hollywood, on 6 September, the cortège was met by André Daven, Douglas Gerrard, Paul Ivano and Robert Florey. All four were inconsolable, and wept unashamedly as they unloaded Rudy's casket from the train – no one else was allowed to touch it until they had placed it in the hearse. The funeral-proper, attended by a veritable *Who's Who?* of Hollywood luminaries, took place the next morning at the Church of the Good Shepherd, in Beverly Hills, outside which lay stretched an ocean of flowers from just about every showbusiness personality in America. From England came a huge wreath from Gerald du Maurier, and others from Damia and Jacques Hébertot in Paris. Flowers had also been sent by the British royal family. Rudy's casket was draped with another blanket of red roses from Pola Negri, this time without her name, on top of which lay a white cross of roses and gardenias from Alberto.

The entombment, for which Charlie Chaplin was one of the pall-bearers, was attended by a crowd of 10,000, and thousands more lined the route between the church and the cemetery as a plane flew overhead, scattering a huge shower of rose petals – Luther Mahoney's final tribute to the employer who had become his closest friend. Prior to this ceremony, too, there had been objections from Alberto Guglielmi because Paul Ivano and André Daven had exercised their right to walk at the front of the cortège with the chief mourners. This time it was Pola Negri who overruled him, declaring that Rudy had loved *them* much more than he could possibly have loved a brother he had only seen a handful of times in the thirteen years since his arrival in America.

Stars and movie moguls alike fought to deliver the sharpest, most heartfelt and of course most publicity-attracting tributes to the press. 'Valentino's death is one of the greatest tragedies that has occurred in the history of the motion picture industry,' declared Chaplin, as if no one had known this, whilst Gloria Swanson wept, 'He was a real artist, a charming gentleman, a true sportsman and a darned good friend.' Rudy and his co-star from *Beyond The Rocks* had detested one another! The *Chicago Tribune*, which many people had actually blamed for Rudy's death – Dick Dorgan's article had certainly aggravated his ulcer, though neither he nor anyone else involved with the publication could have known that the feature would be taken so to heart, let alone that Rudy only had weeks to live – now paid tribute to him with an obituary that was infinitely touching. It concluded:

> We loved him because he was a weaver of dreams, because he brought colour, romance and thrills into our lives. Valentino embroidered our drab moments – he smiled into our eyes, and for a little while we too became storybook people, and everyday worries were things that were very far away.

Pola Negri, whose grief certainly appears to have been genuine, had promised her 'fiancé' an elaborate monument, but for the time being he was placed in the wall-vault near June Mathis's mother, one of the pair she had reserved for herself and her husband, Sylvano Balboni.

The tributes continued for months, filling newspapers with tales of Rudy's so-called love life . . . the women he had promised to marry, most of whom had not even met him . . . those who *had* met him, since he had passed to the other side. Accolades came from people he had hated, such as Jesse Lasky, Robert Z Leonard and Mary Pickford.

According to André Daven and Jacques Hébertot, the 'tribute' Rudy would have appreciated more than any other took place very discreetly in a Los Angeles gay club which Rudy had often visited. For this, many of his admirers and several lovers, including Daven, turned up in sheik, matador and Cossack costumes, and after a full religious service followed by a two-minute silence, the assembly of two hundred had let rip with the Argentinian tango, led by a handsome Latino and a dragged-up Rambova. The event was described as 'deviate' by Chaw Mank, who nevertheless relished writing about it in some detail:

> The 'eulogy' for the service was delivered by a dancer who claimed to have known Valentino 'very well'. He described an

oral sex incident with Rudy as 'divine communication with the Godhead', and wore about his neck a locket in which he allegedly kept 'several hairs from The Master's loin'.

At the time of his death, Rudy's assets were estimated at around $2 million, and as his debts were only put at $160,000, few of his creditors foresaw problems getting their money back. Throughout his entire career, Rudy had lavishly spent money he had borrowed from studio bosses: the wherewithall for his cars, his horses and his houses, not to mention the wealth of antiques and jewellery, had all come from the likes of Jesse Lasky, J D Williams and Joseph Schenck, who, of course, had expected a better return for their investment than to suddenly have a dead idol on their hands. Pola Negri, who during Rudy's final illness had declared how she would have yielded her last cent to see him well again, lost little time putting in a claim for the $15,000 she had loaned him during the last month of his life. On top of this, he had recently borrowed a staggering $21,000 from United Artists for his partying in New York, and George Ullman was still owed the $50,000 surplus to her budget that he had advanced Natacha Rambova for the as yet to be released *What Price Beauty?*

Rudy had taken out an insurance policy for $50,000, naming his brother and sister as his chief beneficiaries, and United Artists had insured him for $200,000. 'All that money,' Paul Ivano later scathed, 'and it didn't buy poor Rudy a decent grave!' George Ullman, therefore, as Rudy's sole executor, had no option but to arrange an auction of his effects, and this took place at the Hall of Art Studios, in Hollywood, on 10 December 1926.

In all, 2,385 items went under the hammer, though hardly anything of Rudy's realised its actual value. His Isotta Fraschini brought in $7,400, but his beloved Voisin with its gold-plated coiled Cobra radiator-cap was sold for just $2,300. When last heard of, early in 1980, it had been resold for $25,000 and was still roadworthy. George Ullman himself bought Rudy's clothes – some fifteen-hundred items in all. He told the press, 'I had to remove them from the catalogue. Those clothes almost talked to me. I just couldn't do it.' Falcon Lair was purchased for $145,000 by Jules Howard, a New York diamond merchant. Rudy's cabin-cruiser, the *Phoenix*, fetched a mere $6,000, even less than his dogs. His Arab horses – Firefly, Ramadin, Yaqui and Haroun – brought in $3,250 and Adolphe Menjou, who had appeared in *The Sheik*, bought Rudy's antique Spanish shower screen and gold toilet for $1,000.

What happened to Natacha Rambova's platinum slave bracelet is not known. Ullman listed it in the auction catalogue as Item 727, which suggests that the bracelet which Rudy was buried in *was* Jean Acker's, unless of course he was buried wearing *both*. In this respect there are two theories. Luther Mahoney, who had rescued Rudy's jewellery stash from a strongbox hidden under the stairs at Falcon Lair, maintained that it had never been sold . . . whilst Jacques Hébertot, to whom André Daven returned after Rudy's death, believed that it had been stolen and disposed of by someone at the Polyclinic Hospital, most likely by Acker herself who, believing that she had been acting in his best interests, had wanted to rid Rudy of this most potent reminder of Rambova, once and for all.

Rudy's will was to the point: save for a few bequests to friends and lovers, everything was to be divided equally between Alberto, Maria, and Aunt Teresa Werner. Rambova was to receive the so-called 'insultory' one-dollar, and Jean Acker nothing at all – though many of his friends believed that, had his will been signed *after* the beginning of August 1926 when she had re-entered his affections, Jean Acker could quite easily have inherited everything . . . Rudy had changed his will on 1 September 1925, one week after reading a newspaper report that Rambova was 'about to tell all' in a biography she was writing, and his illness had prevented him from changing it again.

Rudy's decision to appoint George Ullman as the administrator of what remained of his wealth, once his debts had been settled, was virulently opposed by the Guglielmis, who contested it through their lawyers. Ullman, who in a professional sense had done more for Rudy than anyone save perhaps June Mathis, was unfairly accused of fraud – simply because he had, quite legally, withheld some of the money raised by the auction in case anyone else made a claim on the estate. In July 1930, the courts ruled in the Guglielmis' favour, and the administration of the Valentino estate passed to the Bank of Italy, though it would take another seventeen years to sort out Rudy's affairs.

It was in May 1930 that the notorious 'Woman In Black' made her first appearance at Rudy's tomb, her face heavily veiled so as to conceal her identity. The occasion was the dedication by Dolores del Rio of Roger Noble Burnham's statue of Rudy, 'Aspiration', which was erected in Hollywood's DeLongpre Park. Many of Rudy's friends regarded the bronze structure of a near-naked man, which looked like no one in particular, as an insult to his memory and in 1954, having been vandalised several times, it was taken down and put into storage.

Exactly who the *original* 'Lady In Black' was will perhaps never be known, and in subsequent years she would have several emulators. One of these was a former Ziegfeld chorus girl named Marian Brenda, who told reporters that she had borne Rudy two children following their clandestine marriage in New Jersey in 1925! The press merely declared her insane, covered her innumerable publicity-courting breakdowns and suicide-attempts over the next two decades, and were not surprised when at the end of 1951, having been 'summoned' by Rudy, she finally succeeded in killing herself.

Natacha Rambova's threatened 'tell-all' biography, *Rudy: An Intimate Portrait Of Rudolph Valentino By His Wife Natacha Rambova* was published just a few months after Rudy's death, but it was not as revealing as he had dreaded – more than anything, it was a badly-written exercise in self-vindication for all that had happened to him because of her machinations. At the end of November 1926, she arrived in New York, where she delighted in telling reporters that she and Rudy had 'communicated' through a spiritualist friend named George Wehner. In a questionnaire submitted to *Photoplay*, Rudy's grieving fans were told of how their idol had watched his own funeral, only to be 'torn with unhappiness' over the scenes outside Campbell's Funeral Home, but that his spirit had since been comforted by those of Wallace Reid, Caruso, and Barbara La Marr, one of the most beautiful women in Hollywood who had recently died of a drugs overdose, aged twenty-six, after boasting to friends that *she* had been intent on making Valentino her Husband Number Seven. Rambova now told his admirers;

> Rudy wandered the film theatres where his last film was being shown to sorrowing audiences. He walked his old haunts on Broadway, where he used to spend many hours of his old penniless dancing days . . . He shouted, 'I am Rudolph Valentino!' but they did not hear. It was hard for him to understand. He was just as alive, but in a different vibration . . . He has a message for everybody. He wants earth-people to know and to realise that there is no death and no separation . . . He wants them to realise and believe in the beauty and perfection of this after-life.

In 1934, after several more moderately successful appearances on the stage, Rambova married Alvaro de Urzáiz, a young Basque she had met during a trip to Mallorca. The union proved farcical: Urzáiz, like Rudy before him, wanted children and Rambova did not. After a lengthy separation, the marriage was annulled in 1957. By this time, she had become recognised as a gifted Egyptologist who had published several theses with the Princeton University Press. She died of a heart-attack in Los Angeles, aged sixty-nine, on 5 June 1966.

A few months after Rudy's death, André Daven returned to France, where he moved in with Jacques Hébertot for a while, before disappearing without trace. Douglas Gerrard collapsed and died in a Los Angeles street in 1950, and Nita Naldi died destitute in 1961, ravaged by alcohol after the failure of her marriage to the millionaire, J Searle Barclay.

Richard Arlen and George O'Brien – who during their pinnacle years had risked being 'outed' by the press by conducting more or less open homosexual affairs, whilst refusing to submit to the hypocrisy of studio-organised dates – both married soon after Rudy's death, and so far as is known ceased sleeping with other men. Arlen wed his *Wings* co-star, Jobyna Ralston, in 1927. O'Brien married his leading lady from *The Riders Of The Purple*

Sage, Marguerite Churchill, in 1931. Both actors lived well into their seventies. Ramon Navarro met a grisly end on 31 October 1968 when he was murdered by two hustlers who, having learned that he always kept a large stash of money in his bedroom, ransacked his Hollywood home before choking him to death – with the Art Deco phallus given to him by Rudy as a token of love.

Paul Ivano, who subsequently worked on *Blonde Venus*, with Marlene Dietrich, and *Queen Kelly* with Gloria Swanson, went on to enjoy a lengthy career as a cinematographer. He died in April 1984, aged eighty-three.

George Ullman, whose more credible *Valentino, As I Knew Him* had hit the shops before Rambova's tome, and who went to his grave still cursing her and the Guglielmis, died in 1975, aged eighty-nine.

Pola Negri, whose Hollywood career more or less petered out with the advent of sound, enjoyed phenomenal success in Europe as a film star and a *chanteuse*, recording dozens of *chansons-réal-istes* in French, German, Russian and English. Many of their titles spoke only of her love, real or imagined, for Valentino: 'Mes Nuits Sont Mortes', 'L'Heure de la Tristesse', and Peter Kreuder's 'Je Sens En Moi', which Damia also recorded in memory of Rudy. Negri died in August 1987, when the obituaries estimated her age between 86 and 103! Her memorial to Rudy never saw the light of day.

Aside from his mother, the *most* important woman in Rudy's life, June Mathis, collapsed and died in a New York theatre in July 1927, aged forty-six. The suddenness of her demise, in the midst of the Ullman-Guglielmi feud, meant that Rudy's casket had to be transferred to the adjoining crypt, the one Mathis had reserved for her husband. Here he lies still . . . identified only by a paltry if not patronising cheap plaque bearing just the names RUDOLPHO GUGLIELMI VALENTINO and his dates, flanked by two equally cheap-looking flower holders.

He certainly deserves better than this.

Appendix I
The Films of Rudolph Valentino

1. Extra/Bit Parts

1918

ALIMONY (First National). Director: Emmett J Flynn.
With Josephine Whittel, Lois Wilson, Ida Lewis, George Fisher.

A SOCIETY SENSATION (Universal). Director: Paul Powell.
With Carmel Myers, Alfred Allen, Fred Kelsey, Harold Goodwin, Zazu Pitts.

ALL NIGHT (Universal). Director: Paul Powell.
With Carmel Myers, Charles Dorian, Mary Warren, Wadsworth Harris, William Dyer, Jack Hall.

1919

THE DELICIOUS LITTLE DEVIL (Universal). Director: Robert Z Leonard.
With Mae Murray, Harry Rattenbury, Ivor McFadden, Bertram Gassby, Richard Cummings. Valentino played the part of Jimmie Calhoun.

A ROGUE'S ROMANCE (Vitagraph). Director: James Young.
With Earle Williams, Herbert Standing, Brinsley Shaw, Katherine Adams, Maude George. Based on short story by H H Van Loan.

THE HOMEBREAKER (Ince-Paramount). Director: Victor Schertzinger.
With Dorothy Dalton, Douglas Maclean, Edwin Stevens.

VIRTUOUS SINNERS (Pioneer). Director: Emmett J Flynn.
With Wanda Hawley, Norman Kerry, Harry Holden, Bert Woodruff.

THE BIG LITTLE PERSON (Universal). Director: Robert Z Leonard.
With Mae Murray.

OUT OF LUCK (Griffith-Artcraft). Director: Elmer Clifton.
With Dorothy Gish, Ralph Graves, George Fawcett, Raymond Canon, Peter Strong, Emily Chichester.

EYES OF YOUTH (Equity). Director: Albert Parker.
With Clara Kimball Young, Milton Sills, Gareth Hughes, Edmund Lowe, Ralph Lewis, Pauline Starke.
Based upon the stageplay by Max Marcin and Charles Guernon.

1920

THE MARRIED VIRGIN (Fidelity). Director: Joseph Maxwell.
With Vera Sisson, Frank Newburg, Edward Jobson, Kathleen Kirkham, Lillian Leighton. Valentino's *second* film appearance, its release was delayed on account of litigation.
Re-issued in 1922 under the title **FRIVOLOUS WIVES.**

AN ADVENTURESS (Rep Dist Co). Director: Fred J Balshofer.
With Julian Eltinge, Leo White, Virginia Rappe.
Re-issued in 1922 under the title **THE ISLE OF LOVE.**

THE CHEATER (Metro). Director: Henry Otto.
With May Allison, King Baggott, Harry Van Meter, Frank Currier.
Adapted from the stageplay, *Judah*, by H A Jones.

PASSION'S PLAYGROUND (First National). Director: J A Barry. With Norman Kerry, Katherine MacDonald, Edwin Stevens, Nell Craig, Alice Wilson, Virginia Ainsworth.
Adapted from the novel by C N and M A Williamson.

ONCE TO EVERY WOMAN (Universal). Director: Allan J Holubar.
With Dorothy Phillips, Margaret Mann, Wr. Ellingford, Elinor Field, Emily Chichester, Robert Anderson.

STOLEN MOMENTS (Pioneer). Director: James Vincent.
With Marguerite Namara.

THE WONDERFUL CHANCE (Selznick). Director: George Archainbaud.
With Martha Mansfield, Eugene O'Brien, Tom Blake, Warren Cook, Joe Flanagan.
Adapted from story by H H Van Loan.

2. *Leading Roles*

1920

THE FOUR HORSEMEN OP THE APOCALYPSE (Metro). Eleven reels.
Director: Rex Ingram. Adapter: June Mathis. Cameramen: John F Seitz, Walter Mayo, Starrett Ford. Battle-scenes adviser: Paul Ivano. Art director: Walter Mayo. Titles: Jack Robson.
Julio Desnoyers: Rudolf Valentino. Marguerite Laurier: Alice Terry. Centaur: Pomeroy Cannon. Marcelo Desnoyers: Joseph Swickard. Karl von Hartrott: Alan Hale. With José-Ramon Samaniegos (Ramon Novarro), Mabel van Buren, Bridgetta Clark, Nigel de Brulier.
Adapted from the novel by Vicente Blasco Ibanez. Premièred 6-3-21.

1921

UNCHARTED SEAS (Metro). Six reels.
Director: Wesley Ruggles. Adapter: George Edward Jenks. Cameraman: John F Seitz. Art director: John Holden.
Frank Underwood: Rudolph Valentino. Lucretia Eastman: Alice Lake. Senator Eastman: Carl Gerard. With Fred Turner, Charles Mailes, Rhea Haines.
Based on the short story by J H Wilson. Premièred 25-4-21.

CAMILLE (Metro-Nazimova Productions). 7 reels.
Director: Ray C Smallwood. Adapter: June Mathis. Cameraman: Rudolph Bergquist. Art director: Natacha Rambova.
Camille: Nazimova. Armand: Rudolph Valentino. With Arthur Hoyt, Patsy Ruth Miller, Rex Cherryman, Edward Connelly, William Orland, Zeffie Tillbury, Consuelo Flowerton.
Adapted from the novel/screenplay *La Dame Aux Camélias* by Dumas. Premièred 26-9-21.

THE CONQUERING POWER (Metro). Seven reels.
Director: Rex Ingram. Adapter: June Mathis. Cameraman: John F Seitz.
Charles Grandet: Rudolph Valentino. Eugénie Grandet: Alice Terry. Père Grandet: Ralph Lewis. Victor Grandet: Eric Mayne. With Edna Demaury.
Adapted from the novel, *Eugénie Grandet*, by Balzac. Premièred 8-7-21.

THE SHEIK (Famous Players-Lasky, Paramount). 7 reels.
Director: George Melford. Adapter: Monte Katterjohn. Cameraman: William Marshall.
Sheik Ahmed Ben Hassan: Rudolph Valentino. Lady Diana: Agnes Ayres. Raoul de St Hubert: Adolphe Menjou. Omair: Walter Long. With Patsy Ruth Miller, George Wagner, Lucien Littlefield, Loretta Young, Paul Ivano, Natacha Rambova, Richard Arlen.
Adapted from the novel by E M Hull. Premièred 30-10-21.

1922

MORAN OF THE LADY LETTY (Famous Players-Lasky, Paramount). 7 reels.
Director: George Melford. Adapter: Monte Katterjohn. Cameraman: William Marshall.
Moran: Dorothy Dalton. Ramon Laredo: Rudolph Valentino. Captain Sternersen: Charles Brindley. Captain Kitchell: Walter Long. With Maude Wayne, George O'Brien, William Boyd, Cecil Holland, George Kuwa. Adapted from the novel by Frank Norris. Premièred 12-2-22.

BEYOND THE ROCKS (Famous Players-Lasky, Paramount). 6,740 feet.
Director: Sam Wood. Adapter: Jack Cunningham. Cameraman: Alfred Gilks.
Lord Bracondale: Rudolph Valentino. Theodora Fitzgerald: Gloria Swanson. Lady Bracondale: Edythe Chapman. Captain Fitzgerald: Alec B Tranis. With Gertrude Astor, June Elvidge, Mabel Van Buren.
Adapted from the novel by Elinor Glyn. Premièred 7-5-22.

BLOOD AND SAND (Famous Players-Lasky, Paramount) 8,110 feet.
Director: Fred Niblo. Adapter: June Mathis. Cameraman: Alvin Wyckoff.
Juan Gallardo: Rudolph Valentino. Carmen: Lila Lee. Dona Sol: Nita Naldi. El Nacional: George Field. Plumitas: Walter Long. With Rose Rosanova, Leo White.
Adapted from the novel by Vicente Blasco Ibanez.Premièred 5-8-22.

THE YOUNG RAJAH (Famous Players-Lasky, Paramount). 7,710 feet.
Director: Philip Rosen. Adapter: June Mathis. Cameraman: James C Van Trees.
Amos Judd: Rudolph Valentino. Molly Cabot: Wanda Hawley.

Austin Slade: Jack Giddings. Narada: Joseph Swickard. With Maude Wayne, Pat Moore, Fanny Midgely, George Periolat, Richard Arlen, Charles Ogle, William Boyd, Spottiswoode Aitken, George Field.
Adapted from the novel, *Amos Judd*, by John Ames Mitchell. Premièred 12-11-22.

1924

MONSIEUR BEAUCAIRE (Famous Players-Lasky, Paramount). 9,930 feet.
Director: Sydney Olcott. Adapter: Forrest Halsey. Cameraman: Harry Fischbeck. Art director: Natacha Rambova.
Duc de Chartres/Beaucaire: Rudolph Valentino. Princess Henriette: Bebe Daniels. King of France: Lowell Sherman. Queen of France: Lois Wilson. Lady Mary: Doris Kenyon. Duc de Nemours: André Daven. With Paulette Duval, Flora Finch.
Adapted from the novel by Booth Tarkington. Premièred 18-8-24.

A SAINTED DEVIL (Famous Players-Lasky, Paramount). 8,630 feet.
Director: Joseph Henabery. Adapter: Forrest Halsey. Cameraman: Harry Fischbeck.
Don Alonzo de Castro: Rudolph Valentino. Carlotta: Nita Naldi. Dona Florencia: Dagmar Godowsky. Julietta Valdez: Helen d'Algy. With Louise Lagrange, Jean del Val, George Seigmann, André Daven.
Adapted from the Rex Beach story, *Rope's End*. Premièred 15-11-24.

1925

COBRA (Ritz-Carlton productions, Paramount). 7 reels.
Director: Joseph Henabery. Adapter: Anthony Coldeways. Cameramen: Harry Fischbeck, J D Jennings. Sets: William Cameron Menzies. Costumes: Adrian.
Count Torriani: Rudolph Valentino. Elise van Zile: Nita Naldi. Mary Drake: Gertrude Olmstead. Jack Dorning: Casson Ferguson,

André Daven. With Eileen Percy, Hector V Sarno, Rose Rosanova, Lillian Langdon, André Daven.
Adapted from the stageplay by Martin Brown. Premièred 30-11-25.

THE EAGLE (United Artists). 7 reels.
Director: Clarence Brown. Adapter: Hans Kraly. Titles: George Marion Jr. Cameramen: George Barnes, J Devereaux Jennings. Art director: William Cameron Menzies. Costumes: Adrian.
Vladimir Dubrovsky: Rudolph Valentino; Mascha Troekouroff: Vilma Banky. Catherine II: Louise Dresser. Judge: George Nichols. Aunt Aurelia: Carrie Clark Ward. Kyrilla: James Marcus. Kuschka: Michael Pleschkoff. Dubrovsky's father: Spottiswoode Aitken. With Gustav von Seyffertitz, Mario Carillo, Frank (Gary) Cooper, Albert Conti.
Adapted from the novel *Dubrovsky*, by Pushkin. Premièred 8-11-25.

1926
SON OF THE SHEIK (United Artists). 7 reels.
Director: George Fitzmaurice. Adapters: Frances Marion, Fred de Gresac. Titles: George Marion Jr. Cameraman: George Barnes. Art director: William Cameron Menzies.
Ahmed/The Sheik: Rudolph Valentino. Yasmin: Vilma Banky. André: George Fawcett. Lady Diana: Agnes Ayres. Gabah: Montague Love. With Bull Montana, Karl Dane, André Daven, Mario Cavillo.
Adapted from the novel, *Sons Of The Sheik,* by E M Hull. Premièred 9-7-26.

Appendix II
Valentino-related Films and Plays

VALENTINO (Columbia Pictures-1951). Director: Lewis Allen. With Anthony Dexter, Eleanor Parker, Richard Carlson, Patricia Medina, Otto Kruger, Joseph Calleia, Dona Drake, Lloyd Gough.

After considering 75,000 applicants and conducting 400 screen-tests, the producers settled on an unknown, Anthony Dexter, to portray Valentino. Dexter certainly ressembles the idol, dances well, and has the right amount of muscles, charm, and reptilian glare. Unfortunately, he has absolutely no Italian accent, and when he emulates one of Valentino's obligatory undressing scenes, everything sags.

The story is a hotch-potch of fact and fantasy. Natacha Rambova threatened legal action should she be portrayed in the film, as did the Guglielmis, Mae Murray and Alice Terry. The hero arrives in America already known as Valentino, with a troupe of dancers. He gatecrashes a party to secure the part of Julio in *The Four Horsemen Of The Apocalypse*, which is directed by a Mark Towers, and the order of his subsequent films is changed: *Moran Of The* Lady Letty, *A Sainted Devil*, *Blood And Sand*, *The Young Rajah*. Then – in June 1921, before any of these were made – he moves into Whitley Heights before completing *The Eagle*, *Monsieur Beaucaire . . . then The Sheik*, directed by Bill King and co-starring the equally fictitious Joan Carlisle. One finds it hard to ascertain who these two are supposed to be – Robert Z Leonard and Mae Murray, or Rex Ingram and Alice Terry. The latter sued Columbia because the film depicted 'her' having a pre-marital affair with Valentino, who in the closing scenes elopes to New York with his *real* sweetheart, Lila Reyes, only to succumb to appendicitis on the eve of his wedding, telling his *Italian* manager in the sick-room, 'Pull up the shade and let the sun shine in!'

The film was not a success, and shortly after making it, Dexter gave up acting and became a schoolteacher.

VALENTINO (Ken Russell Production-1977). Director: Ken Russell. With Rudolph Nureyev, Michelle Phillips, Leslie Caron, Felicity Kendall, Alfred Marks, Seymour Cassel, Carole Kane, Linda Thorson, Huntz Hall, David de Keyser, Anton Diffring, Peter Vaughan, June Bolton, Anthony Dowell.

A truly inspired film with first-class acting, direction, sets and costumes. Unlike the earlier 'biopic', Russell manages to incorporate most of the characters in his subject's life, *and* give them their real names. On the face of it, Nureyev the ballet star would appear to have been woefully miscast, yet throughout the scenario, told largely in flashback by mourners at Valentino's funeral, he shines, acting with just the right amount of irony, and like Valentino never really taking himself seriously. The dancing, needless to say, is exquisite.

Michelle Phillips is excellent as the humourless, domineering Rambova, and a more sympathetic June Mathis could not have been found than in the British actress, Felicity Kendall. Leslie Caron steals every scene she is in as a flagrantly over-the-top Nazimova – indeed, one may even excuse Russell's oversight that the Russian star did not attend the funeral, that it was Pola Negri who sent the blanket of roses and repeatedly 'fainted' for the benefit of the press. Negri was in fact still alive when the film was made, and is thought to have requested not to be portrayed in it. The film was based on the biography by Brad Steiger and Chaw Mank.

VALENTINO (BBC Radio-1995). Written and directed by Bob Sinfield. With Alan Cumming, and Lorelei King, Denise Coffey, Dick Vosburgh, Rebecca Front and Mark Caven interpreting Bianca and Jack de Saulles, Bonnie Glass, Robert Z Leonard, Mae

Murray, Carmel Myers, Nazimova, Jean Acker, June Mathis and Natacha Rambova.

'It's true, I *can* speak,' Rudy tells a press-conference in this work which was broadcast on the actor's centenary. Cumming, a Scots actor known mostly for his comedy roles, portrays Valentino with a voice and accent said to be replicas of the real thing. If this is so, this exercise leaves little doubt that the star would have lost none of his popularity with the advent of sound. As June Mathis (Denise Coffey) declares in the closing moments of this excellent drama, 'He was still a boy, and one whose best work lay ahead of him – or would have done.'

Bibliography: Primary and Secondary Sources

ANGER, Kenneth: *Hollywood Babylon* (Straight Arrow, 1975)

BROWNLOW, Kevin and KOBAL, John: *Hollywood, The Pioneers* (Collins, 1979)

FLOREY, Robert: *Rudy, Inoubliable-Inoublié* (unpublished, 1956)

MADSEN, Axel: *The Sewing Circle* (Robson Books, 1996)

MAHONEY, Luther: *Memoirs* (unpublished, 1967)

MANK, Chaw and STEIGER, Brad: *Valentino* (Corgi, 1976)

MORRIS, Michael: *Madame Valentino, The Many Lives of Natacha Rambova* (Abbeville, 1991)

NORMAND, Roger: *Le Ring* (unpublished, for Hébertot, Daven, Ivano)

RAMBOVA, Natacha: *Rudy, An Intimate Portrait of Rudolph Valentino by his Wife* (Hutchinson, 1926)

ROEN, Paul: *High Camp, A Gay Guide to Camp and Cult Films Vol I* (Leyland, 1994)

SCAGNETTI, Jack: *The Intimate Life of Rudolph Valentino* (Jonathan David, 1976)

ULLMAN, S George: *Valentino, As I Knew Him* (Macy-Massius, 1926)

VALENTINO, Rudolph: *Daydreams* (Hurst & Blackett, 1923)

VALENTINO, Rudolph: *Diaries 1923–1926* (unpublished)

VERMILYE, Jerry: *The Films of the Twenties* (Citadel, 1985)

WALKER, Alexander: *Rudolph Valentino* (Hamish Hamilton, 1976)

PUBLICATIONS

Pictures & Picturegoer; Le Théâtre; Photoplay; New York Times; Los Angeles Times; Movie Weekly; Chicago Tribune; Bonsoir; Motion Picture Classic; Bioscope; Liberty; Variety; Newark News; Herald-Examiner; New York Evening Journal; New York Daily News.

Index